D0466755

The Future of Immortality

Other Books by Robert Jay Lifton

The Nazi Doctors: Medical Killing and the Psychology of Genocide

The Broken Connection: On Death and the Continuity of Life

Death in Life: Survivors of Hiroshima

In a Dark Time (with Nicholas Humphrey)

Indefensible Weapons: The Political and Psychological Case against Nuclearism (with Richard Falk)

Six Lives/Six Deaths: Portraits from Modern Japan (with Shuichi Kato and Michael Reich)

The Life of the Self: Toward a New Psychology

Living and Dying (with Eric Olson)

Home from the War: Vietnam Veterans—Neither Victims nor Executioners

History and Human Survival

Boundaries: Psychological Man in Revolution

Revolutionary Immortality: Mao Tse-tung and the Chinese Cultural Revolution

Thought Reform and the Psychology of Totalism: A Study of "Brainwashing" in China

THE FUTURE OF IMMORTALITY

and Other Essays for a Nuclear Age

ROBERT JAY LIFTON

Basic Books, Inc., Publishers

NEW YORK

Library of Congress Cataloging-in-Publication Data

Lifton, Robert Jay, 1926–
The future of immortality and other essays for a nuclear age.

Bibliographical notes: p. 279.
Includes index.
1. Civilization, Modern—1950– —Psychological aspects. 2. Immortality. 3. Nuclear energy—Social aspects. 4. Technology and civilization. I. Title.
CB430.L54 1987 909.82'01'9 86–47763
ISBN 0–465–02597–8

Printed in the United States of America
Designed by Vincent Torre
86 87 88 89 HC 9 8 7 6 5 4 3 2 1

To Fritz Redlich

who made it all possible

. . . in the end it's the end that is the worst . . . you must go on a little more, you must go on a long time more. . . .

—SAMUEL BECKETT

CONTENTS

PART III
REFLECTIONS

ACKNOWLEDGMENTS

I HAVE DEDICATED these essays to Fritz Redlich, who some time ago was rash enough to create a chair for an idiosyncratic young psychiatrist at Yale, where most of the essays were written, and who has remained a close and generous friend. The essays also, in one way or another, reflect the influence on my work in very different ways of Erik Erikson, David Riesman, and Leslie Farber. Much of their content was discussed, at early stages, with members of the Wellfleet Psychohistory Group. At later stages I had valuable exchanges with my new colleagues (but old friends) at The City University of New York, Jack Geiger and Chuck Strozier.

Jo Ann Miller, my editor at Basic Books—with sure sensitivity and (considering the bulk of the reading) stoicism as well—helped me make demanding choices about which writings to use, and about the structure of the book. Phoebe Hoss once again provided a lesson in creative manuscript editing.

Lily B. Finn, my long-time assistant at Yale, prepared most of the original typescripts. Lucy M. Silva, my assistant at John Jay College, prepared portions of the book and wove together many loose ends.

My wife, Betty Jean Lifton, has contributed a great deal to the content of these essays, and still more, on so many planes of love, to the life of their author. Kenneth Jay and Natasha, our children, constantly reminded me what the essays were for.

The Future of Immortality

Introduction

AFTER COLLECTING these essays, my feeling was: "So *this* is what I have been doing for the past fifteen years!" There are surely more pleasant ways to spend one's time than worrying about war, mass murder, and nuclear threat, but I seemed to have made a choice to spend much of mine doing just that.

So much so that I first learned of the Soviet nuclear disaster at Chernobyl during a question period following a talk I gave on the subject of Nazi doctors. The questioner had herself heard of the accident on a television news report just an hour or two earlier, and wanted to know how it was possible—given the human potential for evil she had just heard me describe, together with our misguided relationships to technology—for us to retain a sense of hope for the future. I had no easy answer at the time, nor do I now. But the beginnings of such an answer lie in exploring the ramifications of the question—which is what this book attempts to do. The exploration includes a great deal of darkness but also significant glimmers of light. That is one of the reasons I decided to take the title from the essay "The Future of Immortality"—a phrase that is my way of speaking of our efforts to maintain ourselves as part of the great chain of being.

The mildly playful paradox contained in the phrase seems just right.

People often ask me how and why I became involved with these destructive events, and here too I have no clear answer. I could make a logical argument for the necessity of addressing such events, or I could mention personal psychological tendencies from early in life that contribute to that stance. Yet both of these explanations seem to me beside the point. It is not that they lack truth but rather that each misleadingly concretizes a kernel of truth. A more accurate kind of explanation, I believe, has to do with my evolving a personal and professional sense of self in connection with probing these extreme questions, so that decisions to do so come to feel appropriate and inwardly right. Then, in opening oneself to these destructive forces and their human consequences, one takes on a survivor's imperative to bear witness. I do so not as an actual survivor but as an investigator struggling toward a level of psychological (or psychohistorical) penetration that might inform the moral imagination. In that way, the investigator and the activist in me are never completely separate. While each demands its own rigor and its own passion, my goal is always to press toward their inner unity. As subjectively experienced, of course, little of this occurs in clear, logical ways. It was more a matter of waking up one morning to find I had, willy-nilly, embarked on a particular course that had become more or less a life mission.

That mission is quite absurd. Who, after all, can stand up to these destructive forces—politically, existentially, or even investigatively? One expression of my own sense of absurdity is the drawing of bird cartoons in which my avian protagonists wallow in gallows humor. More generally, I argue (in chapter 1) that a sense of absurdity pervades and sometimes informs contemporary experience. That sense, which surely predates nuclear threat, is radically intensified by the specter of species self-annihilation.

An event like Chernobyl takes place within the context of contemporary dislocation and absurdity. That context includes the nearly universal embrace of a nuclear technology that, in its ostensibly benign use, can endanger the lives of hundreds of thousands of people and instill in millions a lifelong fear of deadly radiation effects; and then the interplay between Soviet claims of having the situation under control and American attribution of the accident to unreliable Soviet arrangements (or some form of Soviet evil) in contrast to ostensibly safe American nuclear technology. Most absurd of all is the worldwide official refusal to accept the true lessons of Chernobyl: our universal vulnerability to nuclear technology, especially to the weapons; and our shared fate in connection with the human future. More hopeful is the response to Chernobyl of large numbers of ordinary people throughout the world who seem ready to grasp these truths. An important question now is how much Chernobyl can contribute to a rejection of that general context of absurdity in favor of life-enhancing alternatives.

Inevitably, there is a dangerous psychic edge to contemporary absurdity, which I would locate in a longing for the nuclear "end," as well as in the resigned acceptance of that end (see chapters 9 and 11). Since writing these essays, I have come to recognize an awesome spiritual battleground in responses to nuclear threat, sometimes involving contending groups of people and sometimes struggles within individual minds. Put most simply, the issue is whether ultimate virtue derives from preserving the world or from destroying it.

Those we may call the world-destructionists (or Armageddonists) are not always clear on exactly *who* would be committing the ultimate act of annihilation (it is sometimes man, sometimes God). Yet that does not so much matter to them because ultimately God would be responsible: he, and he alone would be carrying out his promise, as prophesied in Revelation and other biblical texts. However dubious the theology, it conjoins nuclear holocaust with the evangelical Christian impulse toward world cleansing in the name of achieving the ultimate spiritual moment (the Second Coming or the Kingdom of God). Integral to that world cleansing is *self*-cleansing. What takes on greatest moral urgency for the Armageddonist is not the prevention of nuclear holocaust but the individual's spiritual preparation for his or her transport (via the "Rapture") to a higher state. One is urged to make that religious preparation immediately, "while there is time to do it, not put it off"—and then (as A. G. Mojtabai quotes an "end-time" minister) one will be literally carried away in joy: from one's automobile ("Good-bye, you piece of junk!"), one's home ("Good-bye, old shack!"), and, as one proceeds on up, from everything else ("Good-bye, Dallas! good-bye, Houston! good-bye, Los Angeles! good-bye, World! good-bye!").[1] Though I speak of an absurd psychic extreme, one should not underestimate the broader appeal of end-time ideology as a perverse vision of hope.

There is also a clear intra-Christian alternative (as put forward by the Catholic bishops as well as Methodist leaders and those of other denominations), which more wisely identifies the evil to combat as nuclear mass murder and genocide, and looks to principles of mutuality and love in the struggle to prevent that evil from manifesting itself.

But the spiritual battle extends well beyond Christianity or any other religion. There is a strange secular version of it involving technocratic nuclear strategists. Some of those strategists combine the ideology I call "nuclearism" (exaggerated embrace and even near-worship of the weaponry [see chapters 9 to 12]) with polarized imagery of Soviet evil and American virtue. They can then experience a secular version of the lure of Armageddon, as observed by the psychologist Steven Kull in certain of his interviews with nuclear strategists, and given dramatic expression in Arthur Kopit's recent play *The End of the World.* That secular lure could come close to the theological longing. And even when the lure of Armageddon is not discernibly present, aggressive impulses associated with what is called "challenge" or "risk" can play a similar role. I have in mind, for instance, promoting a "madman theory" (intentionally conveying the sense of being "crazy enough" to plunge the world into nuclear holocaust unless one's adversary backs off); or related inclinations toward playing "nuclear chicken" (displaying increasingly provocative stances in the assumption that one's opponent will be the *first* to back off—the term taken from the male adolescent "game" of driving cars full speed at one another to determine who is "chicken" and turns away first). Such images and impulses, along with many others, undoubtedly contribute to strategists' contradictory projections of a "limited nuclear war" which they know (in another part of their minds) cannot be depended upon to stay limited.

There is, then, a real sense in which we can speak of "secular Armageddonists," who, like their religious counterparts, renounce responsibility for the holocaust they anticipate and, in some cases, press toward bringing about. They may view that holocaust as an inevitable outcome of our time and technology, or they may consider it preferable to an assumed alternative of "giving in" or of "surrendering to the Russians." Still another parallel between religious and secular forms of Armageddonism is the continuum from fringe tendencies of welcoming the end to more muted manifestations of that attraction which can reverberate much more widely through American society, and undoubtedly elsewhere as well.

It would be no exaggeration to view the struggle as one between love of this life and hatred for it—between responsibility toward the lives of others as opposed to vitriolic renunciation of the "other" as a carrier of evil. A related duality is the acceptance of the fallibility of earthly connections, as opposed to the violent destruction of all such connections in the name of wildly imagined absolute perfection that is both infallible and other-worldly. There is a disturbing parallel here between Armageddonism in general and the Nazi vision of killing in the name of healing (see chapters 6, 9, 11, and 14).

But I would be wary of dividing the world neatly into Armageddonists and life-enhancers. Either or both tendencies could be present in large numbers of people. Indeed, a sense of, or even desire for, the end of the world is part of a general human psychological potential (see chapter 11), and can be strongly evoked by combinations of inner terror and desperate need for regenerative hope. Apocalyptic ideologies reflect and usually intensify that terror, while providing their own version of hope. Similarly, Armageddonist tendencies can quickly diminish if there are alternative images of hope and of human continuity. Clearly this is a time to explore and cultivate love for our world and hope for its future.

In comparing these essays to an earlier collection (*History and Human Survival*, published in 1970), I find them to be more urgent in tone, and at the same time more conceptual and reflective. The urgency has to do not only with deepening threat but with my increasing personal inclination to inject what I consider to be appropriate passion into whatever interpretive principles I can offer. The reflectiveness may well be an aspect of aging, but I would like to think that its accompanying hopefulness has something to do with broadening vision. I do know that hopeful tendencies in me are related to my increasing awareness, even as I explore the most vicious human actions, of the beauty and wonder of human life.

The conceptual tendency has to do with deepening commitment to certain kinds of theory and form. My Hiroshima research (beginning in 1962) represented for me a crossing of a threshold conceptually no less than morally. My work there, coming after an earlier study of Chinese thought reform conducted in Hong Kong, made two large principles clear to me: the necessity of connecting psychological theory to historical forces; and the inadequacy of prior theory, psychological or otherwise, for unprecedented events. Yet a new theory put forward for such events may—probably must—reach back to the oldest human concerns and principles. That is very much the case with my model (or paradigm) of life continuity or symbolization of life and death (see chapter 1), which provides common intellectual structure to these essays. I have not included somewhat more technical essays pertaining to this model—"From Analysis to Formation" and "On Psychohistory"—as both have been incorporated into a short book, *The Life of the Self: Toward a New Psychology.* Then in a more recent study, *The Broken Connection,* I extended these conceptual principles in order to examine their broadest possible application: to fundamental human emotions, the life cycle, the major psychiatric syndromes, and larger historical process with specific focus on nuclear threat. Among the satisfying responses I have had to that book include recognition that it is the work of a child of Freud who has felt impelled toward certain investigative and conceptual explorations quite different from those of that estimable parent.

The order of the essays here has a certain arbitrary logic. The first, "The Future of Immortality," lays out some of the major themes of the volume, and can be considered almost a continuation of this introduction. These themes include the symbolization of larger human connectedness (or the *sense* of immortality), a contemporary individual-psychological (or "protean") style, the threat to larger human continuity, and some of the psychological and social possibilities for renewing that sense of continuity. (For the most part, the essays appear in their original form, but I have made changes here and there for better integration and to avoid repetition.)

In part I, the essays follow the sequence of my own encounters with the events discussed. The Hiroshima and Vietnam essays (chapters 2 to 5) do not attempt to recapitulate those destructive experiences in detail (as I did in my books *Death in Life: Survivors of Hiroshima* and *Home from the War*) but focus more on their legacies. Painful as those legacies are for us today, they also have profound potential value in furthering our possibilities for wisdom. The essays on Nazi behavior also stress lasting issues; but one, "Medicalized Killing in Auschwitz" (chapter 6), provides an overview of that work (recorded in much greater detail in my recently published *The Nazi Doctors: Medical Killing and the Psychology of Genocide*). The other two essays raise specific human issues: one deals with the perils of maintaining a profession (in this case psychoanalysis) under an evil regime (chapter 7), and the other evokes the magnificent achievement of Alexander and Margarete Mitscherlich as anti-Nazi physician-psychoanalysts (chapter 8).

Part II contains more recent expressions of a preoccupation with psychological aspects of nuclear threat so longstanding for me as to feel a bit like a chronic illness. But I would insist that the illness in question is the world's—the various national and international arrangements that contribute to the possibility of species annihilation. Much of my focus has been on what I call "imagery of extinction," and on what the imagery does to us. My two most recent essays in this group (chapters 9 and 11) extend that exploration to some of the far reaches of Armageddonism. One of them, "The New Psychology of Human Survival" (chapter 9), looks at what I call the "Grand Illusion" of the Strategic Defense Initiative, or Star Wars, which I see as replacing the series of separate nuclear illusions I summarized a few years earlier in a book written with Richard Falk, *Indefensible Weapons.* In these essays I am also concerned with the dangerously false criteria laid down by influential groups in this country concerning what I call "nuclear normality"—what is "normal" or "sane" in thinking about nuclear weapons—a matter now being looked at by other scholars from a semantic point of view (as in the work of James Skelly of the University of California at San Diego), and one that bears a great deal more scrutiny.

In part III, I explore specific psychological and ethical principles as affected by their nuclear-age context. Inevitably, the figure of the survivor looms large, in terms of personal pain as well as possibility for insight and illumination, psychological and artistic (chapters 17 to 19). I also return to my earliest research concern, that of totalism, in an essay on cult formation (chapter 15), an essay also related to patterns of nuclear-age fundamentalism that reverberate throughout the volume. The essays on dreaming (chapter 13) and on suicide (chapter 16) apply my life-continuity paradigm to these two issues. I decided to include a statement on "doubling," the formation of a functionally separate self (chapter 14), because work with Nazi doctors led me to the concept and taught me the wider danger of doubling as enabling people to adapt to, and further, the work of an evil environment.

The essay with which I end the book, "Toward a Nuclear Age Ethos," explores ways of living and feeling not only hopeful but, in my view, fully available to us in the immediate present.

With it all, these essays speak in quiet tones. I think often of Freud's moving Enlightenment dictum: "The voice of the intellect is a soft one, but will not rest until it has had its hearing." I would like to think that the old master would look sympathetically at this late-twentieth-century effort to infuse that soft intellectual voice with elements of fierce feeling, a sense of absurdity, and an insistence that we all (in Beckett's phrase) "go on a long time more."

1

The Future of Immortality

So the sea wind wakes desire.
My body shimmers with a light flame.

I see in the advancing and retreating waters. . . .
The eternal one, the child, the swaying vine branch,
The numinous ring around the opening flower. . . .

I, who come back from the depths laughing too loudly,
Become another thing;
My eyes extend beyond the farthest bloom of the waves;
I lose and find myself in the long waters;
I am gathered together once more;
I embrace the world.

—THEODORE ROETHKE
"The Long Waters"

This essay was originally a talk I gave at the Harvard Divinity School in the fall of 1985 as the annual Ingersoll Lecture on Immortality, and I have essentially retained its spoken style. Though I knew my work was being taught at the Harvard Divinity School, I was surprised by the invitation, and wondered whether the school had run out of lecturers who, when talking about immortality, would mean the real thing. Of course I mean the "real thing" as well, in the sense that symbolization is at the heart of human psychic function, and our only path to what we call reality. I had to be a bit playful because the subject is so grandiose, but I used the occasion for a somewhat systematic look at the impediments to, and the possibilities for, our experiencing a sense of human continuity.

In combining questions of nuclear threat with the possibilities and dislocations of the contemporary psychological or "protean style," this essay puts forth the two fundamental components of my work—holocaust and transformation—to set the tone for the rest of the volume. Though I claim no theological credentials and hold no specific religious beliefs, the setting had a certain appropriateness. What comes to mind here is a conversation I once had with Erik Erikson about the relationship of much of our work to religious issues. Erikson said that he gravitated naturally to those issues simply by raising fundamental psychological questions. I replied that the events I attempted to engage took me to the same place. But I would also point to a certain sensibility in each of us that causes us to be drawn to religious issues. In my case the sensibility includes inclinations to take seriously questions of immortality and at the same time to bring those questions into a psychological and secular frame of larger human connection, a frame of natural history.

That sensibility requires one to reject the traditional ostrich-like professional psychological attitude of avoiding all such large questions because they are "unscientific" and "a question of personal belief." I would counter, in the spirit of this essay, by saying that matters of what Paul Tillich called "ultimate concern" come as much under the purview of science—that is, science broadly defined—as do any other manifestations of the human mind. Moreover, with such questions put before us at almost every moment, this is hardly a time for ostriches.

HAVING HEARD something about the distinguished history of this lectureship, I have the feeling that I have come in through the back door. Certainly it takes a little more than fool's courage—maybe one would say hubris, or in another idiom, *chutzpah*—for a secular psychiatrist like myself to address the students and faculty of the Harvard Divinity School on the subject of immortality. But so be it. My response to that situation is to share with you another one of my interests. I draw bird cartoons. I have no talent in an artistic sense, but these birds can sometimes say things more directly than can my formal writings. One such bird cartoon seems relevant for this moment particularly: a small, enthusiastic young bird looks up and says, "All of a sudden I had this wonderful feeling, 'I am me.' " An older, skeptical, jaundiced bird looks down and says, "You were wrong." On that note I begin.

Even a fellow as rash as I wouldn't address you on this subject without having in mind a certain view, or really a certain image, of immortality—one that will not sound completely unfamiliar and yet will, I think, differ from much that is generally said and meant certainly by psychologists and probably by theologians, too, in speaking of immortality. The place for me to start is Hiroshima. My thoughts about what I call the sense of immortality, the necessity for it, began with my work in 1962 with the survivors of Hiroshima. I found in talking to these survivors that after this experience of extraordinary devastation they sought not only to re-establish their lives in their families, in their work, in the immediate world around them, but also to recover something else they had lost—something on the order of trust or faith in human existence. Trust or faith in the flow of generations in the expressions of the human spirit. That quest for a sense of immortality was, as I thought more about it, by no means unique to Hiroshima survivors, but was rendered especially palpable, almost visible, among them and to me by the sea of death and the sense of a human end to which they had been exposed in that city.

Now let me leave Hiroshima, at least for the moment, and turn to two sets of quotations—the first from Thomas Merton and the second from William Faulkner. Merton said: "We cannot give an irresponsible and un-Christian consent to the demonic use of power for the destruction of a whole nation, a whole continent or even the whole human race. Or can we? The question is not being asked."[1] Then Faulkner, more personally: "The writer's only responsibility is to his art. He will be completely ruthless, if he is a good one. He has a dream. It anguishes him so he must get rid of it. He has no peace until then. Everything goes by the board—honor, pride, decency, security, happiness—all to get the book written. If a writer has to rob his mother, he will not hesitate."[2] Faulkner went on in another place: "Really the writer doesn't want success. . . . He knows he has a short life span. The day will come that he must pass through the wall of oblivion and he wants to leave a scratch on the wall—Kilroy was here—that someone a hundred or a thousand years later will see."[3]

Clearly Faulkner was talking about what I call the symbolization of immortality, of larger human connectedness; and Merton, about the threat to all such connectedness, to all of history and memory, and even to the claim to immortality, symbolic or other.

It is useful, I think, in considering the symbolization of immortality to turn to what two of the early great psychoanalysts, Freud and Jung, had to say and to how they looked upon the issue of immortality specifically. Freud thought that death itself was unimaginable, psychically unavailable. He thought that modern man, at great cost, had held to a denial of the annihilation that death really signifies; and, in that sense, that all talk of immortality, or of the immortal soul, was an expression of denial of death. Freud, then, takes the position that I call "rationalist-iconoclastic."

Carl Jung took an opposite position. He was very sensitive to myths of immortality and to the existence all through world mythology of beliefs about life after death. He said that these are hidden maps of our own psychic terrain, "hints to us from the unconscious." He was concerned with what he called the "personal myth" and "archetype" in connection with immortality. But then he said something odd: "As a physician I am convinced that it is hygienic to discover in death a goal toward which one can strive." And he went on, "I therefore consider the religious teaching of a life hereafter consonant with the standpoint of psychic hygiene."[4] Jung enables us to recover powerful mythological truth, but at the expense of intellectual or scientific rigor. I characterize Jung's position as "mythic-hygienic."

We can say, then, that Freud, the secular Jew carrying the torch of the Enlightenment, insisted upon death as the annihilation of self, the end of everything. Yet Freud was enormously preoccupied with his own immortality. He said things like, "What will they do with my theory after my death? Will it still resemble my basic thoughts?" And at the age of thirty-eight when he thought he was having cardiac symptoms, one of his main preoccupations was that he would not be able to prove the sexual theory of neurosis; and he added, "After all, one does not want to die either immediately or completely."[5]

Jung, the Protestant visionary, brought his tough-minded, obscurantist, medieval imagination to a reassertion of a principle of immortality. His ingenuity in combining a modern therapeutic ("hygienic") ethos with pre-modern Christian hope takes us closer to important principles of symbolization. But he hedges and mystifies in that combination.

There is a third position which I call a "formative-symbolizing" perspective. It insists upon the wisdom of the symbolizing philosophers, notably Ernst Cassirer and Susanne Langer, in teaching us that the constant re-creation of all experience is the essence of human mentation. From this standpoint, I would focus on the symbolizing process in the experience of collective life continuity. We require symbolization of that continuity, imaginative forms of transcending death, in order to be able to confront the fact that we die. The sense of immortality is by no means mere denial of death, although there is lots of that around. But it is a corollary of the knowledge of death itself. It is our need for a symbolic relationship toward that which has gone on before, and that which we know will go on after, what we realize to be our own finite individual lives. And in that sense, the symbolization of immortality is an appropriate expression of our biological, cultural, and historical connectedness.

Otto Rank also made a considerable contribution to this way of thinking with his assertion that "man creates culture by changing natural conditions in order to maintain his spiritual self."[6] Rank was very much preoccupied with his claim that fear of death equals fear of life, and spoke of the universal inclination toward "immortality ideologies." One difficulty in Rank's work, as with Freud, is that he still held to a Cartesian dualism—the near absolute distinction between the irrational and the rational. And Rank did indeed consider these immortality systems irrational, but an irrational dimension that human beings require.

I would say that, within the formative-symbolizing perspective, the sense of immortality is neither rational nor irrational; it is symbolically appropriate, and can be understood in several modes. In the biological mode, we have the sense of living on, psychologically speaking, *in* our sons and daughters and their sons and daughters. This mode is perhaps given its most intense expression in traditional Chinese culture, in the Chinese family system as articulated in Confucianism with the mystical stress—even part religion—of filial piety. Thus Mencius, Confucius's greatest disciple, speaks of several forms of unfilial acts, and says that among these, lack of posterity is the greatest. One finds, though, that this biological mode of symbolic immortality is also extremely important throughout Western civilization, not just in East Asia. One need only look at the Roman *paterfamilias* as both family monarch and priest of the family ancestor cult.

Now because the human being is the cultural animal, that biological mode always moves outward toward group, tribe, organizations, subculture, people, nation, or even species. And we will have advanced, indeed, when we can feel in dying that we live on in humankind.

A second mode of symbolic immortality is the one that most comes to mind in many cases—the theological or religious mode. Sometimes that can include the idea of a life after death, as a form of "survival" or even as a release from profane burdens into a higher plane of existence. But the theological mode need not necessarily rely upon the concept of an immortal soul, and in most Jewish and Buddhist belief, this concept is weak or absent. Here in Cambridge I talked a great deal about these issues with Paul Tillich toward the end of his life. He always stressed that the literal insistence upon an afterlife was "vulgar theology" generally put forward for the common people, as opposed to symbolized and sensitive "higher theologies" more concerned with spiritual attainment and spiritual continuity. So that seems to be a major vision in Christianity as well. Here the idea of the theological or religious mode, and perhaps of religion itself, has to do with spiritual power, with life power, with moral energy and vitality, which is very much a central theme in my work. The Japanese have the word *kami*—often translated as "god" or "spirit." There is also the Polynesian term *manna* and the Roman idea of *numen;* the Greek idea of *areté* and even the Christian image of grace, all of which have something of this in common.

A third mode of symbolic immortality is the creative mode, that of individual works, whether great works of art, literature, or science or more humble influences on friends, lovers, families, teachers upon students or vice versa. And this mode is of enormous importance as we feel it threatened as well. Now here the larger enterprise or tradition becomes something beyond the individual practitioner whether he or she be scientist, artist, or theologian. One could say that for physicians and psychotherapists the quest for symbolic immortality is expressed partly in one's influence on one's patients.

The fourth mode of symbolic immortality has to do with nature itself, symbolized as eternal nature in virtually all cultures. This stress is notable in Japanese culture and Shinto belief: survivors of Hiroshima, in the struggle to absorb and recover from their holocaust, could reassert a sense of human continuity in an old Japanese (originally Chinese) saying, "The state may collapse, but the mountains and rivers remain."[7]

Now there is a fifth mode of symbolized immortality—that of experiential transcendence—the direct psychic experience, so intense that, within it, time and death disappear. This, of course, is the classical mode of the mystics. Not only can it be experienced in the contemplation of God or of the universe; but, as Marghanita Laski in particular has written, it can have a number of expressions in such things as song, dance, battle, sexual love, childbirth, athletic effort, mechanical flight, contemplation of the past, or artistic or intellectual creation.[8] In other words, in any activity where we feel ourselves outside ourselves (which is the meaning of the word *ecstasy*), we can experience that quality of transcendence. In sexual experience there is a kind of everyday mode of transcendence, which is one reason sex carries such special intensity, in some ways a greater burden, and also greater possibilities, in humans as compared with other animals.

Freud spoke of this mode as the oceanic feeling. But he wanted to take it back to childhood unity. It may indeed have such a model, but I would stress the *presentness* in the experience of transcendence. Laski, and also William James in his classic work on religious conversion,[9] see this experience of transcendence as an opening out to the world toward new forms of mental creation.

Now one can articulate this symbolization of immortality only if one has a more nitty-gritty dimension as well. In the model or paradigm that I use, there is the larger principle of the symbolization of immortality, which is somewhat unusual in psychological work, as well as the more immediate or proximate dimension that is always part of psychological study. For this dimension one requires some beginning feeling of death, through experience from the moment of birth, before one knows what death is. Earliest emotions having to do with separation, stasis, and disintegration—as opposed to connection, movement, and integrity—in this way serve as "death equivalents." These polarities—more accurately, dialectical patterns—are first physiological (connection begins with attachment or proximity to the mothering figure), then become imaged (as the infant comes to recognize its parents), and can ultimately become highly symbolized (as connection takes the form of various love relationships and loyalties). Similarly, integrity, beginning with a sense of the body holding together, can eventually take on the kind of profound ethical and psychological dimension that contributes to the greatest achievements of the individual self. The "death equivalents" first prepare one for actual imagery of death (beginning during the latter half of the second year), and later interact with that death imagery, so that, for example, experiences of separation become associated with death no less than the reverse.

The sense of immortality is bound up with these struggles. It both depends upon and contributes to the self's experience of vitality at the positive or life-enhancing side of the dialectic (connection, movement, and integrity)—even as it contends with and helps overcome the death equivalents.

So this approach turns the classical psychological assumption on its head. Rather than denial of death, the concept of immortality, at least in this symbolized form, is our best avenue toward acceptance of death and the confronting of our own finiteness. It is consistent with a Jewish reinterpretation of the Adam and Eve story, according to which the extrusion from the Garden of Eden was not a "fall" but a "rise," because it was (in the terms we have been using) an exchange of literal for symbolic immortality—or, as Nahum Glatzer puts it, "giving up immortality for knowledge" and thereby "becoming human."

One can extend these principles to the historical process, because the human being is not only the cultural and symbolizing animal but also the historical animal. Much of history can be understood as the struggle to achieve, maintain, and reaffirm a collective sense of immortality under constantly changing psychic and material conditions. In other words, groups are always collectively seeking modes or combinations of modes of immortality and will celebrate them endlessly, fight and die in order to affirm them or put down rivals who threaten their immortality system. One can also understand historical change as shifts in these modes as some of them lose their viability and must be replaced or altered with the formation of new modes or new combinations. Certain major historical turning points can be interpreted in this way. The Darwinian revolution of the nineteenth century, for example, was a shift from a more or less religious mode toward the natural and biological modes. The shift is never complete but only partial, and the problem is not so much the shift itself as what is literalized and is therefore deadened, and what in contrast is more vital and symbolized and active. One could also look at the Chinese revolution, an extraordinary upheaval, as a transformation of the filial son or daughter to the filial Communist, a shift from the biological family mode of symbolic immortality to what I call "revolutionary immortality." Immortality becomes invested in the revolution and can articulate several of those other modes—including the experience of transcendence, its own version of works and even the biological and natural modes, and certainly a kind of religious process as well.[10]

Of course, there are difficulties and impediments to immortality quests and immortality systems. One of the ways to get at some of the contemporary difficulties and quests is to look at the struggles of the contemporary self. And one version of the contemporary self I have called "protean style" or "protean man and woman." In protean man and woman I believe we can find embodied some of the struggles with symbolic immortality that face us at this time.

Again, a quotation. This can only be from James Joyce, from *Finnegan's Wake:* "You were bred, fed, fostered and fattened from holy childhood up to this two easter island. . . . and now forsooth, a nogger among the blankards of this dastard century, you have become of twosome twiminds forenenst gods, hidden and discovered, nay condemned fool, anarch, egoarch, hiresiarch, you have reared your disunited kingdom on the vacuum of your own most intensely doubtful soul."[11] This is the joyous cry of the modern or postmodern self, and if despair lurks beneath it—as indeed it does—that despair is subsumed to a wallowing in multiplicity and, of course, absurdity—multiplicity and absurdity being two cornerstones of the protean style.

Now by protean style I mean a series of explorations of the self in which one tries out various involvements and commitments toward people, ideas, and actions; and shifts from them, leaves them for new ones at relatively minimal psychological cost. Another dimension of the protean style is simultaneous multiplicity of images so that one can hold in one's head, and does frequently and in a great variety of ways, images that are contradictory and seem to take one in opposite directions simultaneously.[12]

I encountered what I identified as the protean style originally in working in Japan with young people, university students back in the 1960s who had been through an extraordinary array of involvements having to do with traditional Japanese culture, emperor worship, and then democracy, Marxism, and a great variety of additional cultural and psychological immersions.

But I came quickly to see that the protean style was by no means a purely Japanese phenomenon. There is a sequence in the psychiatric and the broadly psychoanalytic approach to the mutability of the self from Freud through protean style: for Freud, the self was relatively fixed, as formed in the first few years of life; there was an archeological character to the self with different levels and layers. Erik Erikson's concept of identity has been, among other things, an effort to open out the self or the person into the historical process and allow for more fluidity. But even that model of identity requires an assumption of relative sameness within the individual, which may depend in turn on forms of stability within the social and historical structure, and these are often lacking. So we need even more fluid concepts.

In Greek mythology, as we know, Proteus was a sea god, some say a minor one, but above all a shapeshifter who could change his shape with relative ease from wild boar to lion to dragon to fire to flood: that is, he could assume these various animal or human or natural shapes but found it difficult to commit himself to a single form and would not do so unless seized and chained—that form being his own function of prophecy. At least one interpreter—though his is an unusual interpretation, as well as an authoritative one—Ernst Gombrich, the noted art historian, sees another side of Proteus: the ability to remain constant in every metamorphosis. Gombrich captures the protean struggle for coherence and integration of the self, in the midst of the shapeshifting process.

Now the protean style does not come out of the blue of the sea or sky. It has historical origins along the following lines: First of all, a certain historical or psychohistorical dislocation (see chapter 15, pages 216–17)—that is, the breakdown of traditional symbols, in a sequence from premodern to modern to postmodern experience. To some extent, the whole modern experience from the late eighteenth century on has to do with the expansion of the self; but in postmodern experience—let's say through much of the twentieth century or at least the last thirty to fifty years of it—there has been a further self-expansion and breakdown of symbols. Here I mean the fundamental symbols involving religion, authority, family life—the symbols around which life has been organized.

A second important historical source, insufficiently recognized, is the mass-media revolution. Marshall McLuhan was correct, surely, in focusing on the importance of the medium. But what he did not say was that we need to look at the psychological and symbolic soil encountered by that revolution—the dislocations already taking place in the individual selves the media bombard. In any case, the bombardment is formidable: with only slight exaggeration, it may be said that the mass-media revolution can make available to us, at any time, virtually any image from any culture in our present world or from the historical past, as well as any projection into the imagined future. We have hardly begun to recognize what this totally unprecedented image accessibility might be doing to us.

The third important historical influence is that of imagery of extinction—associated primarily with nuclear weapons, but including Armageddon-like imagery from other sources as well—destruction of the environment, widespread famine, depletion of natural resources, and memories of past genocides, especially that perpetrated by the Nazis, along with an ominous sense of genocide rendered more feasible by high technology.

I view this concept of the protean style as an aspect of the study of the self. In elaborating it, I do not quite subscribe to what might be called the non-self or anti-self school of Sartre and R. D. Laing. For Sartre what we call the self is no more than a flow of consciousness, with the implication that there is no psychic entity that, with any consistency, functions as an agent for the individual. In the assumption that there is such an entity, the protean concept relates to the work of not only Freud and Erikson but also of Harry Stack Sullivan and his concept of the self-system; of Heinz Kohut and his self-psychology; and Otto Rank and his concept of the will in an actively changing self. But the protean style encompasses more radical forms of experimentation with self-process—still in the service of maintaining a measure of coherence and connection.

Throughout Sartre's life and work, there are constant, often brilliant expressions of proteanism. For many he has epitomized twentieth-century man as being "constantly on the go, hurrying from point to point, subject to subject . . . as he endeavors to lose and find himself in his encounters with other lives, disciplines, books, and situations."[13] Of great psychological importance is Sartre's celebration of fatherlessness: "There is no good father, that's the rule. . . . Had my father lived, he would have lain on me at full length . . . and crushed me. . . . I left behind me a young man who did not have time to be my father, and who could now be my son."[14] In referring to his liberation through his father's early death, Sartre raised fundamental contemporary questions not only of fatherlessness but of mentorship and authority and reversals in both, questions that are central to the protean style.

These and related protean elements are prominent in the work of contemporary American novelists—for instance, John Barth, Don Delillo, Kurt Vonnegut, Erica Jong, and before them, Brian Donleavy and Jack

Kerouac. Saul Bellow is particularly notable for the protean characters he has created. In the *Adventures of Augie March,* for example, Augie says, "I touched all sides, and nobody knew where I belonged. I had no good idea of that myself."[15] For, as one critic put it, "Augie indeed celebrates the self, but he can find nothing to do with it."[16]

European novelists also come to mind: for example, Günter Grass (whose *The Tin Drum* is a breathtaking journey through much of German-Polish culture and experience prior to, during, and after the Nazi era), Heinrich Böll, and Italo Calvino. In Japanese literature also—the novels of Kobo Abe and Öe Kenzaburo—and in the emerging brilliance of Eastern European literature, notably the work of the Czech novelist Milan Kundera, one finds powerful expressions of the protean style. While each culture handles the style differently, the extent to which virtually all require it tells us that much of contemporary history is shared history.

One can also see it in art movements—not only in "action painting," which is already an "old" element; but in the rapid sequence of change in art movements, from action painting to kinetic art to pop art to conceptual art to periodic disappearances and reappearances of the human figure, to destructive art, to large wrappings of coastlines with cloth or canvas, to various forms of minimalism—the movements themselves shifting so rapidly that the artist can hardly begin to dig into one of them before feeling in some sense outmoded.

Concerning autobiography, Jerome Hamilton Buckley, in an interesting study called *The Turning Key,* describes the assertion and establishment of the self from the late eighteenth and early nineteenth centuries, developing into an elaboration and expansion of self, and then culminating in the twentieth-century tendency toward inventing the individual self by means of the protean pattern of radically imagined extensions, re-creations, and mocking caricatures of actual experience.[17]

There is also a protean struggle with ideas and beliefs. The problem becomes less the capacity to embrace a particular ideology or belief system than to maintain it over long periods. Until relatively recently, no more than a single major ideological shift was likely to occur in a lifetime, and that one would be long remembered for its conflict and soul searching. But today it is not unusual for several such shifts to take place within a year or even a month, whether in the realm of politics, religion, aesthetic values, personal relationships, or style of living. Quite rare is the man or woman who has gone through life holding firmly to a single ideological vision. More usual is a tendency toward ideological fragments, bits and pieces of belief systems that allow for shifts, revisions, and recombinations.

Bound up with proteanism is the movement from irony to absurdity and mockery. Irony requires a relatively clear position on the part of the self, not characteristic of the protean style. Absurdity and mockery, in contrast, reflect perceptions of surrounding activities and beliefs as strange and inappropriate—a loss of "fit" between internal and external worlds. Mockery can express that loss through mimetic ridicule, without requiring a clear voice of one's own. While absurdity as a concept has a considerable existential tradition in representing modern spiritual homelessness, it has, in recent decades, come to penetrate much of cultural experience. Consider such contemporary terms for a segment of life activity as "bit," "caper," "game," "scene," "show," "scenario," or "schtick"—and the language is ever renewed. What is to be experienced, these terms tell us, is too absurd to be taken at face value; one must either keep much of the self aloof from it or else lubricate the encounter with mockery. This linguistic "lubrication," and a general spirit of mockery, has important musical roots—in the sound and lyric of jazz as well as in the otherwise very different rock.

One can speak of a literature of mockery, pointing again especially to Grass but also to Vonnegut and a whole school of "black humorists"—constituting an American literary consciousness that Richard Lewis has described as a "joining of the dark thread of apocalypse with the nervous detonations of satiric laughter." For ultimately it is death itself, and particularly threats of the contemporary apocalypse, that protean man and woman mock. A politics of mockery emerged dramatically in the late 1960s and the 1970s: the sequence of the Berkeley Free Speech Movement of 1965 to a "Filthy Speech Movement"; the 1968 slogan of rebellious Columbia University students, "up against the wall, motherfucker"; and that same year, the cry of the French students, "We are all German Jews!" The gifted black comedian Dick Gregory caught the spirit of those times with his blend of mockery, self-mockery, and protest. Now Richard Pryor, mostly on film, brings less protest but more pervasive mockery and self-mockery to the heart of American popular culture. Whether we are protesting or seeking laughter, or (perhaps at our best) both, we seem to require a deep strain of absurdity and mockery for an authentic representation of our inner condition.

Of great importance in the protean style is a struggle with the rites of passage associated with birth, entry into adulthood, marriage, and death. Whatever of these rites remain can seem shallow or inappropriate to protean man or woman, who may in turn seek to modify them or improvise new ones. The ceremonial innovation so publicly visible during the late 1960s and 1970s (hippie weddings, Hindu incantations, multimedia church services) have by no means disappeared but have resurfaced in the cultural mainstream in the form of more modest but still significant alterations in these rites undertaken by people who do not consider themselves rebels or radicals. For what is at stake in these struggles over rites of passage is a culture's arrangements for asserting its symbolizations of immortality—its ritual principles that enable individuals, families, and members of particular religions, political groups, or professions to feel part of something much larger than themselves.

The young people who, in the late 1960s and early 1970s, went off to Oregon or Vermont to form a commune and find new ways of family or group life, were experimenting in the biological mode of symbolic immortality. They were experimenting with spiritual combinations (the theological mode), and with human relationships and with products of imagination (the creative mode), and with a "return to nature" idea (the natural mode). And I need not emphasize how much they have experimented with, and still do experiment with, "high states" or the direct experience of transcendence in whatever form, often with the help of drugs or altered states of consciousness.

Today, in the United States, the protean style, while active, is going more and more underground as it interacts with what seems to be its opposite: the constricted style, which can be represented by Holdfast, a lesser-known mythological deity, a "tyrant-monster" and "keeper of the past."[18] Indeed, the interaction between Proteus and Holdfast is at the core of much of what goes on in American society today. The constricted style is evident in the self of many people who seek one place to be, one set of dogmatic truths—a kind of absolute, which they seek to have imprinted on a permanent immortalizing process or mode. The constricted style is also evident in the resurgence of fundamentalism, in expressions like the Moral Majority in this country. There are, moreover, various admixtures of the protean and the constricted styles. They are perhaps brothers and sisters under the skin, two sides of the same coin; both are likely to take intensive forms under the stress of historical change, which itself is related to the kinds of dislocation that I have been describing. And there is a back-and-forth process, a swing from one to the other and back again: and sometimes under the proteanism is a longing for stability; and underneath the exaggerated stability of the constricted style is a longing for newness and change.

While the protean style carries the danger of diffusion, there is a much more profound threat to any sense of larger human connectedness: that is, our technology of destruction, the nuclear instruments of genocide, and the pseudoreligious phenomenon I call "nuclearism." If we ask what is our overall psychological response to nuclear weapons, I would answer with two words: *fear* and *futurelessness*. The fear, of course, has to do with our own death, the deaths of family members—people close to us; fear of bodily assault; fear of disfiguring burns and keloid scars; fear of invisible contamination, as I call it in my Hiroshima work—that is, a deadly substance that enters one's bones, that one cannot see or smell or taste or touch; and finally, fear of the amorphousness and the mystery and the totality of the impact. The fear extends to profound doubts about our personal future as well as the larger human continuity associated with the symbolization of immortality. For should the weapons be used and a holocaust result, who can be sure of living on in one's children, or one's works, or even in nature or in some form of spiritual survival or continuity? Concerning the last, theologians face a greater crisis than most have recognized: they must ask themselves not only whether it is feasible, but whether it is moral to advocate a theology of spiritual continuity in the absence of living human beings.

The responses of children to nuclear threat have been made much of in recent years, and rightly so. Indeed, there is a kind of false debate or non-debate about whether children are really affected by nuclear threat or whether it is really just activists like myself who have put these bad ideas in children's heads. The question is not whether they are affected, but in what way and how much: this question can be studied and should be studied very carefully. But we recognize in children, as in ourselves, a double life: children preparing for adult life, studying, and imagining marrying and having children of their own, but, in another part of their minds, doubting that this will ever come to pass.

And children for us represent not only young people whom we love and feel responsible for, but also a symbolization of our own future, of that process of being part of the great chain of being and the flow of generations. They represent as well our judgment on our claims to virtue as a culture within an immortality system or a claimed immortality system. That's why Anne Frank—the Jewish adolescent who, after hiding in Holland for years with her family, was captured by the Nazis and killed in Bergen-Belsen—moves us as she does. In her diary she wrote that she felt that people are essentially good—a generous conclusion that we who know of the massive victimization of her and millions of others by adult evil have difficulty sharing.

Less known is a Japanese Anne Frank named Sadako Sasaki, who experienced the bombing of Hiroshima at the age of two, seemed to be untouched, and became an outstanding athlete. Ten years later, at the age of twelve, she began to show symptoms of leukemia. Then she began—as the true story became legend—to fold paper cranes, because the legend in Japan has it that if you fold a thousand paper cranes, you cure yourself of all illnesses. Sasaki, it is said, folded only 946 before she died. Then the children of Hiroshima raised money to build a monument to Sasaki and other children killed by the bomb—a monument that is tended by children and garlanded with paper cranes.[19] Sasaki, too, tells us that children are our human future.

The prospect of nuclear winter (see pages 112–13) clarifies our existential situation by concretizing the idea of the nuclear end and thereby helping us to free ourselves from illusion. The grim message is that, if even a modest amount of nuclear weapons are used—maybe as few as one hundred megatons or a number not exactly known—the sun's rays would be so blocked with dirt and debris as to lower the temperature throughout the world and make it unable to sustain human and other forms of animal and plant life. Nuclear winter tells us loud and clear that hope does not lie in preparation for nuclear war; hope lies only in prevention. Nuclear winter tells us that the only form of survival in nuclear war is imaginative survival—or, one might say, pre-emptive imagination.

The illusions from which nuclear winter liberates us include those of preparation, protection, and recovery. While I won't go into the absurdities that have been written about these matters (although our task as students of human behavior is to expose these illusions as illusions), what is interesting here is that the people of the Soviet Union and the United States—as we all struggle for viable immortality systems—do not believe in the false official claims that their governments will protect them somehow with something called civil defense. There is a joke (by now well known but highly relevant here) told by Soviet doctors, which goes the rounds of the Soviet Union: " 'Comrade, what are our instructions should nuclear air raid sirens go off?' And the other man answers, 'Well, you should know that, Comrade. Our instructions are to put a sheet over your head and walk very slowly to the nearest graveyard.' The other man asks, 'Why very slowly?' And the answer: 'So as not to cause a panic.' " Well, isn't this exactly the same as the American counterpart, those posters that tell you what to do in a nuclear attack: you open your shirt and you take off your glasses, and then you bend your head and put it low between your legs—and kiss your ass good-bye. There you have examples of Soviet and American folk wisdom, which tell us the truth, a kind of truth that the two governments are only gradually and reluctantly learning.

Nuclear winter propels our imagination in its quest for immortalizing concepts and immortalizing commitments; it also propels our imaginations in the direction of nothingness. In a later essay (chapter 11) I will discuss expressions of nothingness in Hiroshima and in Auschwitz. Here I want to stress the paradox that imagery of nothingness poses for us: it is on the one hand crucial to our grasp of our predicament, but on the other, a formidable impediment to our psychic struggles to maintain a sense of human continuity. The paradox can be at least partly resolved if we are aware that we bring our moral imagination to bear on nothingness in order to find ways to reject that fate; that we look into the abyss in order to see beyond it. There are dangers, of course: the lure or longing for that nothingness discussed in the introduction in connection with secular and religious Armageddonists—that attraction given brilliantly grotesque expression in Dr. Strangelove's joyous "nuclear high."

Less dramatic but more threatening because more pervasive is the overall constellation of nuclearism, the exaggerated dependency on the weapons to the point of worship, which seeks from them precisely what they cannot give—security, safety, even salvation—the means of keeping the world going. Here the mind refuses responsibility for applying itself to genuine expressions of human continuity and instead renders the weapons themselves immortalizing objects. After all, the weapons can do what in the past only God could do: destroy the world. And the expectation from them is that, like every self-respecting deity, they should also be able to re-create the world. Well, they can do the first, but not the second.

Of course, this ultimate form of idolatry—worshiping a technological object as a god—creates its own immortality system, so that the very objects that could destroy human civilization and the human species are embraced as a basis for symbolizing the endless continuity—the immortality—of that species.

What I have called the "retirement syndrome"—or the retirement *wisdom* of certain political and military leaders previously committed to nuclearism—reveals much about that idolatrous nuclear-weapons–centered immortality system. For instance, when Admiral Hyman Rickover, the father of the nuclear navy, retired some years ago, he declared that the weapons endanger all of us, and will destroy us unless we do something about them; and he expressed regret about the role he had played in building them up. At the moment of retirement, he seemed to reverse the stand he had taken during his entire professional career—and he was not the first to do so. President Dwight Eisenhower's eloquent warning about the dangers of the military-industrial complex—after his administration had built up that same complex—was also a retirement speech. Such retirement wisdom goes back to Henry Stimson who, as secretary of war, had most to do with the decision to drop the two atomic bombs on Japan: he sent a moving document to President Harry S Truman advocating internationalization of nuclear weapons for the sake of the human future. In all these cases, retirement wisdom suggests a tacit recognition of having been bound by the institutional nuclearism of high public office, and, upon one's leaving that office, a capacity to allow prior doubts to surface and become part of a reasoned, often eloquent critique of the nuclearistic ideology one knew so well. But retirement wisdom also contains a condemnation of the idolatrous immortality system constructed around the weapons, as a means of extricating from that system first oneself, then one's country, and ultimately the world. Those who bring us such retirement wisdom—I think especially now of a group of anti-nuclear admirals—are prophets who have known, and in varying degrees succumbed to, deadly temptation and, in rejecting that temptation, articulate its true nature to their people.

In doing that, they begin to take on a very different relationship to symbolic immortality: one based on committing themselves to what becomes for them the newly precious principle of identifying with the human species and its larger continuity. In precisely that kind of commitment lies the future of immortality.

The protean style expresses a struggle to revitalize modes of immortality—a revitalization, I would stress, that depends upon some confrontation of nuclear threat. The protean style is very much part of the nuclear-age ethos (discussed in chapter 20). That relationship between protean style and commitment to human continuity is better understood if examined briefly for each of the modes of symbolic immortality. For the biological and biosocial mode, consider the very important lived definitions of maleness and femaleness, of appropriate or acceptable gender behavior. Prominent in American culture now is an extreme version, a near caricature of a male ideal of a tough, brutal, violent, tight-lipped sexual conqueror (the Rambo or Rocky phenomenon). But side by side with that ideal, and only slightly beneath the surface, is protean experimentation with a more gentle ideal, that of an open, noncombative self-explorer, willing to inhabit formerly "female" areas and aesthetic concerns. Similarly, even as we encounter newly prominent expressions of the traditional, self-sacrificing, family-immersed woman helpmate, there are being crafted various versions of psychically and physically assertive, self-assured proponents of a very different female ideal. In either case, the experiments take on profound cultural significance and great human power only when they can contribute to overcoming violence ultimately related to nuclear threat. (There may be certain differences in men and women in relation to the protean style, with women more able to remain bound in human continuity, and men provided more opportunities for protean experience, though prone to anxiety associated with diffusion. This is a particularly important area for additional study.)

Similarly, for the theological mode, the most urgent experimental tasks involve the creation of principles that contribute to the shared-fate side of the intra-Christian struggle (mentioned in the introduction) and combat fundamentalist expressions of Armageddonism. Concerning the creative mode, various important critiques of existing American and world institutions take on lasting significance only as alternatives to the threat of human extinction. And the natural mode is significantly realized only when the self's relation to nature becomes a means of articulating and combating the potential consequences of dangerous uses of technology, especially nuclear technology. Even protean quests for the experience of transcendence are best realized when part of a flow of larger connectedness, part of a sustained commitment to humanity associated with reverberations of a species self (see chapter 9).

In sum, our cultural innovations take on genuine significance only insofar as they contribute to maintaining the planet. Above all, the future of immortality, if it and we are to have a future, exists within us now, here—at this moment and this place.

PART I

IN EXTREMIS

What happened—really happened.
What happened—really happened.
What happened—really happened.
I believe with perfect faith
That I will have the strength to believe that
What happened—really happened.

—T. Carmi

2

Is Hiroshima Our Text?

I was recently told that a prominent Zen Buddhist leader in this country has made a vow to himself that, in any conversation he enters into, he must bring up the subject of nuclear threat. That includes—so the story goes—the most casual social conversations, talks with taxi drivers, brief exchanges with strangers, whatever. The vow did not sound strange to me. Without being quite aware of it, I had, in effect, made a similar, if much more modest, vow to myself: that in any public statement I make on nuclear threat, I will bring up the subject of Hiroshima.

My strong impulse is to convey to everyone Hiroshima's indelible impact upon me. And I also have come to sense, as both psychiatrist and anti-nuclear activist, the special power of specific Hiroshima or Nagasaki images for those able to receive them. Images that extreme are best described in relatively quiet, understated tones that encourage reflection on our contemporary situation. The themes put forward in this essay (originally from a chapter of mine in a book co-authored with Richard Falk, Indefensible Weapons*) are meant to portray Hiroshima not as an event of the past, but as a source of necessary knowledge for the present and the future.*

Those Hiroshima images continue their insistent claim on me: the searing details of survivors' experiences; the moving scenes, collective pain, and ultimate inadequacy of the 6 August day of commemoration; our own bittersweet family celebration, with a few Hiroshima friends, of our son's first birthday. Put most simply, the six months spent in

Hiroshima in 1962 have formed in me a special constellation of truth that, when I am wise enough to draw upon it, informs everything I have to say about nuclear threat and much else.

I ARRIVED in Hiroshima in the early spring of 1962. I intended no more than a brief visit. But very quickly I made a discovery that I found almost incomprehensible. It had been seventeen years since the dropping of the first atomic weapon on an inhabited city—surely one of the tragic turning points in human history—and no one had studied the impact of that event. There had of course been research on the physical aftereffects of the bomb, and there had been brief commentaries here and there on behavior of some of the survivors at the time of the bomb and afterward. But there had been no systematic examination of what had taken place in people's lives, of the psychological and social consequences of the bomb.

I came to a terrible, but I believe essentially accurate, rule of thumb: the more significant an event, the less likely it is to be studied. Again, there are reasons. One reason, certainly relevant to Hiroshima, has to do with the fear and pain the event arouses—the unacceptable images to which one must, as an investigator, expose oneself. To this anxiety and pain I can certainly attest.

But another source of avoidance is the threat posed to our traditional assumptions and conventional ways of going about our studies. We would rather avoid looking at events that, by their very nature, must change us and our relation to the world. We prefer to hold on to our presuppositions and habits of personal and professional function. And we may well sense that seriously studying such an event means being haunted by it from then on, taking on a lifelong burden of responsibility to it.

I was able to stay in Hiroshima and conduct interview research with people there over a six-month period. The best way I know to describe a few of my findings that might be of use to us now is to look at the Hiroshima experience as taking place in four stages.

The first stage was the immersion in the sea of dead and near-dead at the time the bomb fell. This was the beginning of what I have called a permanent encounter with death. But it was not just death: it was grotesque and absurd death, which had no relationship to the life cycle as such. There was a sudden and absolute shift from normal existence to this overwhelming immersion in death.

Survivors recalled not only feeling that they themselves would soon die but experiencing the sense that *the whole world was dying.* For instance, a science professor who had been covered by falling debris and temporarily blinded remembered: "My body seemed all black. Everything seemed dark, dark all over. Then I thought, 'The world is ending.' " And a Protestant minister, responding to scenes of mutilation and destruction he saw everywhere, told me: "The feeling I had was that everyone was dead. The whole city was destroyed. . . . I thought all of my family must be dead. It doesn't matter if I die. . . . I thought this was the end of Hiroshima, of Japan, of humankind." And a writer later recorded her impressions:

> I just could not understand why our surroundings changed so greatly in one instant. . . . I thought it must have been something which had nothing to do with the war, the collapse of the earth, which was said to take place at the end of the world, which I had read about as a child. . . . There was a fearful silence, which made me feel that all people . . . were dead.[1]

As psychiatrists, we are accustomed to look upon imagery of the end of the world as a symptom of mental illness, usually paranoid psychosis (see chapter 11, page 148ff). But here it may be said that this imagery is a more or less appropriate response to an extraordinary external event (see chapter 4, page 53).

In referring to themselves and others at the time, survivors described themselves as "walking ghosts," or, as one man said of himself: "I was not really alive." People were literally uncertain about whether they were dead or alive, which was why I came to call my study of the event *Death in Life* (1968).

Indicative of the nature of the event is the extraordinary disparity in estimates of the number of people killed by the bomb. These vary from less than 70,000 to more than 250,000, with the City of Hiroshima estimating 200,000. These estimates depend on who one counts and how one goes about counting, and can be subject at either end to various ideological and emotional influences. But the simple truth is that nobody really knows how many people have been killed by the Hiroshima bomb, and such was the confusion at the time that nobody will ever know.

The second stage was associated with what I call "invisible contamination." Within hours or days or weeks after the bomb fell, people—even some who had appeared to be untouched by the bomb—began to experience grotesque symptoms: severe diarrhea and weakness, ulceration of the mouth and gums with bleeding, bleeding from all of the body orifices and into the skin, high fever; extremely low white blood cell counts when these could be taken; and later, loss of scalp and body hair—the condition often following a progressive course until death. These were symptoms of acute radiation effects. People did not know that at the time, of course; and even surviving doctors thought it was some kind of strange epidemic. Ordinary people spoke of a mysterious "poison."

But the kind of terror experienced by survivors can be understood from the rumors that quickly spread among them. One rumor simply held that everyone in Hiroshima would be dead within a few months or a few years. The symbolic message here was: none can escape the poison; the epidemic is total—all shall die. But there was a second rumor, reported to me even more frequently and with greater emotion: the belief that trees, grass, and flowers would never again grow in Hiroshima; that from that day on, the city would be unable to sustain vegetation of any kind. The meaning here was that nature was drying up altogether. Life was being extinguished at its source—an ultimate form of desolation that not only encompassed human death but went beyond it.

These early symptoms were the first large-scale manifestation of the invisible contamination stemming from the atomic particles. The symptoms also gave rise to a special image in the minds of the people of Hiroshima—an image of a force that not only kills and destroys on a colossal scale but also leaves behind in the bodies of those exposed to it deadly influences that may emerge at any time and strike down their victims. That image has also made its way to the rest of us, however we have resisted it.

The third stage of Hiroshima survivors' encounter with death occurred not weeks or months but years after the bomb fell, with the discovery (beginning in 1948 and 1949) that various forms of leukemia were increasing in incidence among survivors sufficiently exposed to irradiation. That fatal malignancy of the blood-forming organs became the model for the relatively loose but highly significant term "A-bomb disease." Then, over decades, there have been increases in various forms of cancer—first thyroid cancer, and then cancer of the breast, lung, stomach, bone marrow, and other areas. Since the latent period for radiation-induced cancer can be quite long, and since for many forms it is still not known, the results are by no means in. Researchers are still learning about increases in different cancers, and the truth is that the incidence of virtually *any* form of cancer can be increased by exposure to radiation.

An additional array of harmful bodily influences have been either demonstrated, or are suspected, to be caused by radiation exposure—including impaired growth and development, premature aging, various blood diseases, endocrine and skin disorders, damage to the central nervous system, and a vague but persistently reported borderline condition of general weakness and debilitation. Again, the returns are not in. But on a chronic level of bodily concern, survivors have the feeling that the bomb can do anything, and that anything it does is likely to be fatal. Moreover, there are endless situations in which neither survivors themselves nor the most astute physicians can say with any certainty where physical radiation effects end and psychological manifestations begin. There is always a "nagging doubt." For instance, I retain a vivid memory of a talk I had in Hiroshima with a distinguished physician who, despite injuries and radiation effects of his own, had at the time of the bomb courageously attempted to care for patients around him. He spoke in philosophical terms of the problem of radiation effects as one that "man cannot solve"; but when I asked him about general anxieties he smiled uneasily and spoke in a way that gave me the strong sense that a raw nerve had been exposed:

> Yes, of course, people are anxious. Take my own case. If I am shaving in the morning and I should happen to cut myself very slightly, I dab the blood with a piece of paper—and then, when I notice that it has stopped flowing, I think to myself, "Well, I guess I am all right."[2]

Nor does the matter end with one's own body or life. There is the fear that this invisible contamination will manifest itself in the next generation, because it is scientifically known that such abnormalities *can* be caused by radiation. There is medical controversy here about whether genetic abnormalities have occurred: they have not been convincingly demonstrated in studies on comparative populations, but abnormalities in the chromosomes of exposed survivors have been demonstrated. People, of course, retain profound anxiety about the possibility of transmitting this deadly taint to subsequent generations. For instance, when I revisited Hiroshima in 1980, people said to me: "Well, maybe the next generation is okay after all, but what about the third generation?" The fact is that, scientifically speaking, no one can assure them with certainty that subsequent generations will not be affected. Again, nobody knows. So there is no end point for possible damage, or for anxiety.

No wonder, then, that a number of survivors told me that they considered the dropping of the bomb to be a "big experiment" by the United States. It was a new weapon; its effects were unknown; American authorities wanted to see what those effects would be. Unfortunately, there is more than a kernel of truth in that claim, at least in its suggestion of one among several motivations. More important for us now is the idea that any use of nuclear warheads would still be, in a related sense, "experimental."

The fourth stage of the Hiroshima experience is its culmination in a lifelong identification with the dead—so extreme in many cases as to cause survivors to feel "as if dead" and to take on what I spoke of as an "identity of the dead." Hiroshima and Nagasaki survivors became, in their own eyes as well as in those of others, a tainted group, one whose collective identity was formed around precisely the continuous death immersion and the invisible contamination I have been discussing. The identity can include what we may think of as paradoxical guilt—the tendency of survivors to berate themselves inwardly for having remained alive while others died, and for not having been able to do more to save others or to combat the general evil at the time of the bomb. In connection with the latter, the sense of "failed enactment"[3] can have little to do with what was possible at the time or with what one actually did or did not do.

More than that, survivors underwent what can be called a second victimization in the form of significant discrimination in two fundamental areas of life: marriage and work. The "logic" of the discrimination was the awareness of potential marriage partners (or families and go-betweens involved in making marriage arrangements) and prospective employers that survivors are susceptible to aftereffects of the bomb, making them poor bets for marriage (and healthy children) and employment. But the deeper, often unconscious feeling about atomic bomb survivors was that they were death-tainted, that they were reminders of a fearful event people did not want to be reminded of, that they were "carriers," so to speak, of the dreaded "A-bomb disease."

At the end of my study of these events, I spoke of Hiroshima, together with Nagasaki, as a last chance, a nuclear catastrophe from which one could still learn. The bombs had been dropped, there was an "end of the world" in ways I have described, yet the world still exists. And precisely in this end-of-the-world quality of Hiroshima lies both its threat and its potential wisdom.

Is Hiroshima, then, our text? Certainly as our *only* text, it would be quite inadequate. We know well that what happened there could not really represent what would happen to people if our contemporary nuclear warheads were used. When the Hiroshima and Nagasaki bombs were dropped, they were the only two functional atomic bombs in the world. Now there are approximately fifty thousand nuclear warheads, most of them having many times—some a hundred or a thousand or more times—the destructive and contaminating (through radiation) power of those first "tiny" bombs. While those early bombs initiated a revolution in killing power, we may speak of another subsequent technological revolution of even greater dimensions in its magnification of that killing power. The scale of Hiroshima was difficult enough to grasp; now the scale is again so radically altered that holding literally to Hiroshima images misleads us in the direction of extreme understatement.

Yet despite all that, Hiroshima and Nagasaki hold out important nuclear-age truths for us. The first of these is the *totality of destruction.* It has been pointed out that Tokyo and Dresden were decimated no less than was Hiroshima. But in Hiroshima it was one plane, one bomb, one city destroyed. And the result of that single bomb was incalculable death and suffering.

A second Hiroshima truth for us is that of the weapon's *unending lethal influence.* Radiation effects were (and are) such that the experience has had no cutoff point. Survivors have the possibility of experiencing delayed but deadly radiation effects for the rest of their lives. That possibility extends to their children, to their children's children, indefinitely into the future—over how many generations no one knows. And we have seen how the physical and psychological blend in relation to these continuing effects.

A third truth, really derived from the other two, has to do with Hiroshima and Nagasaki survivors' identification of themselves as *victims of an ultimate weapon*—of a force that threatens to exterminate the species. This sense had considerable impact on Hiroshima survivors, sometimes creating in them an expectation of future nuclear destruction of all of humankind and most of the earth.

And there is still something more to be said about Hiroshima and Nagasaki regarding our perceptions of nuclear danger. The two cities convey to us a sense of *nuclear actuality.* The bombs were really used there. We can read, view, and, if we will allow ourselves, *feel* what happened to people in them. In the process we experience emotions such as awe, dread, and wonder (at the extent and nature of killing, maiming, and destruction)—emotions surely appropriate to our current nuclear threat. Such emotions can transform our intellectual and moral efforts against nuclear killing into a personal mission—one with profound ethical, spiritual, and sometimes religious overtones. Hiroshima, then, is indeed our text, even if in miniature.

The argument is sometimes extended to the point of claiming that this sense of nuclear actuality has prevented full-scale nuclear war; that, in the absence of the restraining influence of Hiroshima and Nagasaki, the United States and the Soviet Union would have by now embarked upon nuclear annihilation. The claim is difficult to evaluate; and while I feel some of its persuasiveness, I do not quite accept it. In any case, one must raise a countervailing argument having to do with another dimension of Hiroshima and Nagasaki's nuclear actuality: namely, the legitimation of a nation's using atomic bombs on human populations under certain conditions (in this case, wartime). Once a thing has been done, it is psychologically and in a sense morally easier for it to be done again. That legitimation can then combine with an argument minimizing the effects of the Hiroshima bomb: the claim that one has unfortunately heard more than once from American leaders that Hiroshima's having been rebuilt as a city is evidence that one can fight and recover from a limited nuclear war.

Here I may say that part of Hiroshima's value as a text is in its contrasts with our current situation. One crucial contrast has to do with the existence of an outside world to help. Hiroshima could slowly recover from the bomb because there were intact people who came in from the outside and brought healing energies to the city. Help was erratic and slow in arriving, but it did become available: from nearby areas (including a few medical teams); from Japanese returning from former overseas possessions; and, to some extent, from the American Occupation. The groups converging on Hiroshima in many cases contributed more to the recovery of the city as such than to that of individual survivors (physically, mentally, or economically). But they made possible the city's revitalization and repopulation.

In Hiroshima there was a total breakdown of the social and communal structure—of the web of institutions and arrangements necessary to the function of any human group. But because of the existence and intervention of an intact outside world, that social breakdown could be temporary.

Given the number and power of our current nuclear warheads, can one reasonably assume that there will be an intact outside world to help? I do not think so.

Like any powerful text, Hiroshima must be read, absorbed, and re-created by each generation searching for its own truths.

3

The Hiroshima Connection

> A man's real possession is his memory. In nothing else is he rich, in nothing else is he poor.
>
> —ALEXANDER SMITH

This essay belongs to the memory of Robert Vas, the filmmaker whom I worked with during the Hiroshima revisit described in this essay. Vas was a Hungarian Jew who had known too many persecutions and dislocations. He survived the Nazis during the Second World War, the Soviets during the Hungarian Revolution of 1956, then a decade of living and working in an alien English culture. An artist within the documentary mode, he was able to infuse his work with his own survivor sensibility and made a brilliant film on Hiroshima (To Die, to Live—Survivors of Hiroshima). *A year later he killed himself. I remember the anger toward him my wife and I felt, mixed with our pain, when we learned of his suicide. We felt he had no right to terminate so gifted a life, or to shut off a talent so hard won and so desperately needed.*

It is all a question of memory: survivors' thirty-year-old memories, sometimes fading only to reassert their enduring claim; Vas's sensitive perceptions of the bomb experience mediated through memories of his own survivals; my own memories of the city from 1962—and now my memories of Vas. One learns that, even as memories seem to have receded, they can powerfully assert themselves, whether malignantly or illuminatingly. The Hiroshima connection is a bridge of memory between what we human beings have already done, and what we might do to change our course.

THE NIGHT before leaving Tokyo for Hiroshima, where I was to spend most of the month of May 1975 collaborating on a BBC film based on my book *Death in Life,* I had a vivid and disturbing dream. I was the head of a team of doctors about to examine a desperately ill child. We knew that the little boy would die, but our examination seemed important for some obscure humanitarian purpose. The child's father, also a doctor, stood protectively at the bedside as I approached, introduced myself and my colleagues, and reassured the little boy that I would not hurt him. Beginning the examination, I observed a large swelling that protruded from around his eye and asked, "Does your eye feel as though it is swollen?" Before the child could answer, his father responded in a pained, angry voice, "Of course, it feels as though it is swollen—you can see that!" Though I knew there was a good reason for conducting my examination, I nonetheless felt upset by the father's answer, very uneasy toward both father and son, as the dream faded away. It was uncertain whether I had completed the examination.

The dream expressed, among other things, my own painful uncertainties about approaching Hiroshima once more. After all, we *know* that people died in the tens or hundreds of thousands, suffered from grotesque immediate radiation effects, and are still suffering from deadly delayed effects; and that survivors' psychological suffering, compounded of fear and taint, reflects their uniquely intense, many-layered, and, above all, *unending* encounter with death. As the father of the little boy in the dream—the other doctor, Hiroshima's own spokesman—said to me, in effect: The distortion and death are fully visible to anyone. Additional examinations—more questions—these only humiliate further.

At the heart of the dream is my inner question about the "humane purpose" justifying the examination—or, in more general terms, the possible connection between Hiroshima and humanity.

For me, involvement with the city (beginning in April 1962) transformed the question of that connection from a vaguely troubling image in the back of my mind to a continuous and still more troubling personal and professional preoccupation. I was aware of considerable uneasiness at now returning to Hiroshima, eight years since my last visit and thirteen since my original six-month study. The images in the dream reflected conscious anxieties about again approaching survivors, or *hibakusha* ("explosion-affected persons"), having doubts as I did concerning their capacity and inclination to convey any more about their experience than they already had; about spending my energies going "backward" rather than "forward" in time while wondering whether *I* had anything more to say about Hiroshima; about the vicissitudes of historical memory—in them, in me, and in everyone else. How could I not question this further pursuit of a thirty-year-old memory—of what Elie Wiesel has called "a memory of a memory"—in death-haunted witnesses to the ultimate form of mid-twentieth century technological slaughter?

A discussion of some of these issues with Tokyo friends, a sociologist-historian couple long committed to peace efforts, did not dispel these anxieties but did give them more specific contemporary reference to Japan and Hiroshima. Working with a small citizens' group (which they and others had come to prefer to the mass political organizations that had made use of atomic-bomb issues for their own aggrandizement), my friends were struck by how little students and young adults in Tokyo knew about Hiroshima: the war in Vietnam had long been for them, as for us, a much more immediate issue. Only recently had some of them begun to think seriously about nuclear weapons—brought back to them, so to speak, indirectly by issues raised in the Vietnam War, in protests of deaths from environmental poisoning, and with plutonium-based nuclear-energy programs. But, by and large, Hiroshima and its related "victim consciousness" has been out of step with the expansive, forward-looking Japanese mood that has accompanied the country's decades of spectacular economic and technological achievements. Whether all that would be changed by recent economic reversals and political reassessments remained to be seen.

Arriving in Hiroshima, I found that there, too, the "Don't look back" impulse was strong. The dynamism of the rebuilding process had been clear enough during my two earlier stays, but now the city seemed to have taken off into the postmodern future—high-rise, automated buildings everywhere; frantic vehicle and human traffic; a glittering consumerism propagated by the large department-store chains; and a greatly enlarged amusement section, with attractive bars and restaurants and gaudily beckoning nightclubs, strip shows, and sex stores featuring "toys for adults." All this may not be the "real Hiroshima," but when one looks at it together with its business-industrial underpinnings, one can begin to understand how the atomic-bomb experience can (and for many in the city has) come to be viewed as an embarrassment, best ignored. As for the survivors themselves, they are, as a group, aging, dying off, becoming an increasingly small minority (90,000 in a city of 500,000), whose special history must begin to fade even where it is not actively swept away.

Beyond the atomic-bomb experience itself, I felt the strangeness of my meetings with survivors—thirteen years of silence between two intense encounters. It was like stepping out of a time machine—young men projected into balding middle age, teen-aged girls into settled housewives and mothers (they did not tell me what they made of my own graying temples and slightly increased girth around the middle). Part of that time-machine effect was the dramatic change at least some had experienced in economic status. One man, who had shown unusual dedication in helping people and keeping things going at the time of the bomb and whom I had known as a middle-aged laborer, now appeared before me as an old man in a comfortable sitting room lined with the golf trophies of his son, an independent businessman in whose house the laborer was living out his retirement. Another man, with injuries affecting the use of one hand and extensive keloid scars, whom I had known as a street vendor of postcards and atomic-bomb mementos, now proudly demonstrated his small, aesthetically pleasing, and well-stocked bar. Like many *hibakusha* I talked to, they told me of having focused for some time upon everyday existence—being comfortable, earning a living, getting on. While not without resentment toward the more favored Hiroshima majority who had never known their pain, they nonetheless felt their own need to join in with the message of the milieu to let go of the past. Or at least to concentrate sufficiently on the present to try to make up for what they had lost. One woman, also still carrying a keloid scar but proud of all she had done to reconstitute her life, expressed a general sentiment when she said, "I would like my mind and spirit to be the equal of yours."

None of this is surprising. One could hardly expect people to wish to remain fixed in time for thirty years on an event that signifies only pain in the extreme. The change over the thirteen years of my particular time machine was exemplified by a survivor who, as a young clerk during my first stay in Hiroshima, spoke disapprovingly of the children swimming in a nearby river whom he had observed on the way to one of our meetings: "Those who went through the bomb would never swim there. I remember passing that spot and seeing dead bodies floating on the water—burnt and black dead bodies. Whenever I see that part of the river, I recall that scene." Now, however, "My thinking has changed. I have three children myself and I often go to the Peace Park with them, where we play together with the pigeons." The symbolic shift is from the survivor's indelible image to a state in which pleasure and play become permissible on the very ground of holocaust.*

Yet something more nags at each of them—something having to do with the meaning of their experience and the possibility of connecting it with a world outside (and yet not outside) of that experience. Even those

* For my distinction between *holocaust* and *The Holocaust,* see pages 231–32.

most adamant about leaving the memory behind would always express qualifications. One woman spoke bitterly of her disappointments and missed opportunities for marriage because of her keloid scars and insisted, "I don't want to touch the past." But a little later, she said sadly and softly, "And yet, having stayed alive for thirty years, I would somehow like to make use of my experience. I would like to leave something behind me, some trace."

We all, of course, have similar desires. The need to leave a trace is part of the universal aspiration toward continuity and connectedness, toward symbolic immortality. But for Hiroshima survivors the trace one seeks to leave behind—the means of achieving what I am calling the "Hiroshima connection"—becomes mostly the story of one's exposure to nuclear annihilation. That story, or rendition, of the human actuality of the atomic-bomb experience is precisely the rare commodity they possess. They and others sense the universal value of that commodity, but for *hibakusha* its potential for human connectedness (even recognition) is inseparable from something close to ultimate pain. The very combination, as a survivor explained to me some time ago, creates an added source of humiliation: "I always say, if anyone looks at me because I received the Nobel Prize, that's okay, but if my only virtue is that I was a thousand meters from the atomic-bomb center and I am still alive, I don't want to be famous for that." To the perils of this double-edged historical memory and its double humiliation must be added that of repetition and "performance" in the telling of the story. The human actuality so desperately sought (and avoided) turns out to be as difficult to re-create as it is invaluable. The whole process is maintained by the survivor's profound need to find meaning in his or her death immersion on the one hand and the world's need for the Hiroshima story on the other—the latter always expressed ambivalently, fearfully, and often aversively. Has there ever been a historical memory so complex and difficult in its constellation of "trace"?

Certain survivors, of course, give considerable energy and substance to that "trace." For me one of the most memorable experiences in Hiroshima was a visit to an orphanage headed by a *hibakusha* social worker. His preoccupation with helping abandoned children stemmed directly from an indelible image from the time of the bomb of a dying child with its dead mother, both almost totally burned, and of his own failure to rescue the child. Next to a small shrine he called "the sacred place of the orphanage," mother and child were represented by an exquisitely simple sculpture consisting of two rounded pieces of stone, next to which was still a third, somewhat more elongated stone representing a dying man to whose plea for water the survivor had not responded. Part of his daily ritual consisted of pouring water over each of the three stones, as if to offer now what he had been unable to offer then. One has the impression that this ritual helped energize his "survivor mission," his "Hiroshima connection" with the needs of the people of that city.

Others sought active connection beyond their city. An elderly poet, whose young son had died in the bomb, told me how, thirty years later, "the dead still live in my mind." In one poem he described how "the blood of men and women has soaked into . . . every grain of sand." He saw himself as a witness whose mission was to make it possible for others to "feel close to these [atomic-bomb] experiences." He sought to make his poetry available to Hiroshima schoolchildren, as well as for translation into other languages; and one could feel his frustration—the survivor's built upon the writer's—at the limitations he encountered in dissemination and response.

Another man (whom I had previously described as a "zealot saint") has been conducting for the full thirty years an uninterrupted one-man campaign (following the death of a twelve-year-old girl from leukemia) against the bomb and its evil—organizing and leading a children's group devoted to peace and to helping survivors; initiating a campaign that resulted in a monument, now standing in the Peace Park, to children killed by the atomic bomb; writing letters to world leaders; and distributing paper cranes (symbolizing peace and long life) to Hiroshima visitors and correspondents throughout the world. All this he did in his spare time, required as he was to gain his livelihood by working as a janitor in a school. Though undoubtedly a force in the city, his efforts were somewhat scattered and always desperate. Now he told me he was busy collecting atomic-bomb accounts of the most neglected group of survivors, the Koreans, long victims of severe discrimination at the hands of the Japanese; and I was touched to hear him say that he had been influenced in doing this by observing (participating in) my own interviews with survivors thirteen years before. A visit to his tiny apartment told everything: a mountain of clutter of atomic-bomb memorabilia—newspaper stories, pictures, albums, books, boxes with unspecified contents, and, above all, hundreds of thousands of paper cranes. Clearly he would never relent, and I wondered when the absolute requirements of his kind of atomic-bomb connection would literally crowd him out of his living space, just as it had already excluded everything else from his psychic space.

And then there was the retired professor of ethics who has become an almost legendary figure in Hiroshima, conducting his "sitting protest"—cross-legged, straight-backed, silently—whenever any country is revealed to have made a test explosion of a nuclear weapon. Concerning memory, he commented with the utmost simplicity, "I remember because I can't forget." His Hiroshima connection also begins with and remains grounded in the dead on whose behalf he sees himself sitting. But it must be hard for him to sustain his faith in the forward-looking purpose of his protest: to initiate what he called "a chain reaction of spiritual atoms to overcome the chain reaction of material atoms." While neither international politics nor contemporary physics provides much evidence for the realization of that purpose, the sitting protest nonetheless disseminates its own human currents. I can attest personally to that, as, upon encountering him at the Hiroshima Peace Park during one such protest, I sat down beside him.

One Hiroshima journalist made the metaphorical distinction between "masculine" and "feminine" *hibakusha* styles (whatever one's actual sex): the masculine style that of actively joining in with the economic boom and looking ahead toward renewal; the feminine style that of remaining preoccupied with the bomb and with helping those in any way wounded by it. There may be a kernel of truth to this metaphor, but most survivors of either sex experienced considerable conflict about where and how to sustain their connection with the world. A truck driver with keloid scars, whose feelings of humiliation and extreme sensitivities had resulted in frequent job changes and considerable personal instability, put it this way: "There are two ways to think about the problem of remembering. One is to appeal to people in some form of peace movement. The other is to be silent and just go on living." His way was more the second, but he was uncertain which was best. Similarly, in one breath he said that, despite indelible images that will never disappear, "I must be a forward-looking man—I can't always go back to the past"; and in another, expressed a considerable resentment at the fact that "people tend to forget."

A professor of sociology was critical of "exaggerations" concerning the bomb and suggested that the Hiroshima connection ought to emphasize "a brighter perspective . . . that so many people can recover from total destruction, can rebuild from ashes . . . which says something about the human capacity for recovery." Yet over the course of our talk, a different sense emerged. Not only did he characterize the atomic bomb as "a weapon of massacre," but his own lingering fears undermined the "brighter perspective" he advocated. Married to another *hibakusha,* those fears seemed to extend endlessly over the generations: "I have always worried about aftereffects in my children. Up till now there have been none. Our first daughter married and had a baby. . . . Both her husband's parents are *hibakusha*—just a normal baby. Everything is okay, I think. But I do worry a bit."

These conflicts find bodily expression in ways that pose particularly poignant dilemmas for Hiroshima physicians. On the one hand, they have witnessed the most grievous suffering in their patients, from burns and radiation effects (including leukemia and many forms of cancer). They have observed as well the death-haunted psychological state induced by the fear of "A-bomb disease." Many doctors, therefore, support ever more comprehensive government programs of medical and other benefits for *hibakusha.* Yet the same doctors cannot help but become aware of the vicious circle of dependency that results. For instance, one doctor, recently retired from the directorship of a leading medical center and known for his compassion for *hibakusha,* told me that he favored these extended benefits but at the same time was saddened by a pattern he frequently encountered: "For some *hibakusha,* especially older ones, the only purpose in life is going early in the morning to a hospital, waiting around for several hours, and spending the whole day in that way, with no other activity or goal." To be sure, this kind of degrading medical immersion can occur under many different conditions; but in relationship to the atomic bomb, it suggests a pathetic effort to achieve the Hiroshima connection through recognition of bodily impairment, through confirmation as a member of a death-tainted group.

No wonder people in Hiroshima constantly spoke of *munashi,* or "emptiness." Used in Hiroshima, the word suggests that nothing has meaning; nothing connects. A professor of English expressed a similar sentiment when he said that, as a result of the bomb, "This is not soil in which things take root. Things do not grow well here." He was referring to every aspect of cultural experience, including the capacity to evolve ideas and images that could connect with the outside. It was as if the original post-bomb rumor that nothing would ever again grow in Hiroshima was proving to be metaphorically true for the vegetation of culture and history.

Probably no *hibakusha* lacks a considerable element of *munashi* (nor is it totally absent in the rest of us), even if combined with pride in recovery and self-assertion. One woman, who reflected all of these feelings, went on to articulate the bodily taint surrounding the Hiroshima connection in its most bitter extreme: "I have no choice but to accept the fact that I am a *hibakusha.* But when I begin to face the idea of death, at least there I want to be spared from A-bomb disease. I don't think that I could stand the thought that I will eventually die of A-bomb disease. The thought of dying of an ordinary disease is a consolation to me."

Another contradiction in the Hiroshima connection is expressed by the angry frustration of many *hibakusha* at the "festival atmosphere" of the annual 6 August commemoration of the bomb, which seems to them to mock their suffering and "insult the dead." A semi-retired professor of history suggested an alternative form of commemoration: "On that day all the doors in the city should be closed. People who visited the city would say, 'I went to Hiroshima on that day. All the stores were shut. No one was to be seen.' Hiroshima should be made into a city of the dead."

But the most intense individual experience of *munashi* that I encountered was in a man I had met thirteen years before as a vibrant and original young writer (not himself a *hibakusha* but, through death and suffering in his family, very close to the experience) and who now appeared before me in despairing, stagnant middle age. He told me that over those thirteen years he had written almost nothing and had spent his time instead "mostly getting drunk." He explained that, until the early 1960s, he found the human struggles in Hiroshima centering on disintegration and renewal important and interesting to write about. But after that the economic boom and the slogans of "doubling personal income and doubling productivity" were considerably less inspiring, and in fact close to sacrilegious: "When we consider those who died, we should not permit ourselves to eat good food, to take sexual pleasure so freely. We should eat sparsely and be celibate. We should not permit ourselves happiness."

Whatever the contribution of pre-bomb psychological conflicts to his present state, we can say that his death guilt, which had in the past been animating—had provided energy for his writing—had now become static and immobilizing. He went on to speak of the futility of continuing to document the horrors of the bomb because, in his judgment, such efforts were taken advantage of by the United States and the Soviet Union in justifying their own continuing world domination with a nuclear monopoly. And he condemned the inauthenticity of most versions of the Hiroshima connection because they suppressed an unpleasant dimension of the city's experience—the stealing, criminality, murder, moral degradation of every kind that took place during the months and years after the atomic bomb was dropped. As his parting shot, an ironic expression of *munashi,* he compared the relatively orderly behavior of survivors at the moment of the bomb with the absolute panic three decades later of the Hiroshima people—now turned "clerks and salaried men"—in response to the recent gasoline shortage. He seemed to be saying that Hiroshima's story was more tainted than generally realized and that neither he nor the city, in any case, had anything sufficiently heroic to convey to the world.

Yet this same man, after his long silence, was preparing to start writing again. He told me he was beginning to organize his thoughts for a story about a man obsessed with the "arrogance"—by implication, hubris—of surviving and for other stories about what becoming a survivor does to human decency. He was, in other words, still struggling with a form of literary expression of the Hiroshima connection.

For the entire city, in fact, the other side of *munashi* was a sense of a new stage in Hiroshima's relationship to the world. That sense was epitomized by a concerted effort being made by Hiroshima University to establish an Institute for Peace Sciences. I talked at length with the president of the university, who strongly supported the plan and likened the city's situation after the bomb to that of the world after the death of Jesus Christ. He was saying that, with a cataclysmic event, everything depends upon the way it is experienced and the way the story is told. I took the comment as less a suggestion of precise historical analogy than of sensitivity to the issue of collective survivor mission following an ultimate death encounter.

This was part of a refreshing emphasis, at the university and elsewhere in the city, upon the universal dimensions of Hiroshima's experience. This atmosphere emboldened me, when asked to discuss my views with the committee responsible for establishing the new institute, to bring up the subject so sensitive that it had in one way or another been virtually suppressed. I mentioned that students of the late Yoshio Nishina, the great Japanese physicist at the time of the Second World War, had recently published a valuable study of radiation effects as both a memorial to their teacher and an expression of their and his post-Second World War commitment to peace. The study mentioned Nishina's horror at what he found upon arriving in Hiroshima two days after the bomb as part of an additional investigating team. But there was no mention, I said, of the fact that Nishina, at the request of the Japanese military, had himself earlier headed a team of physicists in a serious but unsuccessful effort to produce a Japanese atomic bomb. My Hiroshima academic colleagues readily understood my point—the universal impulse toward weaponry of ultimate destruction. Several of them, in fact, said they welcomed this kind of discussion because it helped Japanese to overcome their preoccupation with "victim consciousness." And they went on to talk about exchanges, already initiated, between Hiroshima and Auschwitz. (At another meeting I was pleased to hear a journalist say that my discussion of survivors in my book on Hiroshima, which has been translated into Japanese, had helped him in his understanding of Auschwitz.) And in other discussions I heard *hibakusha* make sensitive connections between Hiroshima and such events as the Vietnam War, India's acquisition of nuclear weapons, the dangers of plutonium reactors for nuclear energy, and major international threats to the physical environment.

A distinguished historian, deeply involved in the Hiroshima experience although not himself a *hibakusha,* told me that the situation sometimes requires a "third person"—by which he meant someone who is neither a *hibakusha* nor, in a sense, a non-*hibakusha*—someone like himself who did not originally experience the bomb but took on the experience nonetheless.

Such a third person, he implied, could combine detachment and concern, what Martin Buber has called distance and relation. In my terms that would be a once-removed "witness," as I myself have tried to become. In a similar vein, the historian observed, "Just as the *hibakusha* are themselves disappearing, this is the time we must make their full story available to all of humankind."

Is the Hiroshima connection being made? Not adequately. Yet in that city, as in Nagasaki, there exists our only collectivity of survivors of ultimate holocaust. Their "memory of a memory" is our own, bound up with our destiny no less than with theirs.

4

Vietnam—Beyond Atrocity

> The landscape doesn't change much. For days and days you see just about nothing. It's unfamiliar—always unfamiliar. Even when you go back to the same place, it's unfamiliar. And it makes you feel as though, well, there's nothing left in the world but this. . . . You have the illusion of going great distances and traveling, like hundreds of miles . . . and you end up in the same place because you're only a couple of miles away. . . . But you feel like it's not all real. It couldn't possibly be. We couldn't still be in this country. We've been walking for days. . . . You're in Vietnam and they're using real bullets. . . . Here in Vietnam they're actually shooting people for no reason. . . . Any other time you think, It's such an extreme. Here you can go ahead and shoot them for nothing. . . . As a matter of fact it's even . . . smiled upon, you know. Good for you. Everything is backwards. That's part of the kind of unreality of the thing. To the "grunt" [infantryman] this isn't backwards. He doesn't understand. . . . But something [at My Lai 4] was missing. Something you thought was real that would accompany this. It wasn't there. . . . There was something missing in the whole business that made it seem like it really wasn't happening.
>
> —American GI's recollections of My Lai
> (personal interview)

This is the angriest essay in the volume. The atrocities were being committed as I wrote it, and images of Vietnamese victims were everywhere. I had long known about American atrocities, had opposed the Vietnam war from its beginnings, and had participated in many protest meetings and university teach-ins. But everything changed for me from the moment in November 1969 when I read the first detailed (New York Times) *account of My Lai. I was on an airplane on my way to Toronto for a talk and radio broadcast, and I can feel even now the shame and rage I experienced.*

A number of things then happened quickly: I was able to gather more data and make a statement before the Cranston Subcommittee on Veterans in January 1970, from which part of this essay derives. In December of 1970, I helped initiate, at the invitation of veterans, a project of weekly "rap groups" at the New York office of the Vietnam Veterans Against the War, and met regularly with one of those groups over a period of three years. Those memorable groups, along with equally memorable interviews with individual veterans, became the basis for my book Home from the War, *depicting their transformation from "warriors" to "antiwar warriors." I was not without conflict about interrupting work on my more general study,* The Broken Connection, *and I can remember the morning on which I literally removed from my desk materials for the latter book in order to devote myself fully to the work with veterans, which I viewed as an urgent antiwar enterprise as well as a form of scholarship. Then, with some affectionate prodding from leaders of the American Friends peace efforts (notably Stuart Meecham and Richard Fernandez), I collaborated with Richard Falk and Gabriel Kolko in editing a collection,* Crimes of War, *in which this piece was published.*

There was still another step. Together with friends, I helped organize a group we called Redress (referring to the First Amendment right of citizens to petition their elected leaders for redress of grievances). On the basis of what is called the Nuremberg obligation (stemming from the trials of Nazi criminals at the end of the Second World War) of ordinary citizens to resist criminal actions of their own government, we performed a couple of acts of modest civil disobedience outside the antechambers of the House of Representatives and the Senate. While one inevitably learns something from spending two separate nights in the Washington lock-up, most of the hundred or so participants on each occasion shared my sense of absurdity at what we came to call "fat cat civil disobedience" (we were mostly professors, writers, and artists with considerable recognition in American society) and at the disparity between our grandiose rationale and modest actions. Dick Gregory came to address us on one of those occasions, and caught that absurdity as no one else could. First he looked around at our frightened, white, upper-middle-class faces, and told us, "It's OK to be afraid. I was, too, my first time, so I just found myself a couple of nuns and walked behind them." Then he added, just a little mischievously, "But remember, this is one time you can't call the police." Anger and laughter—there are times when they are necessary in equal measure.

IN ONE SENSE, no matter what happens in the external world, personal atrocity, for everyone, begins at birth. It can also be said that some of us have a special nose for atrocity. Yet I can remember very well, during the early stirrings of the academic peace movement taking place around Harvard University during the middle and late 1950s—about two hundred years ago, it now seems—how hard it was for us to *feel* what might happen at the other end of a nuclear weapon. Whatever one's concern about atrocities, there are difficulties surrounding the imaginative act of coming to grips with them.

After six months of living and working in Hiroshima, studying the human effects of the first atomic bomb, I found that these difficulties were partly overcome and partly exacerbated. On the one hand, I learned all too well to feel what happened at the other end of an atomic bomb. But on the other hand, I became impressed with the increasing gap we face between our technological capacity for perpetrating atrocities and our imaginative ability to confront their full actuality. Yet the attempt to narrow that gap can be enlightening, even liberating. For me Hiroshima was a profoundly "radicalizing" experience—not in any strict ideological sense but in terms of fundamental issues of living and dying.

Whatever the contributing wartime pressures, Hiroshima looms as a paradigm of technological atrocity. Each of the major psychological themes of Hiroshima survivors—death immersion, psychic numbing, residual guilt—has direct relationship to its hideously cool and vast technological character. The specific technology of the bomb converted the brief moment of exposure into a lifelong encounter with death described in chapter 2.

The experience of psychic numbing, or emotional desensitization—what some survivors called "paralysis of the mind"—was a necessary defense against feeling what they clearly knew to be happening. But when one looks further into the matter, one discovers that those who made and planned the use of that first nuclear weapon—and those who today make its successors and plan their use—require their own form of psychic numbing. They too cannot afford to feel what they cognitively know would happen.

Victims and victimizers also shared a sense of guilt, expressed partly in a conspiracy of silence, a prolonged absence of any systematic attempt to learn about the combined physical and psychic assaults of the bomb on human beings. Survivors felt guilty about remaining alive while others died and also experienced an amorphous sense of having been part of, having imbibed, the overall evil of the atrocity. The perpetrators of Hiroshima (and those in various ways associated with them)—American scientists, military and political leaders, and ordinary people—felt their own forms of guilt—though, ironically, in less tangible form than that of victims. Yet one cannot but wonder to what extent Hiroshima produced in Americans (and others) a guilt-associated sense that, If we could do this we could do anything; and, Anyone could do anything to us—in other words, an anticipatory sense of unlimited atrocity.

If these are lessons of Hiroshima, one has to learn them personally. My own immersion in massive death during investigations in that city, though much more privileged and infinitely less brutal, will nonetheless be as permanent as that of Hiroshima survivors themselves; as in their case it has profoundly changed my relationship to my own death as well as to all collective forms of death that stalk us. I had a similarly personal lesson regarding psychic numbing. During my first few interviews in Hiroshima, I felt overwhelmed by the grotesque horrors described to me; but within the short space of a week or so, this feeling gave way to a much more comfortable sense of myself as a psychological investigator, still deeply troubled by what I heard but undeterred from my investigative commitment. This kind of partial, task-oriented numbing now strikes me as inevitable and, in this situation, useful—yet at the same time potentially malignant in its implications.

By entering into the experience of survivors, while at the same time remaining an American, I shared something of both victim's and victimizer's sense of guilt. This kind of guilt by identification has its pitfalls,* but I believe it to be one of the few genuine psychological avenues to confrontation of atrocity. For these three psychological themes are hardly confined to Hiroshima: death immersion, psychic numbing, and guilt are a psychic trinity found in all atrocity.

Hiroshima—along with Nazi genocide—also taught me the value and appropriateness of what I would call the "apocalyptic imagination." The term offends our notions of steadiness and balance. But the technological dimensions of contemporary atrocity seem to me to require that we attune our imaginations to processes that are apocalyptic in the full dictionary meaning of the word—processes that are "wildly unrestrained" and "ultimately decisive," that involve "forecasting or predicting the ultimate destiny of the world in the shape of future events" and "foreboding imminent disaster of final doom" (see chapter 9).

Psychological wisdom seems to lie not in wallowing in apocalypse but in putting to use our imagining of it to prevent it (see chapter 12). For we

* In chapter 5, I discuss the distinction between "animating" and "static" forms of guilt.

live in the shadow of the ultimate atrocity, of the potentially *terminal revolution*—and if that term is itself a contradiction, the same contradiction is the central fact of our relationship to death and life.

We perpetrate and experience the American atrocity at My Lai* in the context of these apocalyptic absurdities and dislocations. The GI's quoted description suggests not only that atrocity can be a dreamlike affair—what he described as "missing" was a sense of reality—but that it is committed by men living outside of ordinary human connection, outside of both society and history. My Lai was acted out by men who had lost their bearings, men wandering about in both a military and a psychic no man's land. The atrocity itself can be seen as a grotesquely paradoxical effort to put straight this crooked landscape, to find order and significance in disorder and absurdity. There is at the same time an impulse to carry existing absurdity and disorder to their logical extreme, as if both to transcend and to demonstrate that aberrant existential state.

The average Vietnam GI was thrust into a strange, faraway, and very alien place. The Vietnamese people and their culture were equally alien to him. The environment was not only dangerous and unpredictable but devoid of landmarks that might warn of danger or help him to identify the enemy. He experienced a combination of profound inner confusion, helplessness, and terror.

Then he saw his buddies killed and mutilated. He experienced the soldier-survivor's impulse toward revenge, toward overcoming his own emotional conflicts and giving meaning to his buddies' sacrifices by getting back at the enemy. And in an ordinary war there is a structure and ritual for doing just that—battle lines and established methods for contacting the enemy and carrying out individual and group battle tasks with aggressiveness and courage. But in Vietnam there was none of that: the enemy was everyone and no one, never still, rarely visible, and usually indistinguishable from the ordinary peasant. The GI was therefore denied the minimal psychological satisfactions of war; and, as a result, his fear, rage, and frustration mounted.

(The "pep talk" given by the company commander just prior to My Lai was actually part of a funeral ceremony for a fallen sergeant. GIs remember being told to "kill every man, woman, and child in the village"

* My Lai 4 was the designated name of a small hamlet in which, on 16 March 1968, the officers and men of the American unit known as "Charlie Company" massacred between 450 and 500 Vietnamese civilians, many of them children, women, and old people. There was an extensive military and political cover-up of the event, but it was finally exposed through collaboration between a few of the American soldiers who had been there and investigative reporters, notably Seymour M. Hersh. In *Home from the War,* I discuss at some length the operative psychological factors at My Lai.[1]

so that "nothing would be walking, growing, or crawling" when the company left. They recall also to have been urged to "let it out, let it go." Which they did.)

This dehumanization of the Vietnamese by the individual GI was furthered by his participation in such everyday actions as the saturation of villages with bombs and artillery fire, and the burning of entire hamlets. Observing the death and injuries of Vietnamese civilians on such a massive scale, and the even more massive disruptions of village life and forced relocations, he could not but feel that the Vietnamese had become more or less expendable.

That is why Vietnam combat veterans I talked to were not really surprised by the recent disclosures of atrocities committed by American troops at My Lai and elsewhere. Virtually all of them had either witnessed or heard of similar incidents, if on a somewhat smaller scale. Hence Paul Meadlo's public statement that what he and others did at My Lai "seemed like it was the natural thing to do at the time." Another former infantryman, Terry Reed, who described a similar incident elsewhere, made a public statement of even greater psychological significance. He said: "To me the war was being ambushed every three to five days, being left with scores of wounded GIs. Then come right back at the enemy by going into an innocent village, destroying and killing the people." What these words suggest is how, under the extraordinary stress of an impossible situation, GIs came to see all Vietnamese, whatever their age or sex or affiliation, as interchangeable with the enemy, so that killing any Vietnamese could become a way of "coming right back" at those responsible for wounding or killing their own buddies.

Meadlo went on to say that immediately after killing a number of Vietnamese civilians he "felt good" and that "I was getting relieved from what I had seen earlier over there." Applicable here is an established psychological principle that killing can relieve fear of being killed. But there was something more operating in connection with these massacres: the momentary illusion on the part of GIs that, by gunning down these figures now equated with the enemy—even little babies and women and old men—they were finally involved in a genuine "military action," their elusive adversaries had finally been located, made to stand still, and annihilated—an illusion, in other words, that they had finally put their world back in order.

Other veterans have reported witnessing or participating in killings of civilians without even the need for such an illusion. Sometimes these killings had been performed with the spirit of the hunter or the indiscriminate executioner—potshots at random Vietnamese taken from helicopters, heavy fire directed at populated villages for no more reason than a commanding officer's feeling that he "didn't like their looks." In addition, there have been many accounts of such things as the shoving of suspects out of helicopters, the beheadings of Vietcong or Vietcong suspects, and of various forms of dismembering the bodies of dead Vietnamese. The American infantry company responsible for My Lai, upon first entering a combat zone, had a kind of visual initiation into such brutalization in the form of a weapons carrier the men encountered with its radio aerial strung with Vietnamese ears.

Atrocities are committed by desperate men—in the case of My Lai, by men victimized by the absolute contradictions of the war they were asked to fight, by the murderous illusions of their country's policy. Atrocity, then, is a perverse quest for meaning, the end result of a spurious sense of mission, the product of false witness.

To say that American military involvement in Vietnam was itself a crime is also to say that it was an atrocity-producing situation. Or to put the matter another way, My Lai illuminates, as nothing else has, the essential nature of America's war in Vietnam. The elements of this atrocity-producing situation include an advanced industrial nation engaged in a counterinsurgency action in an underdeveloped area, against guerrillas who merge with the people—precisely the elements that Jean-Paul Sartre has described as inevitably genocidal. In the starkness of its murders and the extreme dehumanization experienced by victimizers and imposed on victims, My Lai reveals how far America had gone along the path of deadly illusion.

Associated with this deadly illusion are three psychological patterns as painful to the sensitized American critic of the war as they are self-evident. The first is the principle of atrocity building upon atrocity, because of the need to deny the atrocity-producing situation. In this sense, My Lai itself was a product of earlier, smaller My Lais and was followed not by an ending of the war but by the American extension of the war into Laos and Cambodia.

The second principle involves the system of nonresponsibility. One searches in vain for a man or a group of men who will come forward to take the blame or even identify a human source of responsibility for what took place: from those who fired the bullets at My Lai (who must bear some responsibility, but were essentially pawns and victims of the atrocity-producing situation, and are now being made scapegoats as well); to the junior-grade officers who gave orders to do the firing and apparently did some of it themselves; to the senior-grade officers who seemed to have ordered the operation; to the highest military and civilian planners in Vietnam, the Pentagon, and the White House who set such policies as that of a "*permanent* free-fire zone" (which, according to Richard Hammer means "in essence . . . that any Americans operating within it had, basically, a license to kill and any Vietnamese living within it had a license to be killed") and made even more basic decisions about continuing and even extending the war; to the amorphous conglomerate of the American people who, presumably, chose, or at least tolerated, the aforementioned as their representatives. The atrocity-producing situation, at least in this case, depends upon what the Japanese social theorist Masao Maruyama has called a "system of nonresponsibility." Situation and system alike are characterized by a technology and a technicized bureaucracy unchecked by sensate human minds.

The third and perhaps most terrible pattern is the psychology of nothing happening. General Westmoreland gives way to General Abrams, President Johnson to President Nixon, a visibly angry student generation to one silent with rage—and the war, the atrocity-producing situation, continues to grind out its thousands of recorded and unrecorded atrocities. To be more accurate, something does happen—the subliminal American perception of atrocity edges toward consciousness—making it more difficult but, unfortunately, not impossible to defend and maintain the atrocity-producing situation. The widespread feeling of being stuck in atrocity contributes, in ways we can now hardly grasp, to a national sense of degradation and to a related attraction to violence. For nothing is more conducive to collective rage and totalism (see pages 212–16) than a sense of being bound to a situation perceived to be both suffocating and evil.

Atrocity in general, and My Lai in particular, brings its perpetrators—even a whole nation—into the realm of existential evil. That state is exemplified by what another GI described to me as a working definition of the enemy in Vietnam: "If it's dead, it's VC*—because it's dead. If it's dead, it *had* to be VC. And of course, a corpse couldn't defend itself anyhow." When, at some future moment, ethically sensitive historians get around to telling the story of the Vietnam War—assuming that there will be ethically sensitive (or for that matter, any) historians around—I have no doubt that they will select the phenomenon of the "body count" as the perfect symbol of America's descent into evil. What better represents the numbing, brutalization, illusion (most of the bodies, after all, turned out to be those of civilians), grotesque competition (companies and individuals vying for the highest body counts), and equally grotesque technicizing

* VC was the term used for Vietcong, itself a fabricated name (meaning Vietnamese Communists) for the revolutionary organization in the South (Communist-dominated but including other groups as well) whose actual name was the National Liberation Front.

(progress lying in the *count*) characteristic of the overall American crime of war in Vietnam.

My Lai is unusual in one respect. It combined two kinds of atrocity: technological overkill (of unarmed peasants by Americans using automatic weapons), and a more personal, face-to-face gunning-down of victims at point-blank range. This combination lends the incident particular psychic force, however Americans may try to fend off awareness of its implications. A participating GI could characterize My Lai as "just like a Nazi-type thing,"[2] a characterization made by few if any pilots or crewmen participating in the more technologically distanced killings of larger numbers of Vietnamese civilians from the air.

The sense of being associated with existential evil is new to Americans. This is so partly because such perceptions have been suppressed in other atrocity-producing situations, but also because of the humane elements of American tradition that contribute to a national self-image of opposing, through use of force if necessary, just this kind of "Nazi-type thing." The full effects of the war in Vietnam upon this self-image are at this point unclear. The returns from My Lai are not yet in. Perhaps they never are for atrocity. But I, for one, worry about a society that seems to absorb, with some questioning but without fundamental self-examination, first Hiroshima and now My Lai.

For there is always a cost. Atrocities have a way of coming home. In 1970, the killings by National Guardsmen of four Kent State students protesting the extension of the war in Cambodia reflect the use of violence in defense of illusion and denial of evil—and the killings of six blacks at Augusta, Georgia, and of two black students at Jackson State in Mississippi reflect indirectly that atmosphere. Indeed, there is a real danger that the impulse to preserve illusion and deny evil could carry America beyond Vietnam and Cambodia into some form of world-destroying nuclear confrontation. In this sense, as well as in its relationship to existential evil, My Lai symbolized a shaking of the American foundations—a bitterly mocking perversion of what was left of the American dream. Like Hiroshima and Auschwitz, My Lai is a revolutionary event: its total inversion of moral standards raises fundamental questions about the institutions and national practices of the nation responsible for it.

The problem facing Americans now is, What do we do with our atrocities? Do we simply try our best to absorb them by a kind of half-admission that denies their implications and prevents genuine confrontation? That is the classical method of governments for dealing with documented atrocities, and it is clearly the method being used by the United States government and military now in its legal trials of individuals. Those who did the shooting and those who covered up the event are being labeled aberrant and negligent, so that the larger truth of the atrocity-producing situation can be avoided. The award of a Pulitzer Prize in 1970 to Seymour Hersh for his journalistic feat in uncovering the story of My Lai and telling it in detail would seem to be a step in the direction of that larger truth. Yet one cannot but fear that such an award—as in the case of the National Book Award I received in 1969 for my work on Hiroshima—can serve as a form of conscience-salving token recognition in place of confrontation. Surely more must be faced throughout American society, more must be articulated and given form by leaders and ordinary people, if this atrocity is to contribute to a national process of illumination instead of merely one of further degradation.

I am struck by how little my own profession has had to say about the matter—about the way in which aberrant *situations* can produce collective disturbance and mass murder. The psychiatry and psychohistory I would like to envisage for the future would put such matters at its center. It would also encourage the combining of ethical involvement with professional skills in ways that could simultaneously shed light upon such crimes of war and contribute to the transformation our country so desperately requires. In dealing with our dislocations, we need to replace the false witness of atrocity with the genuine witness of new and liberating forms and directions.

5

The Postwar War

The conference at which this paper was originally given (at the City University of New York in June 1973) had the interesting general title of "The Ending of Wars"—and was clearly a response to a war that Americans had begun to fear would never end. From that conference and many other discussions of the meaning of the Vietnam War, I began to realize that public expressions of what we call "history" consist of little more than a set of images constructed by groups of people, or by influential individuals, from certain events or nonevents. Moreover, meanings initially given events by actual participants can be quickly taken over by political and historical manipulators, especially in the wake of our mass-media revolution.

Consider, for instance, the efforts of the Reagan administration during the 1980s to re-create the Vietnam War as having been fought in a noble American cause. Consider also the spate of films more or less refighting the war with the idea (as a leading character in a Rambo film says directly), "This time we win!" This essay is a small effort on behalf of a very different historical understanding of Vietnam. While little national discourse has acknowledged the full extent of American participation in slaughter, lessons concerning American military restraint have been at least partially learned by a number of our elected officials, as reflected in resistance to parallel military and political adventures in South and Central America. The Reagan administration would like to label that restraint as a kind of illness—the "Vietnam syndrome"; but there is enough memory around to contest that version of history.

The wiser historical rendering of that war is embodied in the extraordinary Vietnam Veterans Memorial in Washington, completed in 1982, known simply as "The Wall." The stark black granite structure containing nothing but the names of the American dead seems to me to be as morally appropriate a symbol of the Vietnam War as could be imagined. But history making never stops, and wisdom from Vietnam is a fragile dimension of American consciousness. We need to keep on seeking truthful history from that war, including truthful psychological history.

MY TITLE is ambiguous and has at least two levels of meaning. One is the literal fact that the Vietnam War still goes on, and with active American participation. But the postwar war that I want to discuss is that of consciousness, the struggle over the residual meaning of the war as perceived by antagonistic groups in American society. I want to examine contending expressions of survival that can be looked at rather systematically, though they have implications that are enormous and at times unmanageable, both intellectually and politically.

The imagery with which one survives a war has much to do with the way in which one fights it and ends it. The survivor imagery begins to take shape long before the war itself is over. In the previous chapter (as in my study of Vietnam veterans)[1] I have tried to show how extreme and immediate feelings of grief and loss following the deaths of one's buddies have a direct bearing on the commission of such atrocities as My Lai: the only way to justify one's own survival is to render their deaths significant by getting back at the enemy; and, if one is unable to engage him in the manner desired, to create an enemy out of defenseless peasants. In an atrocity-producing situation like Vietnam, where battle lines were obscure and the enemy elusive, survivor imagery actively shaped the quality of the war experience and served to internalize within the GIs the need for constant atrocities.

Survivor imagery arising from wars is self-perpetuating, as is evident, for instance, in the influence of the First World War upon the Second. Concerning French behavior, Marshal Pétain, the "hero of Verdun" in 1916, was undoubtedly influenced by memories of that slaughter in his disinclination to resist the Nazi invasion in 1940. In a different way, Germany's rearmament in the 1930s and chauvinistic demands for revenge also reflected survivor images of humiliation and "betrayal" at the Versailles Peace Conference in 1920.

In my work in Hiroshima on the experience of the survivor,[2] I tried to delineate a general pattern that seemed consistent for virtually all survivors of actual or metaphorical death immersions. That concept of the survivor has served as a theoretical foundation for my subsequent work with Vietnam veterans and has important relevance, I believe, for post-Vietnam America.

The psychology of the survivor involves five patterns of response (see chapter 17). First is the "death imprint," the impact of death and of one's loss of a sense of invulnerability. The death imprint is associated with emotions organized around what becomes an indelible image or set of images. Second, the issue of "death guilt," the classical question of the survivor: Why did he or she die while I remain alive? The guilt is often focused on various things one feels one has had to do in order to survive, on choices one has had to make at the expense of others. The third pattern I call "psychic numbing" or "desensitization": that is, loss of feeling in order to escape the impact of unacceptable images. This numbing, psychologically necessary at the time, can later give rise to despair, depression, and withdrawal. The fourth pattern has to do with a suspicion of the counterfeit in all relationships, and with accompanying anger and rage at one's dependency and vulnerability. Finally, the overall struggle of the survivor is to give form, significance, and meaning to the death immersion, in order to move forward in one's post-holocaust existence.

There is evidence that Americans experienced, in one way or another, all five of these survivor patterns in the wake of the Vietnam War. But I wish particularly to emphasize the last—the struggle for significance, sometimes in the form of a special *survivor mission*—as exemplified in three public scenes. The first was a January 1973 White House evening when President Nixon hosted most of the returned prisoners of war. Irving Berlin was there to lead the singing of "God Bless America." Bob Hope's wife recited a prayer. The President delivered a speech in which he made an unusually belligerent defense of his Vietnam policy (fighting the war as long as was necessary and then achieving "peace with honor") and of his behavior in association with the then increasingly embarrassing Watergate scandal. By making use of the POWs to emphasize America's honor and glory in Vietnam and elsewhere, he in effect issued a call to reactivate the deadly romance of war and to salvage, insofar as that was possible, the synthetic romance of the Vietnam War. The POWs were placed at the center (together with President Nixon) of an attempt to rally the nation around a sense of immortalizing glory and traditional nationalism. The actualities of the Vietnam War were covered over, and the public was offered a message of shallow moralism rather than a genuinely moral response.

The other two scenes suggest the contrast between the peace demonstrations of 1945 and 1973. On the night of V-E Day, 1945, in Times Square, the film clips reflect pure mass joy, which I know to be authentic as I was there in that crowd, a happy nineteen-year-old medical student. The second scene flashed on the television screens after the 1973 ceasefire: Times Square, the area itself now looking seedy, was almost deserted; a few Vietnam veterans gathered in anger, some drinking, others apparently on drugs, most simply enraged, screaming at the camera, at the society, about having been deceived by the war and ignored upon coming back, one especially enraged black veteran shouting, "You can tell that bastard the war isn't over!"

Those three incidents suggest some of the survivor imagery now having an impact on American life. In thinking about the returned prisoners of war, one must begin with the assumption that, even prior to their being received by the Pentagon and the administration, they had the survivor's need to try to give significance to their death immersion, which in this case was twofold—that of the war itself and that of their period of imprisonment in Vietnam. The survivor formulation for these men involves the struggle to find meaning and significance in those lost years (up to seven years for some of them), and to convince themselves and the country that there was some redeeming value in that experience. One way of claiming honor is to call forth the traditional definition of the socialized warrior, within which honor consists of standing up under pressures of imprisonment. This approach has been greatly emphasized, partly because many in this group received their air-force training after the general demoralization of American POWs in the Korean War by means of Chinese Communist thought-reform programs.

I would stress not only the struggle of the Vietnam POWs to achieve significance and honor in their way of formulating their experience but also the survivor mission many of them have assumed: that of restoring national honor and pride in relation to some positive feeling about America's contribution in Vietnam. But beyond the psychological struggles of the men themselves, one must immediately emphasize the enormous embrace, orchestration, and manipulation of survivor imagery by the Nixon administration for political purposes. As a result, the POWs were made into instant heroes. This is probably the first war in human history in which the returning prisoners of war were the national heroes of that war, which in turn points to the absolute absence of American heroes in the Vietnam

War. That combined survivor imagery, then, consisting of psychological needs of many POWs and political needs of the administration, becomes inseparable from an insistence that we learn nothing from the Vietnam War; survivor significance is reduced to simple-minded glorification of the American version of the warrior ethos.

At the opposite pole were the antiwar veterans whom I worked with for three years in rap groups in New York. My work with these veterans was both political and psychological. Over the course of the experience, I attempted to give theoretical form to this approach through the concept of "advocacy research." That concept draws upon and extends earlier principles of participant observation and disciplined subjectivity to suggest an investigative equilibrium between the detachment required for intellectual rigor and the passions of social commitment. While the ethical-political dimension in this experience was especially compelling, I believe that open acknowledgment of advocacies in all investigative work can strengthen, rather than diminish, one's scientific enterprise.[3]

The antiwar veterans sought their survivor formulation by articulating the very absurdity of their war. They found meaning in revealing its meaninglessness. Their survivor mission became one of telling the truth about the war as they perceived it, no matter how unacceptable that truth was or is to the American people. As veterans of a war who mounted a grassroots effort to expose and oppose that war while it was still being fought, these men are unique in American history. Part of the truth as they see it and part of the message they have sought to convey is an understanding of the American military presence in Vietnam as itself an atrocity-producing situation.

I was able to spend ten hours interviewing one man who had been at My Lai but had not fired and, moreover, had not even pretended to fire (the few others in the company who did not fire made that pretense out of fear of group condemnation). There were several elements in the life of this survivor of the My Lai atrocity that seemed important in explaining his refusal to fire and his capacity to risk ostracism from the group. Though he had broken away from his early Catholic teachings in a formal religious sense, he retained from them certain imagery about limits beyond which one cannot go. He grew up a loner, mostly off by himself, living by the ocean as a child, rarely involved in groups; he was consequently less susceptible than most to group influence. Finally, he had loved the military and had embraced it strongly after a somewhat confused young adulthood. He excelled in various training exercises, had planned to make the military his career, but was appalled when he got to Vietnam at the violation of his ideal of military honor. From the beginning, this exceptionally skillful soldier was "maladapted" to the atrocity-producing situation in Vietnam; hence his restraint at My Lai.

Guilt is very much part of the survivor imagery of the antiwar veterans. In the rap groups the men sought to convert guilt from the static, endless self-laceration to what I call "animating guilt," which becomes a vital part of the energy for transformation. That animating relationship to guilt includes examination of its sources as well as imagery of possibility beyond the guilt itself. Guilt then becomes virtually inseparable from a sense of individual responsibility, but I should also emphasize that the men were insisting that their countrymen share that guilt and responsibility for what America did in Indochina.

Anger and rage have also been central to this survivor imagery. We professionals who were in the rap groups with the veterans saw ourselves not as serving a cooling function but rather as exploring with the veterans the roots of anger and rage. Of course, we had plenty of anger of our own about the war, and we had our own struggles with redirecting and using that anger. For the veterans, expressing anger and rage could be a way of dealing with violent impulses they retained from Vietnam and the post-Vietnam experience.

The veterans' survivor formulation also includes a fundamental political critique of spiritual authority in the society. Among the most passionate targets of bitterness and rage in the rap groups were two groups representing that authority: chaplains and "shrinks." While we tried to be alert to the possibility that some of this feeling was indirectly aimed at professionals in the group, we came to see its major source in the way veterans had experienced chaplains and psychiatrists in Vietnam. Often when these men had been in combat over a period of time they reached a point of combined moral revulsion and psychological suffering, the one difficult to distinguish from the other. Seeking some kind of spiritual guidance, they were taken to a chaplain or to a psychiatrist (or the assistant of either), who would then serve the military function of helping the men adjust to combat and to the daily commission or witnessing of atrocities. The men felt that it was one thing to be ordered by command to commit atrocities on an everyday basis in Vietnam but another to have the spiritual authorities of one's society rationalize and attempt to justify and legitimize that process. They felt this to be a kind of ultimate corruption of the spirit.

In sharing this exploration with them I was led to questions about my profession as a psychiatrist, about the relationship of psychiatry to the authorities it serves, and about issues concerning professionalism in general.[4] Most psychiatrists and chaplains serving in Vietnam were reasonably decent men; many understood what was occurring and took steps to enable soldiers to leave the combat area. But they could not avoid excruciating dilemmas having to do with their own position in the military and their assigned mission of doing everything necessary to maintain combat strength. Yet few psychiatrists had refused military service in Vietnam, most being inclined to believe that, whatever the setting and whatever their own convictions on the war, their technical skills as healers would serve essentially humane purposes. The history of the idea of a "profession" reveals that it was originally associated with the religious *professing* or *confessing* of one's spiritual commitment. Gradually, as it became secularized, the emphasis shifted more and more to professional skills and techniques. The premodern image of profession as advocacy based on faith gave way to the modern image of technique devoid of advocacy. What we need is a postmodern model of professions that would include both knowledge and skill on the one hand and specific advocacies and ethical commitments on the other. This would mean divesting ourselves not of technique but of *technicism,* the claim of moral neutrality on the model of the machine. Concerning situations like Vietnam, psychiatrists would be faced with moral questions no different from those of prospective GIs. And those same questions—about what one does, to whose benefit, and on behalf of what mission or project—would apply equally, if less dramatically, to our everyday work as well.

Veterans' survivor struggles included a sustained effort to free themselves from what they call the "John Wayne thing." By that they meant various forms of supermasculine bravado in respect to war and war making and in relationships with other people, especially with women. This was a dominant issue throughout, as many of the men came to feel themselves entrapped within a definition of maleness that required continuous demonstration of toughness and readiness for violence, as well as suppression within themselves of softness, aesthetic sensitivity, and much of their general capacity to feel. The "John Wayne thing" is not without its appeal, as, for instance, in its stress on courage and on absolute loyalty to one's group, so prominent in the survivor imagery of POWs. The veterans also discussed the influence of American cultural attitudes in shaping this kind of maleness; they came to relate their own struggles, however difficult and ambivalent, to those of their girlfriends and wives affected by the women's movement. In making that relationship and in their realization that the "John Wayne thing" is inseparable from the romantic appeal of war, individual psychological explorations became inseparable from involvement in wider social change.

Another aspect of their survivor mission had to do with re-examining their and other Americans' images of the Vietnamese. The veterans discussed ways in which the situation in Vietnam created intense psychological impulses toward victimization and dehumanization, toward group involvement in what I have described as the "gook syndrome." They seem to have to rediscover the Vietnamese as human beings, in order, as they put it, to "become human again" themselves. One of the most poignant moments in the rap groups came with the showing of a slide sequence by one of the men which portrayed the Vietnamese sympathetically in their rhythms of ordinary existence, and then the overwhelming presence of the American military with its vast technology. In the group, the men seemed to feel the humanity of the Vietnamese virtually leaping out at them from the projection screen. The confrontation was painful, but it contributed greatly to eventual insight concerning the "gook syndrome" and to the useful exposure of previously untapped sources of guilt.

In this whole process, the men sought various forms of external association and inner connection with other groups critical of American society, some of them part of the amorphous entities we call "youth culture" or "counterculture." They groped toward animating personal and institutional arrangements that might enhance (and perhaps be enhanced by) their own effort at transformation.

In general, I saw the transformation in their survivor imagery as having three fundamental stages. The first stage is confrontation, and that means confrontation with death in Vietnam. The second stage is reordering, which involves struggles similar to those experienced in therapy or any meaningful individual change, notably the reordering of guilt from its static to its animating forms. The third stage is renewal, a new sense of self—and is likely to include the rediscovery of play. The new sense of self is both introspective and extrospective: the men look *out* at the world in new ways as they reorder their inner imagery.

Most veterans and most Americans are probably somewhere in the middle of that survivor continuum represented by the POWs at one pole and the anti-war veterans at the other. Most Americans identify with much that the anti-war veterans say about the absurdity of the war. They may also identify with the overall sense of betrayal—with the idea of having been, as the men say, "fucked over" by the war. The war has had no satisfactory resolution for anyone. Still, many cringe at the full message of grotesqueness these men brought back. I spoke with a triple amputee who testified movingly before a Senate subcommittee about the difficulties of getting adequate medical treatment. In addition to everything else this man had suffered, he spoke of the doubt he and others had that the experience was worth it, the feeling that a small minority of Americans underwent a sacrifice that was neither meaningful nor shared. As I spoke with this man, he told me of his plans to run for political office in the deep South. I asked him if a dissident like himself could hope to be elected in his state. And he replied, "I'm no dissident! I've got to believe there was some value in that war." That little dialogue taught me a great deal. Here was a man who was deeply impressed with the absurdity of the whole enterprise but had lost so much that he had a strong need to believe there was some value in what he had done. This is a feeling that, I believe, connects with the responses of many Americans, of both veterans and the general population.

In general, the POWs represent an élite military officer group and the antiwar veterans represent mainly enlisted men. Most Americans sense that the heroic image initially created around the POWs is at best fragile and artificially imposed. As more and more conflicts have been revealed in the POWs, they could increasingly be seen as simply human—men subjected to a difficult ordeal in a war devoid of American glory.

Just a few days after the ceasefire, I had the experience of talking with a group of antiwar veterans whom I knew quite well. They called immediately after the ceasefire and wanted to meet because, as one of them put it, "The guys are having some pretty strong reactions." When I spoke to them it was clear that their main reaction was rage. They also experienced a reactivation of Vietnam conflicts and described dreams recalling deaths of buddies in Vietnam or of horrible deaths of Vietnamese. A few expressed a desire to smash into something or just to "take off"; it was the sort of rage that became almost uncontrollable. One of them said, "There's no sense of an ending. A war or anything else has to have a beginning, a middle, and an end. This is a false ending." And he connected that with what he called "the incredible reluctance of the country to face what did go on out there."

These veterans also commented on how much the country seemed to need heroes and how strongly the country was beginning to focus on the POWs. And one of them said, "I'm withholding sympathy for them." He did have a certain amount of sympathy because he felt some affinity with the POWs, who were veterans, too. But he saw quite clearly the manipulative manner in which the POWs had been used all through the war as a rationalization for continuing it.

Some of these veterans had tried to celebrate at the announcement of the ceasefire, but their hearts were not in it. They had gone home from the bar early. Lyndon Johnson's death just before the ceasefire had affected them as well, because, as one of them said, "We had to realize it wasn't just him. It was the whole country." But that realization left them with no place to put the rage. The men were especially embittered by the phrase "peace with honor." Their sense was that the phrase was being used with complete hypocrisy while the war continued in Laos and Cambodia, and while there were still new body counts—"the last man to die before the accords" and "the first man to die after the accords." It was all like baseball statistics, as they put it. One said very simply, "It isn't peace and there's no honor."

The men were also worried about what their own identities would be after the ceasefire. One of them said, "We're no longer dissidents against the war, we're just hippies." They were concerned with losing their stature as *veteran*-dissidents. What they were really talking about, I think, was the government's effort at official termination of their own special survivor mission as antiwar veterans. In other words, their survivor mission required that they confront the war, while the government's way of making peace, ostensibly peace with honor, actually meant refusal to look at what the war had been for this country and for Vietnam. They in fact regarded the ceasefire agreements as a way of shutting out the possibility of illumination and of a new beginning for the country. One veteran said, "Once and for all it closed the door." A survivor in either the POW or the antiwar veteran groups greatly depends upon wider social and national responses for the activation and encouragement of his own survivor mission and his own well-being within that mission.

But the door is not entirely closed. The struggle over consciousness in relation to the two competing survivor images continues on many levels. One of these levels concerns confronting the corpses of the war. In an important book about Vietnam casualties entitled *365 Days*, the sensitive physician-author quotes the instructions given by the military to those who are to accompany bodies on the trip home:

> Each body in its casket is at all times to have a body escort. An effort has been made to find an escort whose personal involvement with the deceased or presence with the family of the deceased will be of comfort and aid. Your mission as a body escort is as follows: To make sure the body is afforded at all times the respect to a fallen soldier of the United States Army. Specifically as follows: To check the tags on the casket at every point of departure. To insist that the tags indicate the remains as nonviewable—that the relatives not view the body. Remember that nonviewable means exactly that—nonviewable.[5]

One could say that the military is being sensitive to family survivors' feelings by insisting that they not view severely mangled corpses of sons and husbands. But the larger symbolism of these instructions lies in the wish of the military and the administration to reinforce the impulse of civilian society to keep Vietnam corpses "nonviewable": that is, to avoid taking a hard look at what we have done in Vietnam to ourselves and to the Vietnamese. In contrast, antiwar veterans insist that we should join with them in viewing the corpses. But our way of ending our Vietnam War meant turning away, thereby raising the large question of the extent to which any country is capable of looking at its corpses in connection with its survivor imagery of that war.

The issue of amnesty raises a parallel question about the American consciousness in connection with our collective survival of the war. Amnesty has enormous significance not only for the one hundred thousand or so young people numbered among the resisters and exiles but also for a far larger group, numbering closer to half a million, including deserters and all those who have received less than honorable discharges. The word *amnesty* itself has roots that connect it with forgetting, with amnesia. And indeed, while much of the country is all too willing to forget what was done in Vietnam, there seems to be little chance that the acts of those who opposed the war will be legally forgotten so that they can freely re-enter society. Were amnesty to be granted to these groups, it would be very much a "confirmation" (in Martin Buber's sense), an acknowledgment of the moral value of having resisted the war. That point was well understood by our former vice president Spiro Agnew, who vituperatively opposed amnesty: "It would mean that we were wrong and they were right." The granting of amnesty would similarly confirm the antiwar veterans in their survivor mission.*

I would like to return to the scene I suggested at the beginning of this essay, that of the President in the White House receiving his POW guests. It was a beleaguered President who welcomed the prisoners of war, upon whom he was depending so heavily. On that occasion, the President was reacting to heavy blows emanating from the Watergate scandal, which each day implicated him further in unprecedented revelations of executive corruption and lawbreaking. In addition to calling forth simple patriotism in and around the POWs, President Nixon made his famous statement that it was high time we stopped making heroes out of those who steal government documents and publish them in the newspapers. In this he seemed to be making reference to Daniel Ellsberg but also, as Ellsberg quite rightly pointed out a few days later, to Nixon's own former White

* *De facto* amnesty was partially granted in a series of steps: the Ford administration's limited "clemency" program of 1974 (after his post-Watergate pardon of Richard Nixon); Carter's January 1977 "pardon" of draft evaders (affecting mostly white, middle-class young men), which he distinguished from "amnesty"; and the Carter program, from March 1977, for review of and upgrading of other-than-honorable discharges (potentially affecting former servicemen, mostly working-class, underclass, and minority).

House counsel, John Dean, who had done something of the same thing.*

What I want to suggest here is that there are important relationships between Vietnam and Watergate. One way to look at these is to consider some of the psychological resemblances between two atrocities, Watergate† and My Lai—a resemblance that is not literal but is rather in the cast of mind expressed in both. My Lai occurred in 1968 during the Johnson administration, which was not made up of the same men who brought us Watergate, but it may be that the patterns involved are deeper in American life and less dependent upon the idiosyncrasies of particular administrations than we like to believe.

Certain analogies between the two events are striking. At My Lai the atrocity involved the killing of five hundred noncombatants. Watergate involved subverting the electoral process—an atrocity of its own—in a way that makes more likely the kind of military atrocity that occurred at My Lai. In both cases, those who carried out the atrocity—the GIs at My Lai, the mostly Cuban team at Watergate—were in a borderline psychological area between following orders and an internalized impulse toward carrying through their action. Both groups had a sense of a higher purpose. Neither group was simply following orders; each had, to a degree, a sense of mission. And in each case, the actions and emotions of the men pulling the trigger, so to speak, were extensively manipulated from above.

One encounters in connection with both My Lai and Watergate a strange American capacity to combine intense idealism and equally intense cynicism. In the figure of H. R. Haldeman, for instance, considered to have been the President's alter ego as well as his top assistant, there is evidence of a strong right-wing idealism as well as of a fairly pragmatic cynicism in the machinations he was willing to undertake in order to maintain that idealistic vision. At My Lai, the idealism had to do with being true to the memory of dead buddies, and the combination of idealism and cynicism was something in the spirit of the famous phrase uttered at a different village in Vietnam: "We had to destroy it in order to save it." This combination of attitudes is characteristic of what I have called "ideological totalism"—an all-or-nothing stance that impels one toward obliterating

* In 1971, Daniel Ellsberg, together with Anthony Russo, copied and released classified documents on the Vietnam War—which became known as the Pentagon Papers—as an act of civil disobedience in the service of ending the war. In 1973, John Dean made use of White House documents in pleading his own case in various places in connection with the Watergate scandal.

† In speaking of Watergate and its analogies to My Lai, I refer mostly to the specific break-in that took place in 1972 in the building bearing that name where the headquarters of the Democratic party was then located, but at times I also adopt the general usage, which extends the meaning of the word to include the entire array of illegalities engaged in by the Nixon administration.

alternative perceptions of reality.[6] Related to that totalism is the insistence—reaffirmed by both recent presidents (and several before them)—that the United States remain, at all costs, the strongest country in the world. America's military hegemony, that is, is held forth to its people as a source of immortalizing power.

One finds in both Watergate and My Lai a simplistic polarization of American virtue and absolute Communist depravity. In the Watergate episode, the notion of Communist depravity was extended to include protesters, among whom were anti-war veterans, viewed as potentially violent disrupters of the Republican National Convention in 1972. It was around this image of the barbarians at the gates (a strong image for those who carried out the Watergate plans) that the required idealism and sense of mission were established and internalized.

There was a self-perpetuating quality in the whole Watergate style. One had to keep on doing more things to prevent a recognition of what one had done from reaching oneself or others. So also in My Lai, where atrocity begot atrocity. And in both situations, there was an elaborate cover-up as serious as the event itself, in that it revealed the depth of corruption and corruptibility within existing institutions. One is also struck by the centrality of illusions in both My Lai and Watergate. At My Lai, the GIs had the illusion that they had finally engaged the enemy and had got him to stand up and fight in ennobling combat; in fact, the enemy was entirely composed of noncombatants. Watergate included a similar illusion of ennobling activity that surrounded "dirty tricks" with an aura of service to the nation and national security.

These illusions, in turn, reflect another common feature—the counterinsurgency theme in both My Lai and Watergate. My Lai expressed that theme in relationship to an Asian revolution, while Watergate extended the counterinsurgency ethos to American protesters of the Vietnam War, to the Democratic party, and (in the sense of violating laws and the Constitution at will) to the American people as a whole. Some observers have thus spoken of the "Vietnamization of America." But the more important point, I believe, is the overall psychohistorical response to change that subsumes both events: the fearful sense that various forces of change threaten to destroy or kill something in the American cultural-ideological essence, a perception that is itself called upon in order to ward off the unacceptable feeling that the process of decay is internal (nationally and individually). Broadly speaking, one could say that Watergate and My Lai were desperate efforts to maintain a faltering cosmology around the American secular religion of nationalism, which was inwardly perceived to be collapsing. At such a moment, as many people (notably Hannah Arendt) have said, there is a greater likelihood of violence or extreme measures of one kind or another—of the kind that occurred at Watergate and My Lai.

The ultimate test of this struggle over consciousness will be in the answers to the question that is always asked after wars and is going to be asked about Indochina, whether today or in ten, twenty, or thirty years: "Daddy, what did you do in the great Vietnam War?" The traditional answer—the answer that all the manipulation around the POWs sought to preserve—is a simple one: "I fought bravely at Khe Sanh or in the Delta." But the answer that would be given within the new consciousness to which the anti-war veterans contribute would be different: "I opposed the war," or "I resisted it," or "I went to prison, or into exile, or in one way or another avoided fighting it," or "I started to fight it and then fled," or "I fought the war and then returned to tell the country the truth about it," or even "I tried to use my professional skills in opposing the war, probing its underlying causes, or contributing to alternative social forms." I think that more and more fathers (and indeed mothers, too) are beginning to be able to answer the question in such words as these.

But the survivor war goes on. And one has to say that, in this kind of struggle over consciousness, there is no such thing as absolute virtue or purity; it is not to be achieved, and I am not even sure its achievement is to be desired. Many possible meanings can be derived from survivor formulation of wars. Too often a meaning is created out of illusion. The Vietnam War, because it has been so unacceptable to virtually everyone, has provided a special opportunity for locating much of that meaning closer to the grim actuality. To the extent that this can be accomplished, Vietnam will have a perverse value in providing insight about war in general.

6

Medicalized Killing in Auschwitz

During the near decade of my work on Nazi doctors, I sustained myself partly by imagining the day on which they would no longer inhabit my desk and my mind. With the completion of the study and the publication of my book The Nazi Doctors: Medical Killing and the Psychology of Genocide *(1986), the first part of that image has been realized. But of course they continue to inhabit my mind; and my question now, to myself, is, In what way?*

What they seem to continue to represent for me is an embodiment of a certain murderous behavior that need not feel *like murder. In that sense they may seem to epitomize what Hannah Arendt called "the banality of evil." But that is not quite the case. Although they were indeed banal to begin with, that was not true of either the evil they did or what they became in doing it. This essay is concerned with the actualization of their potential for evil, and with the context, institutional and ideological, within which the evil took shape. These doctors linger in my mind as illustrations of the relative psychological ease with which*

I wish to thank Prof. Dr. Paul Matussek, Director, Forschungsstelle für Psychopathologie und Psychotherapie in der Max-Planck-Gesellschaft, Munich; and Dr. Friedrich Hacker, Director, Institut für Konfliktforschung, Vienna, for their invaluable help with arrangements. I make fuller acknowledgment of the others whose participation was indispensable to the work in my book *The Nazi Doctors: Medical Killing and the Psychology of Genocide* (New York: Basic Books, 1986).

one can enter a killing process, and at the same time as reminders, in their violations, of questions of human responsibility. (I examine more closely the central psychological mechanism involved, which I call "doubling," in chapter 14.)

I gave the first version of this chapter at an international conference at the Yad Vashem Holocaust Research Center in Jerusalem, and subsequent versions of it as the Messenger Lectures at Cornell University and a keynote address to the American Academy of Psychoanalysis, all in 1980.

While this chapter speaks to general ethical questions in medicine, my deepest concern is with the larger phenomenon of killing in the name of healing, and with the human potential for mass murder.

SINCE LATE 1977, I have been conducting a psychological study of medical behavior in Auschwitz and of Nazi doctors in general. I have been especially interested in the relationship of doctors, SS doctors in particular, to the killing process—in the transformation from healer to killer. I am concerned with the importance of the medicalized pattern for the overall Nazi project of mass murder and have therefore tried to examine the interaction of biomedical ideology, political ideology, and individual behavior. Finally, the work raises questions of more general significance: for doctors and medicine elsewhere; for scientists, other professionals, and institutions of all kinds; for approaches to triage and control over life and death; and for our understanding of human nature and human values.

After describing how I did the study, I will discuss what I call the Nazi "biomedical vision" and its relationship to the killing of mental patients as well as to Auschwitz. Next I will suggest features of the Auschwitz atmosphere, particularly in regard to the psychological factors, or mechanisms, that enabled the Nazi doctors to do what they did. Finally, I will turn briefly to the general problems raised by the study.

I

Much of the study revolves around interviews I conducted in Germany and Austria with twenty-eight former Nazi doctors and one pharmacist. Five of the doctors had at some time worked in concentration camps. Six others had been involved with what was called the "euthanasia" program, which was mainly the killing of mental patients, mostly from 1939 to 1941 but afterward as well. A third group consisted of eight high-ranking Nazis who were involved in linking medical principles with racial ideology, both as theoreticians and as administrators. Another group of six held responsible positions in the Nazi medical hierarchy; their work became tainted by the various projects in which they took part. The three remaining doctors were for the most part engaged in traditional military medicine on the eastern front, but at the same time they were partly aware—and trying to avoid awareness—of the massive killing of Jews by *Einsatzgruppen** troops immediately behind the lines.

Introductions to the doctors were carefully arranged for me, largely by one person—a friend who, as the director of a Max Planck Institute in Munich and a professor of psychiatry, is a person of high standing in German medicine. He wrote an initial letter introducing me as a "prominent American researcher" who had worked on Hiroshima and Vietnam, which conveyed to those with whom I talked a sense of my concern with destructiveness in general.

About 70 percent of those approached in this way eventually agreed to see me, motivated in part by a sense of obligation to me as a "colleague" and in part by an inner inclination that included recognition of an opportunity to affirm their post-Nazi identity. They spoke with varying degrees of candor, indirection, and evasiveness, and I cross-checked much of the information against descriptions by others and various records, especially early ones. Still, I was surprised at how willing they were to see me and how relatively freely they talked. They had a need to explain themselves—to try to justify themselves. In the process, they revealed a great deal, but none really confronted in a moral sense what he had done or been part of. Often the doctor I interviewed would talk as if he were a third person, looking back at events as an observer.

I also interviewed a second group of former Nazis: twelve nonmedical professionals—lawyers, judges, teachers, architects, party officials and organizers—who gave me valuable background on the general Nazi project and how professionals fit into it.

Finally, I interviewed a third and very different group, eighty Auschwitz survivors who had been associated with medical work of some kind, most of them former prisoner doctors. These interviews were held throughout Western Europe (Germany, Austria, France, England, Norway, Denmark) and in the United States, Israel, Poland, and Australia. Survivor physicians provided me with invaluable descriptions of the behavior of

* *Einsatzgruppen,* literally "task forces," were the special mobile formations attached to the SS Security Police, which carried out mass murder of Jews in occupied areas.

Nazi doctors and of the entire pattern of pseudo-medical behavior in Auschwitz.

Most of the interviews in the first two groups were conducted with the help of an interpreter-research assistant, specially trained to facilitate communication.[1] All of these interviews were tape-recorded, which permitted me to work from the original German. The survivor group differed in that many spoke fluent English (including some living outside of English-speaking countries), while others required interpreting from Hebrew, Polish, French, and German. I spent a minimum of two to four hours with most people in all three groups but had much more time with many of them, sometimes thirty hours or more during six or seven interviews, each lasting from a few hours to an entire day.

The psychological paradigm of symbolization of life and death[2] (see chapter 1) is important here in stressing both the ultimate and proximate dimensions. At the ultimate dimension I seek to account for relationships to larger historical experience. These involve the struggle with symbolic forms of immortality: the collective sense of being part of something larger than the self, which will—at least in one's imagery—continue indefinitely, beyond one's own limited life span. This can be a human group, a set of social, political, or spiritual principles, a movement, nation, or institution. Symbolization of immortality was of course central to the Nazi concept of the "Thousand-Year Reich."

The general paradigm applies, I believe, to the widespread individual experience of separation, disintegration, and stasis among many Germans during the period following the First World War. These feelings were described to me repeatedly in connection with general demoralization and confusion in association with military defeat, economic duress, and the threat of revolution. For many Germans, the Nazi movement held out the promise of new human connection, general social integration, and a sense of development and progress—all in the service of a vast national and cultural revitalization.

II

Many students of the Holocaust have rightly stressed the idea of a barrier that has been removed, a boundary that has been crossed: the boundary between violent imagery and periodic killing of victims (as of Jews in pogroms) on the one hand, and the systematic genocide in Auschwitz on the other. My argument here is that the medicalization of killing—the imagery of killing in the name of healing—is one important way of understanding that terrible step. At the heart of the Nazi enterprise, then, is the loss of a boundary between healing and killing.

In the sequence of psychological impressions of the killing process at Auschwitz and other death camps, early reports stressed Nazi sadism and viciousness. But as those attempting to understand the process realized that sadism and viciousness could not in themselves account for the killing of millions of people, the stress shifted to the principle of faceless, bureaucratized killing.[3] This remains a significant and necessary emphasis. Yet my belief is that neither of these emphases is sufficient in itself. We need also to consider motivational principles concerning ideology and the various psychological mechanisms that contributed to the killing.

What I call medicalized killing certainly includes expressions of sadism and depends upon the elaborate bureaucracy and routinization of killing that prevailed in Auschwitz and other camps. But it also focuses upon the psychological motivations of specific individuals involved in the killing.

Medicalized killing can be understood in two ways. One is the efficient or so-called surgical method of killing large numbers of people by a controlled technology using highly poisonous gas. This method becomes a way of protecting the killers from the psychological consequences of face-to-face killing. Nazi documents reveal considerable concern with precisely those psychological consequences among *Einsatzgruppen* troops, a large number of whom apparently experienced incapacitating symptoms in response to their "work." A former *Wehrmacht* neuropsychiatrist, assigned to treat members of the *Einsatzgruppen*, estimated, in an interview with me, that as many as 20 percent of those who did the actual killing had significant psychological difficulties. In other words, there were impediments—human impediments—when applying ordinary military methods to mass murder on this extraordinary scale. What I am calling surgical killing provided a means to overcome these impediments by minimizing the psychological difficulties of the killers.

But there is another dimension of medicalized killing, one that I believe is insufficiently emphasized: killing as a therapeutic imperative. This kind of imagery was dramatically revealed in the words of an SS doctor in response to a question posed to him in Auschwitz by a distinguished survivor physician, Dr. Ella Lingens-Reiner. Pointing to the chimneys in the distance, she asked, "How can you reconcile that with your Hippocratic oath?" His answer was: "When you find a gangrenous appendix you must remove it."[4]* The image here is of the Jews as a gangrenous disease, which

* Dr. Lingens-Reiner had reported the same incident in her book slightly differently. Her question to the SS doctor Fritz Klein was: "Have you, as a doctor, no respect for human

has to be removed from the social or racial body of the German people in order to bring about a cure. Most SS physicians would not have answered that question so absolutely, would not have held such an extreme ideological position. But they were not likely to be entirely free of such "therapeutic" imagery, which was psychologically prevalent in the Auschwitz atmosphere and provided an important basis for the extermination camps in general.

Such imagery recalls the description of Turkey during the nineteenth century as the "sick man of Europe," and more specifically the similar attitude toward Germany at the end of the First World War. Adolf Hitler, writing, in the middle 1920s, in *Mein Kampf* on the German state, said, and italicized for emphasis: "*Anyone who wants to cure this era, which is inwardly sick and rotten, must first of all summon up the courage to make clear the causes of this disease.*"[6] Certainly many Germans felt that way, and one vision of cure involved the extermination of the Jewish people and the extermination or subjugation of Gypsies, Poles, Slavs, and other groups. That vision culminated in specific views of leading Nazi officials. For Hans Frank, jurist and *Generalgouverneur* of Poland, "the Jews were a lower species of life, a kind of vermin, which upon contact infected the German people with deadly diseases." Frank frequently referred to Jews as "lice," and when the Jews were killed in the area of Poland he ruled, he declared that "now a sick Europe would become healthy again."[7] Himmler used similar language in cautioning his SS generals against tolerating the stealing of property that had belonged to dead Jews: "Just because we exterminate a bacterium we do not want, in the end, to be infected by that bacterium and die of it."[8]

Part of this vision includes a religion of the will, in which the will becomes "an all-encompassing metaphysical principle."[9]* What the Nazis "willed" was nothing less than total control over life and death, and, indeed, control of the evolutionary process. Making widespread use of the Darwinian term *selection,* the Nazis sought to take over the functions of nature (natural selection) and God (the Lord giveth and the Lord taketh away) in orchestrating their own "selections," their own version of human evolution.†

---

life?" His answer was: "Out of respect for human life, I would remove a purulent appendix from a diseased body. The Jew is the purulent appendix in the body of Europe."[5]

* The celebration of that religious impulse was epitomized by the gigantic Nuremberg rally of 1934, whose theme, "The Triumph of the Will," became the title of Leni Rienfenstahl's celebrated film. Riefenstahl, in an interview with an assistant of mine, made clear that it was Hitler himself who provided that slogan for the overall Nuremberg rally.

† Stern makes a related point when he speaks of the Nazi and broadly fascist application of the doctrine of "the Will" as existing "within the framework of *Sozialdarwinismus* as that agency of Nature which acts in the social and political sphere with the same absolute validity as the principle of natural selection does among species of animals."[10] But the Nazi version

The therapeutic imperative was a biological imperative. One could call the Nazi hierarchy a "biocracy"—in the sense of the model of a theocracy but with an important difference. In a theocracy, the rulers are the high priests, empowered by their tie to the sacred. In the Nazi biocracy, the political and military leaders—Hitler and his circle—were the rulers, but they ruled in the name of what was held to be a higher biological principle. Among the biological authorities who gave credence to that principle—including physical anthropologists, geneticists, evolutionary and racial theorists of all kinds—it was mainly the doctors who became the activists, the practitioners. Doctors regularly function at the border of life and death. They, more than other biological authorities, are associated with the awesome, death-defying, and sometimes deadly imagery of the primitive shaman, witch doctor, or medicine man.

Hence, manipulative political regimes or their clandestine agencies tend to call upon doctors to use their authority and skills—their shamanistic legacy—in support of the regimes' worldviews and against people perceived as threats to those worldviews. In the Soviet Union, psychiatrists diagnose dissenters as mentally ill and incarcerate them in mental hospitals—a procedure that functions as political repression.[11] In Chile, according to Amnesty International, doctors have been involved in torture for political purposes. In the United States, physicians and psychologists have been employed by the Central Intelligence Agency in unethical medical and psychological experiments involving drugs and mind-manipulation.[12] In the mass suicide and murder of more than nine hundred members of the religious cult known as the People's Temple in Guyana, in November 1978, the group's physician prepared the poison.[13]

To be sure, these examples differ fundamentally from the Nazi practices and are in no way to be equated with them. But their common principle is that of the physician as activist agent for some form of reality control or oppression.

The Nazis' unique intensity of focus on biological salvation gave special emphasis to this perverse use of the physician's power.

III

One may thus say that the doctor standing on the ramp at Birkenau—the division of Auschwitz where initial selections and most of the gassings were performed—represents a kind of omega point, a final common path-

---

of fascism is unique in the extent to which its social Darwinism is bound up with racial theory—what I call the "biomedical vision"—to which the doctrine of the will can be applied.

way of the Nazi vision of therapy via mass murder. In a sense, the doctor takes on the mythical identity of a gatekeeper between two worlds—that of the dead and that of the living.

Doctors were not tried at Nuremberg for performing selections, partly because the full significance of this activity was not yet understood.[14]* I believe, however, that the doctors' role in selections has even greater significance than their participation in medical experiments—for which doctors *were* tried at Nuremberg.

The SS doctors made the initial large-scale selections of arriving Jewish prisoners at the Birkenau ramp.[15] (Only Jews were systematically subjected to selections.) The task was performed quickly, massively, and often according to formula, so that old people, children, and women with children were all automatically selected for gas, while relatively intact young adults were permitted to survive, at least temporarily, in order to work. The great majority of arriving Jews—most estimates are of more than 70 percent—were quickly sent to the gas chamber. Since no medical examination was done and no medical skill was required for this function, the Nazis apparently sought to invest it with medical authority and to represent it as a medical procedure.

After a selection, the presiding doctor was driven in an SS vehicle usually marked with a red cross, with a medical technician (one of a special group of "disinfectors" [*Desinfektoren*] from within the *Sanitätsdienstgrade* or SDG) and the gas pellets, to a gas chamber adjoining one of the crematoria. There the doctor had supervisory responsibility for the correct carrying out of the process, though the medical technician actually inserted the gas pellets, and the entire sequence became so routine that little intervention was required. The doctor also had the task of declaring dead the victims inside the gas chamber, which in some cases meant looking through a peephole to observe them. This, too, became routine, a matter of permitting twenty minutes or so to pass before the doors of the gas chamber could be opened and the bodies removed. The doctor's participation in selections, then, was the first of a series of tasks involving the whole sequence of killing.

SS doctors also carried out two other forms of selection. In the first, Jewish prisoners were lined up on very short notice at various places in the camp and their ranks thinned in order to allow room for presumably healthier replacements from new transports. The other type of selection

* I was also able to discuss the issue with James M. McHaney, chief prosecutor of the medical trial, who confirmed the lack of full appreciation at that time of doctors' participation in the overall killing process. He stressed that the policy then was to prosecute high-ranking doctors (who were not likely to be at the ramp at Auschwitz), considered to have the greatest responsibility for overall medical crimes, and to do so on the basis of stark and convincing evidence such as that associated with medical experiments on concentration-camp inmates.

took place directly in the medical blocks, and is of great significance because it meant, in effect, that the medical blocks—places where people are supposed to be treated for their diseases—became centers for camp "triage." This was not, of course, the usual triage, in which a doctor lets those beyond help die while giving full medical energy to those considered salvageable (this was the meaning given the term as originally used by the French military). Rather, it was triage plus murder, in which the Nazis killed those prisoners judged to be significantly ill or debilitated, or who required more than two or three weeks for recovery. That length of time was apparently set in conjunction with I. G. Farben, the firm that controlled and contracted for much of the Auschwitz work force. When some prisoners had typhus, the inhabitants of an entire block or even of several blocks—sometimes hundreds at once—would be sent to the gas chamber in order to prevent further spread of the disease and an epidemic. In their murderous practices, these medical blocks became microcosms of the overall Auschwitz process.

SS doctors were active as well in determining how best to keep the selections running smoothly—making recommendations, for example, about whether women and children should be separated or allowed to proceed along the line together. They also advised on policies concerning numbers of people permitted to remain alive, weighing the benefits to the Nazi regime of the work function against the increased health problems created by permitting relatively debilitated people to live.

Doctors' technical knowledge was also called upon with regard to the burning of bodies, a great problem in Auschwitz during the summer of 1944, when the rapid arrival and destruction of enormous numbers of Hungarian Jews overstrained the facilities of the crematoria. These technical matters could include questions of physics—problems of maintaining great heat, of evaluating conditions for maximum efficiency in burning, and of overall function of the mechanical facilities of the crematoria.

Doctors also had to witness executions as part of their general function of declaring people dead and to sign various documents certifying that one could proceed with a punitive procedure. The latter function implied that a prisoner could survive the particular punishment ordered—such as a certain number of blows with a whip.

Finally, doctors were involved in killing by injections, usually of phenol, into the heart or the blood system. These were widely employed prior to the complete functioning of the gas chambers and were often used for very debilitated patients or for secret political murders. Doctors occasionally did these injections themselves, but more often they were performed by SDG personnel or brutalized prisoners.

All of these activities, of course, were manifestations of overall Auschwitz structure and function, as dictated from above. I am suggesting, nonetheless, that the doctors were given considerable responsibility for carrying out the entire killing process—for the choosing of victims, for the physical and psychological mechanisms of the process, and for the general equilibrium of killing and work function in the camp.

IV

Although I have been emphasizing the doctors' role in medicalized killing, the medical experiments on human beings have their own importance and can be understood as an aspect of the larger Nazi biomedical vision.[16] Generally speaking, in Auschwitz and elsewhere, medical experiments fell into two categories: those sponsored by the regime for specific ideological and military purposes and those that were done *ad hoc* out of allegedly scientific interest on the part of an SS doctor.

In Auschwitz, the first category consisted mainly of sterilization experiments—injections of caustic substances into the uterine cervix of women by Carl Clauberg, and the use of X rays on the genital organs of men and women by Horst Schumann, followed by surgical removal of testicles or ovaries to study the effects of the X rays. These experiments were actively promoted by Heinrich Himmler, who on the whole was somewhat deceived by the doctors in their claims that they were on the verge of achieving efficient and economic methods for large-scale sterilization of inferior peoples. Experiments were done at other camps on cold immersion and exposure to high pressure (as at high altitudes); on the effects of sulfonamides and other therapeutic agents on artificially created wound infections and gangrene; and on the effectiveness of various serums for typhus and yellow fever.

The second kind of experiment emerged from doctors' desire to do "scientific" work: many SS doctors found the enormous population of helpless victims irresistible from the standpoint of medical research. The largest *ad hoc* experiments of this category in Auschwitz were those undertaken by Josef Mengele and by Eduard Wirths, the chief doctor at Auschwitz. Mengele worked mostly with identical twins, but he also studied dwarfs, and to a lesser extent certain medical conditions, such as noma (tumorlike infectious ulcerations of the mouth and face, which can often become gangrenous). Because Mengele was known to be an ideological fanatic, it is frequently assumed that his study of twins was motivated by a desire to learn how to induce multiple births, in order to repopulate the world with Germans. The evidence, however, does not seem to bear out that assumption, even though his extreme focus on genetic factors did have a strong ideological component. Rather, I think, Mengele was continuing studies he had begun at the racial biology institute at the University of Frankfurt—studies of twins meant to confirm the overriding significance of genetic and racial factors. Mengele's dedication to the Nazi biomedical vision kept him always on the border between science and ideologically corrupted pseudoscience, a border very important to understand—both because it separates the two, and because it can be so readily crossed over.*

At times he stepped clearly over that border, as when he worked on prisoners who had the rare condition of eyes of two different colors, and injected blue dye into a brown eye in order to see whether the eye could be rendered blue like the other one. But according to observations conveyed to me by several prisoner doctors and by a prisoner anthropologist who took bodily measurements for Mengele, in much of his work he was apparently following standard practices of the physical anthropology of his time. His method was descriptive, the amassing of data; and I know of no evidence that he had any significantly original scientific ideas. On the whole, being a twin in his study had enormous survival value, as he tended to protect his research subjects. But it is also well established that on several occasions he had one or both twins—usually children—killed, because he wanted to see the results of a post-mortem examination.

Eduard Wirths's experiments were meant to be a legitimate study of precancerous growths on the cervix in women. The most destructive aspect of these experiments involved the surgical removal of all or most of the cervix, although a small tissue biopsy would have been appropriate to this kind of study under ordinary conditions. But these were hardly ordinary conditions; and in the absence of anything approaching adequate care for the women so "studied," there were of course many complications and deaths. Wirths also became involved in a small experimental trial of a new

* Since writing this essay, I have become still more uncertain about Mengele's motives. In *The Nazi Doctors,* I refer to suggestive evidence that he may have understood himself to be exploring biological ways to create outstanding leaders or gifted individuals. There is also considerable question concerning whether Mengele was always clear about which of his research subjects were identical twins—that is, from the same ovum—since they alone carry the same genetic structure, while non-identical twins have no more similarity in genetic structure than do ordinary siblings.

typhus vaccine: prisoners were first artificially infected with the disease, a procedure that resulted in a few deaths. Such experiments with infectious diseases—especially typhus, because of its danger to German military and civilian personnel—were performed on a much larger scale in other camps.

Other kinds of experiment at Auschwitz combined official purposes with individual interests—such as the use of drugs (probably including mescaline, morphine, and barbiturate derivatives) for purposes of extracting confessions, and the use of poisons, including the development of poison bullets. Smaller *ad hoc* experiments involved tooth extraction in the service of theories of focal infection, and there were relatively conventional bacteriological and microscopic studies. One borderline investigation involved the use of electroshock for mental illness, a project initiated, with the approval and sponsorship of an SS doctor, by an Auschwitz prisoner doctor with some experience in the procedure. Finally, as in many other camps, experimental surgery was done by SS doctors; that is, various operations were performed in order to gain experience in doing them, sometimes but not always under the supervision of more experienced prisoner surgeons.

On the whole, experiments in Auschwitz were perceived as relatively limited, as compared with the extraordinary scope of what I am calling medicalized killing. But in another sense, all of Auschwitz was sometimes viewed—by Nazi doctors as well as by prisoners—as one vast experiment.

V

In the sequence of medicalized killing, one can see a direct medical link between the official compulsory sterilization programs of 1933, the "euthanasia" programs beginning in 1939, and the subsequent Final Solution or concentration camp exterminations.[17] Many of the doctors I spoke to were in favor of the sterilization laws. These were broadly applied to people with conditions considered incurable, most extensively to mental defectives and schizophrenics. Some of the eugenic thought behind the laws extended far beyond Nazi Germany—there were at one time active sterilization laws in many states in the United States; but no country, before or since, has imposed on its people so extensive and systematic a program of forced sterilization.

The key event, however, in the sequence from sterilization to Auschwitz was the program of direct medical killing—loosely and wrongly termed "euthanasia"—that operated in Germany, mostly from the winter of 1939–40 to the late summer of 1941. This project was initiated on a direct order by Hitler and utilized large sectors of the German medical profession, especially psychiatry, to kill more than one hundred thousand German citizens who were defined as suffering from "incurable" mental disorders.

The killing function of Auschwitz-Birkenau was anticipated by that program in at least three ways. First, during that program, the systematic use of deadly gas to kill large numbers of people was developed. The gas chambers were camouflaged as shower rooms to allay suspicions of the victims. Carbon monoxide gas was released into the chambers, with the number killed varying from a few to as many as seventy-five "patients" at a time.

Second, there was a direct "medical" and "psychiatric" link between "euthanasia" and concentration-camp extermination in the form of the program known officially as 14f13. That program involved "physicians' commissions"—mostly psychiatrists, who were sent directly from the "euthanasia" program to some of the camps, including Auschwitz. There they "selected" "mentally ill" prisoners to be sent to "euthanasia" killing centers. Selections soon came to include anyone who was sick, debilitated, or Jewish. The general principle of "life unworthy of life" was thus extended into the camps in this immediate way to include not only medical but racial "unworthiness," as applied particularly to Jews.

Third, when the "euthanasia" program was officially halted in August 1941,* program personnel were sent to occupied Poland to establish and administer the extermination camps in which millions of Jews were killed in gas chambers. The first commandant of Treblinka, the largest of these extermination camps, was Dr. Irmfried Eberl, who had been an early participant in the "euthanasia" program and the director of the Brandenburg killing center, where the initial experiments and demonstrations of the use of gas chambers were undertaken. Eberl was the only physician ever to head an extermination camp, though his reign was brief because he was considered too inefficient.

* The official termination of the program did not actually end the killing. With most of the "euthanasia" gas chambers dismantled, some doctors continued to kill adult mental patients by means of drugs (mostly morphine injections) or starvation. This "wild euthanasia," as it came to be called, was often encouraged by health authorities but also was sometimes done at the initiative of the doctors themselves. The killing of children—at first infants with birth defects, but then older children with less and less incapacitating deformities or illnesses—was done mostly after the official termination of the adult program. For children, drugs (often large oral doses of barbiturates) and various forms of neglect were used throughout.

Auschwitz was planned separately from the "euthanasia" program, but there is a link in the person of Dr. Schumann, who came from a "euthanasia" killing center to Auschwitz in order to conduct the sterilization experiments mentioned earlier.

Nazi political leaders and psychiatrists did not originate the idea of direct medical killing, or "euthanasia." Arguments for killing mentally ill patients considered incurable had been put forward in previous German writings, the most influential of which was a book by Karl Binding, a distinguished jurist, and psychiatrist Alfred Hoche, *The Permission to Destroy Life Unworthy of Life* (*Die Freigabe der Vernichtung lebensunwerten Lebens*), published in 1920.[18] While the Nazis extended their murder of mental patients far beyond the relatively restricted criteria prescribed in that book, it became a bible for their psychiatric argument, most particularly its malignant phrase "life unworthy of life" (*lebensunwertes Leben*).

A special vocabulary was developed in connection with the "euthanasia" and deportation programs. Euphemisms for killing, such as "special treatment" (*Sonderbehandlung**) and "special action" (*Sonderaktion*), were very important and quickly became the vocabulary of the genocidal process. And the idea of "special treatment" for "life unworthy of life" became the realization of the Nazi biological imperative on a long-term basis. Soon the word "selection" was added, giving further verbal form to the spectacle of Nazi manipulation of the evolutionary process.

To understand these developments more fully, one must look for their broader origins. The "euthanasia" program was not solely the whim of Hitler himself, although his direct order initiated it. Rather, it was the incorporation of eugenic principles then having wide currency into the broader Nazi biomedical vision. Also crucial to the medical killing was the merging of the two major strains of European racism (recently described by George Mosse):[19] the older, mystical-medieval form of anti-Semitism and racism, to which Hitler was heavily exposed in Vienna and elsewhere; and the more modern, so-called scientific racism, promulgated by various writers including biological and physical-anthropological theorists during the late nineteenth and the twentieth centuries. Mosse points out that early racism existed in sixteenth-century Spain, for instance, in the concept of "purity of blood" as a justification for victimization of Jews. But, ironically, it was the eighteenth-century impact of the new sciences of the Enlightenment that provided considerable grounding for European racism, along with the Pietistic revival of Christianity.[20]

* The euphemism *Sonderbehandlung* was apparently taken from SS usage, where it meant killing outside of the ordinary legal process—essentially the same meaning carried over into the 14f13 program of "euthanasia" and subsequent mass murder in the death camps.

The doctors, of course, always expressed themselves in terms of "scientific racism." But there is evidence that the two strains merged in them as well: their claim to professional and scientific logic could cover primal impulses toward victimizing Jews and others, which they shared with much of the general population. Moreover, they could connect either or both currents of racism with what was, at least for them, a more fundamental vision of Nazi-linked national revitalization.

Perhaps the ultimate expression of this merger was the infamous collection of Jewish skulls begun in 1942 by an anatomist named August Hirt for study and display at Strasbourg. While most of these skulls were eventually taken from Auschwitz, the original idea, as expressed in a letter to Himmler, was apparently to take the skulls of "Jewish Bolshevik Commissars" to study a particularly evil manifestation of this disappearing and despised race.[21] Hirt thereby brought together the two strains of anti-Semitism. On the one hand, there is the mystical tradition of anti-Semitism and racism, for Hirt's plan recalls the Protocols of the Elders of Zion—the notorious nineteenth-century forgery involving a supposed Jewish world conspiracy, which came to include Jewish Bolsheviks and Jewish capitalists. On the other, his study of the skulls directly reflects "scientific racism."

These patterns were all part of a general approach to the medical profession put forward by the Nazis as a national program. That approach was elaborated by Rudolf Ramm in 1943 in an important book which became a standard guide for medical students and young doctors. In it, Ramm expresses great idealism about the physician's calling and conscience. He describes the new German physician as one who rids himself of materialistic concerns and embraces instead the new "National Socialist idealism," who is no longer concerned primarily with the individual patient but is a "physician to the *Volk*" and the nation; who is a "cultivator of the genes."[22]* While one cannot say that this perspective inevitably led to widespread sterilization, direct medical killing, and finally Auschwitz, it is at least consistent with those developments.

* I do not mean to imply that German medical behavior can be understood simply in terms of this idealism. Indeed, the profession was profoundly corrupted at virtually all levels, and much that doctors did was associated with self-serving ambition of various kinds. But the idealistic claim of the biomedical vision had great significance nonetheless as a baseline that could combine with and facilitate other motivations, including those I will discuss in relation to Auschwitz.

VI

In Auschwitz, too, killing was done in the name of healing. It is not too much to say that every action an SS doctor took was connected to some kind of perversion or reversal of healing and killing. For the SS doctor, involvement in the killing process became equated with healing. This, then, is what I call the "healing-killing paradox," the first of the Auschwitz psychological themes—or mechanisms—I want to suggest. These mechanisms help us to understand the kinds of self-process by which Nazi doctors could abrogate elements of conscience toward commitment to life-enhancement, and thereby minimize their sense of guilt while participating in killing.

Medical control of selections is a key aspect of this paradox, and Eduard Wirths was intent upon maintaining this control. He claimed that if doctors did the selecting, they would be more "humane" and save more people than would nonmedical Nazi personnel, a claim that sometimes had a kernel of truth. Wirths is a pivotal figure within the healing-killing paradox; prisoners who came into regular contact with him were impressed by his relative humanity and decency, but it was he who set up and maintained much of the overall program of medicalized killing in Auschwitz.

The consequences of this healing-killing reversal were also imposed on prisoner doctors,[23] even though their position as prisoners was radically different from that of SS doctors. Many took Herculean measures to save lives—for example, pleading with SS doctors to let certain people pass in selections, warning prisoners to leave the hospital when selections were imminent, replacing the identification numbers of living prisoners on the "selected" list with those of dead prisoners. But saving some prisoners in these ways usually meant that others would be killed in their place. The healing-killing paradox thus permeated all aspects of Auschwitz existence.

For SS doctors the integration into the healing-killing paradox involved a transition period, during which some became anxious and disturbed. Some of those I talked with or heard about had wanted to leave. Some were upset by selections, either expressing hesitation about them or temporarily (and in at least one case, permanently) refusing to do them. This reluctance could reflect fear, stemming from the whole scene of grotesque killing and dying, as much as it did moral restraint; in that kind of atmosphere, the one may be difficult to separate from the other.

One of the doctors I interviewed who had had this kind of response—Ernst B.—was well known in Auschwitz for his relative decency to prisoners—in fact, when eventually put on trial, he was acquitted on the basis of survivor testimony. When he first arrived at Auschwitz, he was appalled and overwhelmed by what he saw and wanted to leave immediately. He approached his superior, who convinced him that he was needed, assured him that he would not have to do selections, and told him that by staying he would help strengthen their unit, which was separate from the main medical division. Dr. B. decided to stay and struggled through the next three weeks—the all-important transition period—during which he made a concerted, conscious effort to overcome his anxiety and traumatic dreams, including guilty dreams about a former Jewish schoolfriend. As part of his struggle to get over some of these symptoms, he succeeded in integrating himself with SS doctors. He also managed to integrate himself to a considerable extent with the prisoner doctors who worked under him. Ernst B. was psychologically functional until the chief camp doctor, because of the extraordinary numbers of Jews arriving in transports, decided to ignore administrative distinctions and ordered him to "ramp duty"—that is, selections. He again became very upset and went immediately to Berlin to speak to the highest medical officer of his own administrative unit. He said that he was unable to do selections, stressing psychological incapacity rather than an ethical objection. The officer listened sympathetically, said he could understand as "I am a family man myself," and arranged for Dr. B. not to have to do any selections.*

To me, Ernst B. went on to describe how a younger man, fresh from an SS medical academy, was then brought in and assigned to do selections instead. The latter also became upset, virtually collapsing at the first selection he witnessed. He was then put through a "rehabilitation program" to ease his transition. One component of the program placed him under the guidance of Josef Mengele, who taught him that he would be "saving lives" through selections, and that it was necessary to do these things in order to solve the "Jewish problem." Dr. B. was also permitted to have his wife stay at the camp, which was very unusual, especially for a young doctor. Further, and most ironically, an older, Jewish prisoner doctor, a distinguished professor from Eastern Europe, was assigned to tutor him for his medical thesis, which he had not yet completed. Dr. B. formed a close relationship to the Jewish doctor, who became, in the opinion of Ernst B., more or less a father figure to him. After several weeks, the younger replacement was "strong enough" to perform selections and continued to do so until the end of the war. When taken into American custody, he killed himself.

Dr. B. feels more guilt, I think, toward his younger colleague than he

* That senior figure was himself extensively involved in human medical experiments, for which he was eventually convicted and hanged.

does about the massive number of Jews killed in Auschwitz. The Jews are more impersonal to him, and he is able to separate himself psychologically from the killing process.[24]

Another mechanism contributing to Nazi doctors' behavior was their relationship to ideological fragments. The great majority of doctors I interviewed—and, I believe, of Nazi doctors in general—were not ideological fanatics. Mengele and a few others were undoubtedly exceptions. Most seemed to believe only in fragments of ideology—fragments that could, however, be very important. For example, the doctors could believe such ideological elements as the importance of the Nazi movement for revitalizing Germany, and the existence of a "Jewish problem" that required a "solution." These ideological fragments could become a basis for resolving ambivalent feelings in the direction of prescribed beliefs and actions. As one former Nazi doctor told me: "It is a lot easier if you either totally believe in them [the Nazis] or you are against them. It is very tough when you are somewhere in between."

A third mechanism was Nazi doctors' contradictory sense of themselves as physicians. Doing virtually no medical work themselves, they could at times take pride in having distinguished prisoner physicians working under them. They would sometimes introduce the latter as the "professor from Prague" or the "professor from Budapest." Although these introductions contained an element of sarcasm or irony, they also served to provide a sense of medical presence and thereby to ward off suppressed shame and guilt at being involved in killing instead of healing.

The doctors could also reinforce their medical self-image by what they understood as "scientific" discussions of racial issues. In another manifestation of the inner struggle to continue to view themselves as physicians, they tended to become involved in what one SS doctor described to me as "hobbies"—such as the medical experiments on prisoners, or special small medical units or laboratories.

Within these struggles around professional identity, the strongest single pattern was the technicizing of everything. As an SS doctor said to me: "Ethics was not a word used in Auschwitz. Doctors and others spoke only about how to do things most efficiently, about what worked best." There can be no greater caricature of modern tendencies toward absolute pragmatism and technicism in place of ethics.

A fourth mechanism involved psychic numbing, diffusion of responsibility, and "derealization"—arrangements for diminished feeling and blunting of the meaning of what one was doing.[25] When doctors killed, they generally did so from a distance. It was usually someone else who injected the phenol and always someone else who inserted the gas pellets.

Heavy drinking—virtually every night and for some during the day—contributed importantly to the numbing. Discomfort felt by newcomers was often expressed, and vaguely put aside, at these drinking sessions, as were questions about Auschwitz in general. This was part of the transition period for newcomers. Their psychic numbing was encouraged—one may say demanded—by virtually everything and everyone around them. Powerfully contributing to that numbing, and to the relatively quick adaptation of most Nazi doctors, was the routinization of all phases of the "death factory." At the same time, the very extremity of Auschwitz transgressions—the sense that one was on a separate planet—contributed to the process of derealization, to the feeling that things happening there did not "count" in terms of the "real world."

A fifth mechanism was a bizarre form of construction of meaning. Auschwitz reminds us that human beings are such meaning-hungry creatures that one will render in some way significant and justified virtually anything one finds oneself doing. Auschwitz doctors went to work in the morning, joked with their secretaries, exchanged greetings with "colleagues," engaged in daily backbiting of their "enemies"—in other words, behaved as though they were in an ordinary place, an ordinary institution devoted to some life-enhancing purpose, instead of a vast killing machine.

The construction of meaning was enhanced by the well-known process of blaming the victim:[26] the Jews did not look human, the Gypsies did not distribute their food equitably, people died in the hospital block because of prisoner doctors' poor treatment. Even Mengele's sartorial elegance and cool pointing of the finger at selections were, in their dramatic staging, part of this extremely important quest for inner significance.

Two additional important mechanisms that I will mention only briefly involve omnipotence and impotence. SS doctors, in their literal life-death decisions, experienced a sense of omnipotence that could protect them from their own death anxiety in the Auschwitz environment. That sense of omnipotence, along with elements of sadism with which it can be closely associated, contributed to feelings of power and invulnerability that could also serve to suppress guilt and enhance numbing.

Yet doctors could feel powerless, consider themselves pawns in the hands of a total institution. That feeling was described to me as follows: "I'm not here because I want to be—but because prisoners come here. I can't change the fact that prisoners come here. I can just try to make the best of it." While doctors in most cases could probably have arranged to leave Auschwitz if they felt strongly enough about doing so,* they had no

* The problem about leaving was that the alternative usually was service on the eastern front, which during the last years of the war often meant death. Most doctors preferred to stay in Auschwitz.

capacity to interfere with the basic functioning of the institution. But that claim of powerlessness was also a means of renouncing individual responsibility and fending off a sense of guilt.

An eighth mechanism was the feeling of these medical victimizers that they *themselves* were undergoing an ordeal. They believed that they were faced with a tough, unpleasant job that they simply had to do, while in the process they could feel sorry for themselves for having to do it. That attitude was encouraged by Heinrich Himmler, who appeared at Auschwitz several times and made speeches similar to his famous declaration to *Einsatzgruppen* leaders about the enormous demands made upon Nazi killers ("Most of you must know what it means to see a hundred corpses lie side by side, or five hundred, or a thousand") and their heroic achievement ("To have stuck this out—and except in cases of human weakness—to have kept our integrity . . . is an unwritten and never-to-be written . . . glory").[27]

Still another mechanism was the attraction of order—the overall appeal of what Mircea Eliade calls the movement "from chaos to structure and cosmology."[28] To Nazis, doctors included, it was important to keep Auschwitz a coherent, functioning world. If things got difficult, doctors could point out how much worse they were before an orderly routine had been established in Auschwitz—or in other camps where no such order existed.

Finally, there was one overall mechanism, which I call "doubling," within which all the others operated. Through doubling (described in detail in chapter 14), a relatively separate "Auschwitz self" could be formed, which drew upon Nazi ideology and the Auschwitz atmosphere in ways that could more or less integrate all of these mechanisms into a functioning whole. One could both participate actively in the killing and remain tender in one's family relationships and even occasionally in certain relationships in Auschwitz.

VII

By way of conclusion, I would like to mention three general areas of concern suggested by the study.

First, the study of Nazi behavior forces us to re-examine relationships between healing and killing. When we do, we find that the distinction—the barrier—between them has always been more fragile than we wish to believe. That fragility is revealed in primitive mythology and ritual, as described in the works of Joseph Campbell, Otto Jensen, and James Frazier. Whether the killing is done by mythological gods, by human medicine men, witch doctors, or shamans, specifically as religious ceremony (as in various forms of human sacrifice), or in connection with hunting or warfare, it is done in the name of a higher purpose—on behalf of a healing function for the tribe or people.

In modern experience, the use of advanced technology radically alters whatever balance might have been maintained between healing and killing in the past. As the Nazis demonstrate, science in general, and biology in particular—however distorted or falsified—can be mobilized on behalf of a murderous claim to healing. So while focusing on what is specific to the Nazi project, we must also begin to raise more general questions about the significance of breakdown, or threatened breakdown, of distinctions between healing and killing—for physicians, scientists, and professionals everywhere, and for the institutions they create and maintain. We must raise the same questions concerning current projections of "triage" policies for combating starvation and disease.

Second, healers—even the highly imperfect healers of modern medicine—did not automatically turn into killers overnight without some ideological justification and motivation for doing so. Human beings and ideology can perform strange and deadly dances, using incomplete choreography as a basis for endless inventive steps. The fact that people embrace only fragments of ideology rather than the total system does not mean the ideology is any less dangerous—especially when it involves the reversal of healing and killing. It can be all the *more* dangerous because one can embrace these fragments in the name of absolute consequences. The Nazis mobilized a peculiar combination of partial, often fragmented ideology and total (comprehensive) ideology, which individuals—here, doctors—lived out. This Nazi blend was never fully coherent, yet held out something for everyone but its victims. The Nazi way of combining political and biomedical imagery suggests the flexibility and intricacy with which ideological elements can be held. If these elements can evoke collective imagery of revitalization, their destructive and contradictory components can be absorbed. Ideological systems can then have even greater significance than previously realized in motivating and supporting murderous behavior.

Third, I believe that a deeper exploration of the Nazi practice of medicalized killing—and of the ideological, historical, and psychological currents around it—takes us closer to an understanding of Nazi genocide. This is not, of course, the only emphasis that can be made in the approach to the terrible question of Nazi mass murder. Rather, it provides an additional dimension to our understanding of how such a program could be instituted, and how individual people could help carry it out. I am suggesting that the elements contributing to mass murder, including extensive sadism and technicized bureaucratic killing, were contained within an overall Nazi biomedical vision of mass murder as a healing process. More generally, we do well to understand much collective violence in terms of a perverse quest for the vitality and immortality of one's own group. We thus encounter the impulse toward mass murder in the name of "more life."[29]

We need to understand that impulse, wherever it occurs, if we are to renew the meaning and spirit of healing, and in the process renew ourselves.

7

"Decent" People and Evil Projects

As I write this commentary, a number of German psychoanalysts and psychotherapists are raising questions about their mentors—their teachers and training analysts. They want to know what those mentors were doing under the Nazis, specifically in relationship to the strange entity known as the Göring Institute discussed in this essay. I include the piece, even though originally a book review (for the New York Times, *of* Psychotherapy in the Third Reich: The Göring Institute *by Geoffrey Cocks), because it focuses on a problem I believe to be at the moral center of professional behavior, or professionalism.*

In earlier work with Vietnam veterans, I discussed a tendency among professionals, especially those in healing professions, to consider any *work they do to be good,* because *it is healing. The implicit assumption is that, as a professional, one functions independently of ideological and institutional forces. That false assumption had grotesque consequences in Nazi Germany for members of all of the professions. What complicated the problem was that people could do humane individual work, as did psychotherapists at the Göring Institute, while actively serving an evil regime.*

I found this phenomenon of the "decent Nazi" to be widespread among doctors I studied. And I would raise the possibility of corollaries among "decent nuclear strategists" in both the Soviet Union and the United States—men and women who may be gentle and considerate in personal relationships, even "balanced" in resisting more extreme positions of vulgar colleagues, and who do most of the work in promoting the nuclear weapons progression toward doomsday. Still more broadly, the moral choices mentioned in this essay apply, in subtle and not so subtle ways, to all of us who claim to be professionals, and affect both our everyday actions and our possible contributions to a human future.

WHEN Matthias Heinrich Göring set up a psychotherapeutic institute in Nazi Germany, it was no disadvantage to have a first cousin named Hermann. But was that institute a help to psychotherapy as a healing profession—or was it a means of placing German psychotherapy in the hands of the Nazis?

Geoffrey Cocks, who teaches history at Albion College in Michigan, argues in his book on the Göring Institute, *Psychotherapy in the Third Reich* (the source of all of the quotations in this essay), for psychotherapeutic achievement. He asks us to question the assumption that the Nazis simply "polluted and destroyed" the field of medical psychotherapy, and to look instead into "the seams, cracks, and niches" of a regime whose contradictions could give rise to surprising professional opportunity. In fact, he tells us, "the Göring Institute represented a unique and significant step in the development of psychotherapy in Central Europe." Mr. Cocks is aware that the claim is a startling one, but he builds a considerable case for it, based on interviews with surviving members of the institute as well as on intensive study of documents and writings of the time. The strange and troubling story reveals much about professionals' experience in Nazi Germany and the moral vicissitudes of psychotherapy there and elsewhere.

Those who formed the German General Medical Society for Psychotherapy in September 1933 chose Matthias Göring as their leader because they believed that his name, his Nazi contacts, and his moderate personal qualities would offer sufficient protection for them to continue to practice their relatively new and fragile profession. They felt threatened not only by the regime itself but by the influence on the regime of the medical-psychiatric establishment, with its strongly organic, bitterly anti-psychological bias.

Göring, a neuropsychiatrist and Adlerian psychotherapist, succeeded beyond their expectations. He created a thriving institute backed financially and politically by various elements of the regime. And by absorbing the Berlin Psychoanalytic Institute, which had lost most of its predominantly Jewish members, Göring brought about what Mr. Cocks considers a doubly ironic situation: a Nazi agency facilitated the survival of the despised "Jewish science" of psychoanalysis; and a group of psychotherapists benefited from association with their old rivals, the Freudian psychoanalysts, who had previously been suspicious of the former's heretical tendencies. Still more remarkable was the spectacle of Jungians, Adlerians, Freudians, independents, and strong advocates of a Nazi-oriented psychotherapy working together under the same roof, at first mainly through separately functioning sections of the institute but increasingly as an integrated faculty carrying out the institute's functions of training, research, therapy, and consultation. Perhaps only the Nazis could have accomplished that.

Göring was the guiding spirit who made it all happen. He was a father protector, known in the institute as "Papi" or "Father Christmas" because of his "long white beard and grandfatherly personality." He took in therapists who were in trouble with the regime because they had Jewish wives, and encouraged ingenious survival arrangements. (One could, for instance, discuss Freudian ideas as long as one did not call them that or use classical Freudian terms.) He even permitted his wife, Erna, to undergo psychoanalysis with a Freudian, Werner Kemper, over the course of which she is said not only to have changed from a "dangerous defender" of Nazified psychotherapy into an admirer of psychoanalysis, but to have passed along information regarding colleagues who were in any danger. Göring also vigorously defended the interests of psychotherapy against the constant attacks of prominent psychiatric critics.

By functioning in this way, the psychotherapists of the Göring Institute were able to help a considerable number of patients, including Jews and others in difficulty with the regime. The institute continued to function until the German defeat, after which its members became a nucleus for the revival of German psychotherapy, mostly in West Germany, but to a lesser extent in East Germany as well.

There is, however, another side of the story that is insufficiently emphasized by Mr. Cocks. It has to do with the Nazi principle of *Gleichschaltung,* which means "coordination" or "synchronization" but was actually a euphemism for purging and assuming control over political and professional groups of all kinds. *Gleichschaltung* included components of terror, idealism, and careerism and was more frequently than not self-imposed. Mr. Cocks is aware that the Göring Institute was a form of *Gleichschaltung,* and even quotes the statement by Martin Bormann (the head of Hitler's party chancellery) that "the Führer holds the cleansing of the medical profession far more important than, for example, that of the bureaucracy, since in his opinion the duty of the physician is, or should be, one of racial leadership." In the author's fascination with the Göring Institute's successful maneuvering within the confusions of the Third Reich, I believe he underestimates the extent to which it became an organizational creature and a servant of the regime.

Matthias Göring had to be eminently acceptable to the regime to become the leader of medical psychotherapists; and he was, in fact, a dedicated Nazi party professional who made *Mein Kampf* required reading for psychotherapists. He was also a strong advocate of what was called a "new German psychotherapy," which equated psychological health with Nazi attitudes and values. Because the new psychotherapy never took clear shape, Mr. Cocks assumes the *Gleichschaltung* was limited and superficial. But loose combinations of ideological fragments could be embraced by various professionals, certainly by many of those psychotherapists, in ways that were useful to the regime. Many of them were motivated to find connections between these ideological fragments and their own prior professional beliefs.

For instance, Adlerians could associate their stress on family and community with the strength of the German *Volk* and the goal of rendering it "rich in creative spirits [rather than producing] hysterics and obsessive neurotics." Matthias Göring himself could declare, "German psychotherapy does not recognize any leveling: it wishes to force all abilities from a person, not for his own sake, but in service to the *Volksgemeinschaft* [community of the people]." When the most rabid Nazi in the clinic declared, "What it is that the Führer appeals to . . . what carries us along, is not rational argument, but the image," we should not dismiss this as mere obeisance but view it as setting a tone that affected others even as they maintained their wariness toward this colleague and his ideas.

Indeed, the Göring Institute needed some of that psychotherapeutic ideology in offering its consultative services to a wide variety of Nazi institutions—the Hitler Youth, the League of German Girls, the military services (especially Hermann Göring's *Luftwaffe*) and various programs of the SS, among others. How much all this contributed to the Nazis and their projects is another matter, but there should be little doubt the Göring Institute was theirs and not, as Mr. Cocks almost seems to imply, a relatively independent body making only necessary gestures toward the regime. Whatever individual therapists' relations with the Nazis—a few were in full sympathy, a few were strongly opposed, and the great majority had mixed sentiments and sought to adapt—the institution's policies could not deviate from Nazi ideology and practice.

Matthias Göring represents an especially important phenomenon among professionals: that of the "decent Nazi"—relatively kind and considerate, opposing from within more primitive Nazis and their brutal policies, but in the end loyal to the regime, necessary to it, and performing most of its specialized intellectual work. He was undoubtedly, as he is described here, a dedicated Lutheran who always carried a Bible, manifested concern for the individual and "the needs of the common man," and was much concerned with love and intimacy. But when the chips were down, he never ceased to be a completely reliable Nazi. The regime made use of men like Göring to a much greater extent than has been appreciated, men who were kind to individual Jews but believed that the Jews in general constituted a threat to the health of the Aryan race, men who brought idealistic impulses to an evil cause.

Consider two crucial situations. When John Rittmeister, the Freudian head of the outpatient clinic and a genuine anti-Nazi, was arrested, accused loosely of treason, and executed, Matthias Göring apparently consulted with his cousin on the matter. But, as Mr. Cocks concludes on the basis of later talks with Matthias's son, "it seems that Rittmeister and his wife (given a prison term) were compromised to the degree of arousing the patriotic wrath of the Institute's director."

Still more fundamental was Göring's relationship to the ultimate scandal of the psychiatric profession, the "euthanasia" project through which psychiatrists and other physicians actively participated in the murder of more than one hundred thousand people, most of them mental patients. Mr. Cocks reports being told by Matthias's son of his father's efforts to save the lives of some individual patients. But there is no mention of his failure to respond to approaches made by several psychiatric colleagues seeking help in opposing the program: notably Professor Gottfried Ewald, who prepared an elaborate memorandum on why he refused to join the inner councils of the project. The fact that Göring was approached reflected his reputation as an influential Nazi with some decent impulses. On the basis of several former Nazi doctors I have interviewed who had similar inclinations, I would suspect he experienced a certain amount of conflict about such matters but managed to suppress that conflict sufficiently to maintain his loyalty and service to the regime.

I am also skeptical of Mr. Cocks's claims about the value of the Göring Institute in reconstituting the German psychotherapeutic profession after the Second World War. We need to know more about the ramifications of the institute's Nazi affiliations, about what the profession has had to overcome or has failed to overcome. Indeed, precisely these questions are at the heart of polemical exchanges now taking place among German psychotherapists and psychoanalysts.

Mr. Cocks has produced a valuable study in an area previously neglected. But if we are to draw important lessons from it, we require more critical ethical and psychological probing than he has provided on questions of institutional collaboration, the political vulnerability of psychotherapy, and the relationship of "decent" individuals to evil projects.

8

The Inability to Mourn: Alexander and Margarete Mitscherlich

I first met Alexander Mitscherlich in the mid-1960s when he came to Yale University as a visiting lecturer. I remember Fritz Redlich, for many years chairman of the department of psychiatry there, saying that for him to be able to welcome and introduce Mitscherlich was one of the great moments of his professional life. It turned out that both Redlich and Mitscherlich were to become key figures for me in my undertaking work on Nazi doctors: Mitscherlich, in his early exposé of Nazi doctors (as described in this essay); and Redlich, in a number of conversations we had concerning former professors of his at the University of Vienna who had taken part in Nazi experiments on human subjects.

Later, the Mitscherlichs were to come to one of our summer psychohistory meetings at Wellfleet (which I have been coordinating for more than two decades), and were to bring their special understanding of historical memory to questions of Vietnam. During my work with Nazi doctors in Germany, I saw them whenever I visited Frankfurt. Even more important to me than the insights they suggested concerning my work was their being at the heart of an anti-Nazi German network of people who became my good friends and offered a very special kind of moral support, derived from a commitment we shared to confront the recent German past. We could also share personal moments of stark and beautiful contrast with everything in that past.

In writing this essay originally as an introduction to the Mitscherlichs' book, The Inability to Mourn,[1] *I was concerned both with the importance of recognizing German anti-Nazi heroes and with the moral significance of historical memory. Alexander Mitscherlich died in 1982; I am very glad to have known him, and to be able now to celebrate his memory.*

THERE IS no love without loss. And there is no moving beyond loss without some experience of mourning. To be unable to mourn is to be unable to enter into the great human cycle of death and rebirth—to be unable, that is, to "live again."

But what if one discovers evil in what one has lost—and, by implication, in oneself? How does one reconcile that evil with the sense of nobility one had originally associated with one's love? Is it then possible to mourn? If so, for whom and for what? What is the relationship of guilt and responsibility to mourning, or not mourning? What are the collective consequences of the inability to mourn? Alexander and Margarete Mitscherlich raise these questions about post-Hitler Germany. How timely they turn out to be for post-Vietnam and post-Nixon America. Beyond Germany or America, these are questions that trouble the sleep of contemporary man and woman.

One is in need of mourning when one has survived a death encounter, actual or symbolic; and the Mitscherlichs view post–Second World War Germany as a nation of survivors. But they are survivors unable to come to terms with the intensity of their love for the leader they lost. Most Americans have never realized—and many Germans prefer to forget—how intense those feelings were, how infused with imagery of shared virtue and of national purification and revitalization. Reading the Mitscherlichs' careful reconstruction of those feelings, on the basis of their clinical work with psychoanalytic patients, I was reminded of very similar emotions expressed to me by Germans (several businessmen and one physician) whom I interviewed in Hong Kong in the mid-1950s in connection with research on Chinese Communist "thought reform" programs. These men, having lived and worked in China at least from the time of the later war years, had been somewhat removed from the massive pattern of denial among Germans immediately following the Second World War. They spoke candidly about the "beauty" and "purity" of the Nazi Youth Movement, the hope Hitler instilled in his people and the love they felt for him, and the noble ideals they continued to associate with the Nazi program even if remaining critical of its "excesses." In their uneasy insistence that they "knew nothing about what was happening to the Jews," the people I interviewed were calling forth the kind of defense the Mitscherlichs observed regularly in their psychoanalytic patients: "the defense against collective responsibility and guilt—guilt whether of action or of toleration." The Mitscherlichs emphasize that virtually *all* segments of German society, notably people in industry and the professions, "had given the regime their definite and enthusiastic support; but with its failure they regarded themselves as automatically absolved from personal responsibility." It is precisely this "intensive defense against guilt, shame, and anxiety" that renders them unable to mourn the loss of the Führer.

Those of us who have worked closely with Vietnam veterans have found that they, too, suffer from sustained grief and an inability to mourn. To be sure they did not lose a Hitler. Figures associated with their war (such as Presidents Johnson and Nixon or General Westmoreland) had invoked powerful feelings in them, but none that could become associated with an equivalent imagery of either total deliverance or absolute evil. Yet those veterans, too, had experienced love and loss. Their love had consisted of an amorphous but powerful faith in American national virtue as well as much more immediate emotions toward comrades (and sometimes Vietnamese) whose grotesque deaths they witnessed. For them, too, guilt has been a barrier to mourning. And, in more muffled and distant fashion, the same can be said of the American people as a whole.

The Mitscherlichs describe the German people's avoidance of intolerable emotions "by breaking all affective bridges linking them to the immediate past." One can say the same of the United States in 1974 as we observe the rapidity with which Vietnam has disappeared from public discussion, its highly significant relationship to the entire Watergate scandal having been all but ignored in the various disclosures that culminated in President Nixon's resignation. The basic issue raised by the Mitscherlichs has to do with the capacity of survivors—and especially survivors who have colluded from a distance in killing—to confront their own psychological experience and its moral consequences. In the absence of such confrontation, a survivor must live in a state of desensitization, or psychic numbing, which keeps locked and silent within the self a potentially explosive conflict. The Mitscherlichs make clear that such a pattern of non-resolution has been characteristic of most adult Germans following the Second World War. And the psychological cost has been high: "A very considerable expenditure of psychic energy is necessary to maintain this separation of acceptable and unacceptable memories; and [that psychic energy] consumed in the defense of a self anxious to protect itself against bitter qualms of conscience and doubts about its own worth is unavailable for mastering the present." The Mitscherlichs are aware of the other, more constructive response: opening oneself up to the pain of the experience in order to derive from it various forms of insight, even what I have called "survivor illumination." That kind of confrontation and probing of a death encounter has probably been the source of many great religious and political advances throughout history. Nor has it been entirely absent in post–Second World War Germany: the Mitscherlichs themselves furnish a case in point.

In the United States of the Vietnam War years, the constructive survivor mode has been much more available, psychologically and politically, to those who would embrace it. In contrast to Nazi Germany, opposition to the Vietnam War could be openly expressed, and, in fact, energized more fundamental probing of American institutions and cultural and political ideologies. Moreover, an organized force of direct survivors of that holocaust, the Vietnam veterans, arose to infuse that confrontation with the special authority of those who had "been there" and returned to tell the tale. The extent of their impact on this country has, in my judgment, not yet been fully appreciated. Indeed, one of our major survivor images of the Vietnam War is that of anti-war veterans standing at the foot of the Capitol building angrily tossing away their medals, literally throwing them in the face of the country that awarded them, while angrily shouting such things as: "This is for Private Jim Smith, killed at Danang, for no goddamn reason at all!" That image took its place beside such related images as the corpses at My Lai, and the American marine setting fire to a Vietnamese hut with his Zippo lighter. These antiwar veterans performed the important historical task of publicly proclaiming the grotesque truth about their war even as it was still in progress, while at the same time (many of them) confronting their own sense of guilt and responsibility and demanding that their silent countrymen do the same.

Still, that form of confrontation, although considerably more widespread than in postwar Germany, has been limited to a small minority of Americans, veterans or otherwise. More characteristic have been the forms of denial the Mitscherlichs describe. Since they associate that denial and numbing with an overall national stagnation in the political and social spheres, Americans reading this book are bound to experience an enlightened concern about their own country's immediate future. It must be added, however, that, despite its considerable demands on the reader, the original German edition had an astounding impact: more than 100,000 copies sold; an extensive intellectual and moral response; and, eventually, the incorporation of passages from it into school textbooks. We may thus say that the Mitscherlichs, by exposing the German predicament, enhanced the capacity of many Germans to begin to break out of that predicament. That exposure could be of similar, if slightly more indirect, service to Americans now.

The Inability to Mourn, then, is a psychohistorical work of extraordinary importance and, at the same time, the expression of a survivor mission. We therefore do well to place the psychohistorians themselves within the work and to consider some of the sources of that illumination.

Alexander Mitscherlich, responsible for the basic conception of the book, was, as a student during the early 1930s, associated with a left-wing anti-Nazi movement. In late 1932, he displayed in the window of a bookstore a pamphlet entitled "Adolph Hitler—Germany's Doom," whose cover consisted of a cartoon depicting columns of SA (*Sturmabteilung* or Storm Troopers) members, their banners raised, marching lemming-like into a mass grave. When the Nazis assumed power the following year, Mitscherlich's house was searched and his library confiscated. He then spent considerable time in exile in Switzerland, but was arrested in 1937, upon returning to Germany to try to arrange for the legal defense of his group's leader. Mitscherlich spent eight months in a Nuremberg jail and, after his release, was required to report to the Gestapo twice a day throughout the remainder of the war. During that time he completed his medical studies, became a neurologist, and joined the staff of the university clinic at Heidelberg.

Dr. Mitscherlich became a minister in the first German government formed by the American Occupation and was shortly afterward selected by a group of German medical societies and reconstituted universities to head the German Medical Commission to the American Military Tribunal at Nuremberg dealing with medical war crimes of twenty-three German physician defendants. Dr. Mitscherlich and Dr. Fred Mielke, the other German representative, sat through seven months of trial as observers with access to all information and documents. Out of that experience, Mitscherlich and Mielke produced three books that have since become essential records not only of Nazi medical crimes but also of the more general human potential for corruption and evil that can exist under the guise of national loyalty and neutral professionalism. The first of these, *Das Diktat der Menschenverachtung,* was published in Germany in 1947, and appeared in the

United States in 1949 as *Doctors of Infamy: The Story of the Nazi Medical Crimes. Medizin ohne Menschlichkeit* was issued in Germany in 1960 and in England two years later as *The Death Doctors.* Rereading the authors' special appendix to the English-language edition of *Doctors of Infamy,* we are (in retrospect) not surprised to find Mitscherlich and his collaborator saying: "Now we must make every effort to help one another to create a common realm of life in which the simplest stirrings of justice are no longer threatened with death. . . . We shall succeed in this effort, which must claim every fiber of our strength, *only if we realize in full clarity the events of the past decades, their chaos as well as the planning behind them*" (italics added). And again: "Only he who traces the disaster back to its historical motivation can get the better of the overwhelming array of awful facts now unfolded in the quiet courtroom. This is the sole permissible impartiality." The authors also spoke of the "twilight . . . space in which all of us lived" and of "the guilt of all of us [that] arises in consequence of our failure to find the strength to air out this murky atmosphere." We may thus say that Mitscherlich and his collaborator were able to do what morally creative survivors have always done: achieve an animating relationship to guilt, transforming it into an anxiety of responsibility, and thus into a survivor mission of illumination. Indeed, the authors explained their task as "not one of indictment or extenuation, but of communicating contemporary history."

I believe that *Doctors of Infamy* was Alexander Mitscherlich's initial intellectual and moral confrontation with his and Germany's survival of the Nazi experience, and *The Inability to Mourn* his and Margarete Mitscherlich's more mature and probing later development of that same confrontation. For, during the time between the two books, Mitscherlich not only underwent psychoanalytic training but also became the leading figure in the re-establishment of German psychoanalysis. After extensive work with psychosomatic disorders, he began to apply psychoanalysis to social thought, his concerns ranging virtually everywhere from politics to architecture. His *Auf dem Weg zur vaterlosen Gesellschaft* (appearing in English as *Society Without the Father*) is a wide-ranging exploration into shifting contemporary patterns of authority, obedience, adaptation, and possibilities for autonomy. He became professor at the University of Frankfurt and director of the Sigmund Freud Institute in that same city, and was recognized as one of Germany's leading intellectual voices.

Dr. Margarete Mitscherlich, also an outstanding figure in German psychoanalysis, brings to this collaboration her clinical astuteness, critical intellectual judgment, and sensitive perceptions of contemporary social experience. In other writings, she has brought psychoanalytic insight to bear on such issues as levels of reality, the holding of ideals, and female quests for autonomy.

The Mitscherlichs are virtually unique in their capacity to combine classical psychoanalytic theory with careful attention to social and historical process. I have elsewhere raised questions about how much of that theory can remain adequate to our increasingly complex understanding of history. But there is no doubt that we can learn much from its sensitive application by the Mitscherlichs in this present volume. Indeed, psychoanalysis itself becomes infused by survivor illumination and reappears as a liberating body of thought that permits us to confront, and derive insight from, the most grotesque episode in human history. The periodic "Hitler boom" in Germany, with its confusing mixture of nostalgia, financial exploitation, identity hunger, and malignant denial, reminds us of the continuing importance of precisely this intellectual and moral task.

There is a sentence in the authors' appendix to *Doctors of Infamy* that has a haunting ring in post-Vietnam America: "We live no longer in the childlike ingenuousness of early history." Around that simple truth Americans and Germans can now better understand one another. In that same appendix, the two German authors acknowledge their debt to the Americans who conducted themselves with such seriousness and fairness at the Nuremberg trials. Now it is *our* turn to learn from the Mitscherlichs. They have much to tell us—about post-Hitler Germany, about the universal potential for evil, and, perhaps most important of all, about the psychological sources of our own painful moral contradictions.

PART II

IMAGINING THE END

The first promise of the atomic age is that it can make some of our nightmares come true. The capacity painfully acquired by normal men to distinguish between sleep, delusion, hallucination, and the objective reality of waking life has for the first time in human history been seriously weakened.

—EDWARD GLOVER, 1946

If this is the best of possible worlds, what then are the others?

—VOLTAIRE

9

The New Psychology of Human Survival

I wrote this essay specifically for this volume. It has two basic purposes. One is to make use of a psychological idiom for questioning fundamental assumptions—wrong ones, in my view, that perpetuate the nuclear arms race. That required a fresh look at cultural definitions, spoken or implied, of what is "normal and sane" and what constitutes "winning." It has always been important to question such assumptions and definitions, but the receptivity to the questioning is greater now than ever.

Second, I wanted to make a broad integrative statement, within which I could bring up to date my own thinking about recent nuclear developments. Inevitably, that meant focusing on President Reagan's "Star Wars" plan—both in itself and as an ultimate cosmic embodiment of the perversions of the imagination that characterize what we call "nuclear strategy."

The brief last section on the "species self" more or less crept in by itself. I do not remember its having been part of the plan. But I needed to explain to myself how the very grimness of scientific findings and official policies has contributed to the emergence of psychologically hopeful tendencies in large numbers of people. This may well be a new version of the old, sometimes Marxist, slogan that "worse is better." But I think of it as a more general expression of a peculiarly human possibility, however partially realized, for significant transformation.

WE LIVE on images. I am not speaking of the perversion of the word in relegating it to forms of self- or group-presentation ("improving my [our] image")—though we certainly live on that variety as well. Rather, I refer to collective mental pictures bound up with powerful psychological and historical forces, mental pictures that tend to construct much of what we consider our reality. These primal historical images can be associated with specific events, or with social and technological developments, and inevitably with new threats and new possibilities.

In the very act of evaluating such imagery, we find ourselves immediately raising issues concerning lived history, or the penetration of the individual psyche (and of large numbers of individual psyches) by historical forces—the fundamental question of that much-maligned (not only by its critics but in another way by some of its proponents), and yet very real, discipline we call psychohistory. When that piece of history concerns nuclear weapons, however, what penetrates the individual mind can be said to be cosmic in all meanings of that word. Such is very much the case when I suggest, as I shall in the first part of this essay, a series of new variations on the fundamental polarity we have been living with since the Second World War: imagery of extinction of the human species versus the creation of a human future. Nor do the dimensions diminish as I move along in this essay to such categories as the "new 'nuclear normality,' " the "new nuclear strategy of winning," the "Star Wars vision," "doubling and genocide," the "new nuclearism," "nothingness," and the "species self." If politicians describe their message as one of the "state of the State" or "state of the Nation [or Union]," then my message here is one of the "state of the cosmos."

Images

The first of these images—the most fundamental of all—is that of nuclear winter. Just what most people imagine in connection with that set of scientific findings is not easy to state and has to do with much of the subject matter of this essay. But collectively sinking into people's minds is *some* image to encompass the idea that the use of relatively small numbers of nuclear devices by *anyone* is likely to bring about the annihilation of *everyone*. It is known, of course, that scientists differ as to how much megatonnage is necessary to create the nuclear-winter effect: sufficient dirt and debris to block the sun's rays and lower the temperature throughout the world to an extent that plant life, and therefore human life, could no longer be sustained.

In one sense, nuclear winter is little more than an extension of imagery of extinction which began, at least in its contemporary form, with Hiroshima and Nagasaki. But as an expression of scientific findings (there are differences among scientists, but these mostly concern necessary megatonnage rather than questioning the principle), that idea of species annihilation becomes more concrete and more credible.*

To be sure, one hears much less about nuclear winter these days than one did a few years ago, during the early 1980s, when scientists first reported the phenomenon. That is partly due to a kind of American (and no doubt international) faddism: nuclear winter was *last* year's subject. But in fact, neither the potential phenomenon nor its historical image has gone away. To the contrary, over the last couple of years, the image has penetrated more deeply into our collective psyche as an organizing principle around which terrible truths, long resisted, become part of the shared knowledge of our time. In that sense nuclear winter marks a significant turning point in human consciousness.

With the image of nuclear winter taking hold, there are glimmerings—sometimes more than glimmerings—of an ethical shift as well: increasing recognition, at whatever level of awareness, that genocide has become self-genocide; murder on an absolute scale has become collective self-murder or suicide; and what we call "nuclear war" (the phrase is misleading without quotation marks) is no more and no less than species suicide, forms of which can be initiated from a variety of places and by a variety of groups on their own or in tandem with others.

The power and credibility of nuclear-winter imagery does something else of great importance: it enhances broader dialogue among various fac-

* Recent scientific findings (mid-1986) have been raising questions about some of the earlier reports on the phenomenon of nuclear winter. While much remains to be learned—and various additional scientific studies will tell us more—there is a danger of using such findings to reassert prior nuclear-weapons policies and to minimize the destructive effects of a nuclear holocaust. In a psychological sense, the issue is not whether we can prove that a phenomenon called "nuclear winter" would destroy all life on earth. Rather, that phenomenon epitomizes the idea of the "nuclear end." Even if it turned out that the nuclear winter effects were unlikely to occur, the rest of the effects of a nuclear holocaust are sufficient to warrant a concept of the "nuclear end." And, as Carl Sagan and others have pointed out, there are always additional possibilities of destructive effects that so far we have been unable to identify.

tions concerned with nuclear weapons, those thought of as "hawks," as "doves," or as somewhere (often obscurely) in-between. The improved dialogue is made possible by newly shared truths—not to mention the equally shared "death chill" of those truths. These partial ethical advances are in keeping with the many paradoxes of nuclear threat: the grimmest of all messages contains powerful possibilities for expanded wisdom and hope.

A second new image current takes us to the edge of psychopathology and evil in our society. I have in mind a certain ideological and organizational marriage from which we can hardly expect healthy offspring.

We have watched the re-emergence of neo-Nazi groups, now known by such names as Aryan Nations and The Order. Partly they do what neo-Nazis have always done: mobilize their hatred and violence toward Jews and blacks (mostly the former in this case) and other groups. Certainly, since the Second World War there have always been neo-Nazis in the wings, ready to exploit social and economic unrest. But these are neo-Nazis with a difference: they are *survivalists* as well. So they position themselves in isolated places, build up their extensive arsenal of small and not so small weapons, which they diligently practice using, anticipating the day—*their* day—of nuclear holocaust. That is the day when they (so their fantasy goes) will be the only, or at least the strongest, survivors, poised to take over the American government, and perhaps more. Nuclear war, that is, will be their special opportunity to realize their Nazi principles.

Perhaps we should not be surprised by the marriage. It is the joining of a murderous and apocalyptic political fundamentalism (the Nazi vision of mass murder in the name of healing and regeneration) with a specific nuclear form of equally apocalyptic fundamentalism (also in the name of regeneration) via an ostensibly powerful and privileged survivor élite.

The marriage bears watching. To be sure, these groups are very much on the social fringe at the moment. But they are serious and they have killed. Moreover, in them we find Nazism infused with, and potentially strengthened by, the most direct and pathological form of survivalist death denial. Nor have the potential combinations of this kind of marriage been exhausted.

We need to be clear that the phenomenon is, at bottom, a product of the apocalyptic currents of the nuclear-arms race: of the end-of-the-world imagery that haunts us all. The pattern bears some resemblance to a response to similar imagery of the "end" during the time of the plagues of the Middle Ages. At that time Jews were frequently accused of poisoning the wells and spreading the plague—and could be massacred or otherwise victimized by fearful perpetrators.

A third and very different image and event: the awarding of the Nobel Peace Prize to the International Physicians for the Prevention of Nuclear War. The award reflects highly significant human hungers. The first thing I want to say, however, is that all of us in the physicians' movement received the award in joy—because it was a joyous event, one that deepened our energies and kindled our hope. There was some confusion about exactly who the award was given to, and I am sure that many people associated with the movement had the same experience I had: friends and well-wishers stumbling over their friendly question: shall I congratulate *you?* I have learned to reply so quickly that my loud "Yes!" precedes the completion of the question—and I advise others in the movement to do the same. The sequence is this: first the decisive "Yes!" and then of course the appropriate show of humility ("Aw shucks, it's really nothing and I hardly did anything")—that step also a brief one—and then the third step: a prompt question to the questioner: "Okay, you have congratulated me, which I appreciate, but what are *you* doing in the way of peacemaking?" The serious point here is that the award was given not to individuals but to an organization that includes many thousands of us throughout the world—and was surely meant to be an invitation to still larger numbers of others, heretofore less active, to join in a quest for peace.

Yet there is another, more problematic, side to the award, which should in no way diminish our joy or pride but does demand our attention. I have in mind of course the uproar that followed in connection with the despicable letter, signed some years before by Eugeny Chasov, head of the Soviet physicians group, denouncing Andrei Sakharov as anti-Soviet. Much of the protest of the Nobel Peace Prize on that basis was, of course, orchestrated by groups that do not wish the physicians' movement well. But friends of ours were troubled also as we should be ourselves. For the issue of human rights is very real and will not go away. Neither the international nor the national American (Physicians for Social Responsibility) movement is a human-rights organization as such. But we cannot carry forth our program on behalf of that ultimate human right—of individual and species survival—while being indifferent to the suppression of our fellow human beings, all the more so if our colleagues in peacemaking are involved in that suppression or if (as is the case in the Soviet Union) some of those whose rights are being violated are also fellow physicians.

We require a politics of peacemaking, one that includes systematic prodding of our Soviet colleagues on this issue, even as we insist upon the absolute necessity to continue working with them for nuclear disarmament. (They might, correspondingly, feel the need to raise with us problems created by the American bombing of Libya—again, ideally, while stressing the need to continue our work together.) We have to an extent been doing this: others and myself have, directly and in writing, expressed strong concern to Soviet colleagues about the psychiatric incarceration of dissidents in mental hospitals, and about the status of Anatoly Koryagin in particular. There is no easy path here, but this politics of peacemaking must include a psychological and political balance, a viable equilibrium between promoting an atmosphere of cooperation with Soviet colleagues on nuclear issues on the one hand and expressing continuously to them our concerns about human rights on the other. We also need to dissociate ourselves from any violations of human rights, wherever they occur—and I think our Soviet colleagues can be made to understand this. We simply cannot retreat into the role of bystanders, any more than we would accept proponents of human rights becoming bystanders on nuclear-weapons issues.

In larger terms of shifting historical and psychological images, we should recognize the extraordinary importance of the Nobel Peace Prize. The physicians' organization was given the award because the value of its specific kind of work was recognized. But the Nobel Peace Prize committee has never been known for its radical impulses or its defiance of social norms. It gave us the prize because our message of nuclear disarmament and peacemaking is increasingly embraced by people and welcomed virtually everywhere. The human hungers reflected by the award, then, include hunger for truth about our nuclear predicament (the physicians' movement has been primarily educational), hunger for an end to nuclear terror, hunger for genuine rather than bogus security and for a clear path to a human future. All this is hardly just a matter of physicians or of any single peace group. The recognition is part of the shift in world consciousness we seek to recognize and to further. The award, then, is part of the collective revulsion toward these murderous devices and those who would use them, part of the collective rebellion of the human mind against an uncontested journey to doomsday.

A fourth new image current is another hopeful one: the universalization of nuclear concern. While nuclear devices have always threatened everyone on the globe, this truth is still in the process of achieving full realization. But increasingly—and the concrete findings of nuclear winter are important here, too—East-West nuclear issues have become North-South issues as well. And in this country there have been beginnings of alliances on nuclear-weapons questions with black and Hispanic Americans and with members of various new immigrant groups. The image of threat is earthwide: one is vulnerable whether one is, say, a black or a white South African, a Lebanese or a Syrian or an Israeli, a Russian or an American.

To further action that reflects this universalization, anti-nuclear activities must in some way combine with immediate survival problems in Third

World countries. Much more work has to be done on the relationships of various levels of deprivation and violence to conditions and policies that favor nuclear violence. We are likely to find that nuclear threat is not unaffected by the victimization of the majority black population in South Africa or by the economic subjugation of minority groups in this country. The pursuit of that connection, moreover, is a step toward integrating what often seem to be contending moral claims.

Here Martin Luther King was, as on many issues, ahead of his time. While fighting for the rights of blacks, he managed to oppose the Vietnam War and could also state, "I refuse to accept the cynical notion that nation after nation must spiral down a militaristic stairway into the hell of nuclear destruction." That statement was made, appropriately enough, in the acceptance speech for *his* Nobel Peace Prize (1964). The sentence that came next was the prophet's version of the human hunger of which we have been speaking: "I believe that unarmed truth and unconditional love will have the final word in reality."

A fifth, still newer image has to do with the radical fallibility of the highest technology. I refer here to the space shuttle disaster of early 1986. Few Americans could avoid participation in the pain of that instantaneous transformation of seven highly visible heroes—represented particularly by an enthusiastic and appealing young woman schoolteacher—into virtual nothingness. Nor did anyone mistake the fact that the technology (including the capacity of human beings to maintain it in absolutely reliable function) had failed, and not the voyagers themselves. Nor was anybody ignorant of the fact that it was *space* technology.

People differ in how much they associate the event with corrupting pressures coming from a weapons–technology-oriented administration, or from a beleaguered National Aeronautics and Space Administration fighting for its resources and bureaucratic hegemony. The point here is the sudden shared national experience of the most sophisticated technology that is in various ways related to the use of, or claimed defense against, nuclear weapons.*

The New "Nuclear Normality"

From the time of the appearance of nuclear weapons, contradictions in claims, frightening truths, and feelings of opposition have all been muted by means of imposed definitions of normality. These definitions must be

* The Chernobyl nuclear accident of 1986, which occurred after this essay had been completed, contributes in special ways associated with *nuclear* disaster (as discussed in the introduction) to a particularly profound and fearful version of technological infallibility.

understood in the context of the kinds of images just mentioned, since they seek to tell us how to judge ourselves in relationship to such images. For instance, in the halcyon days of early nuclear strategy during the 1950s, Herman Kahn and others made judgments in this area that were as bellicose as they were loose, whether made directly or implicitly: The reasonable normal man or woman was to join in "rational" assessment of how to prepare for and win nuclear wars. Above all, one was to remain calm and sensible, as opposed to protestors already on the scene who tended to become "emotional" and "unreasonable."

It may seem surprising in retrospect how generally accepted those judgments were. Indeed, they pervaded most professional environments. I can remember some of the responses that greeted the early efforts of Jerome Frank, a distinguished psychiatrist, to raise psychological and moral questions concerning nuclear threat. There were whisperings about his stability. What was the matter with Jerry? his fellow psychiatrists asked one another. What kind of "problem," early abnormality from childhood, caused him to raise such issues—and with such strong *feeling?*

More than that, recent release of a 1956 document reveals the active role of professionals themselves, especially psychiatrists and other physicians, in imposing nuclear normality. William F. Vandercook, a historian of that period, tells of the formation of a special panel called into being in early 1956 by the National Security Council and the Federal Civil Defense Administration in order to evaluate the willingness of the American people "to support national policies which might involve the risk of nuclear warfare." The panel was charged with determining the human effects of general awareness of a nation's civilian population that an enemy "has the technological capability of annihilating such nation," or of the possibility that the two nations in question "could produce mutual annihilation."[1] The panel was to be made up of "wise and mature individuals" with professional knowledge of human behavior and came to include eleven white males, among whom were five physicians (several of whom had been actively involved either in the Manhattan Project or at later nuclear-test sites), three of them psychiatrists,* the rest either social scientists with a military or morale background or retired military officers.

* I was troubled to find among them Dr. Frank Fremont-Smith, a psychiatrist I had known as the chairman and convener of a series of extraordinary conferences sponsored by the Josiah Macy Jr. Foundation on fundamental questions of the human sciences, several of which I had attended early in my professional life. Fremont-Smith was revered by virtually everyone associated with those conferences—including such prominent participants as Margaret Mead, Erik Erikson, Gregory Bateson, and Jerome Frank. Rarely did one encounter a man as soft and kind in manner and devoted to evoking whatever was creative in individuals and groups around him. But it turns out that Fremont-Smith chaired the original panel, and

In their report, "Human Effects of Nuclear Weapons," which they presented in November 1956, they declared their "firm belief" that it was "possible to prepare effective psychological defenses" for nuclear attack, so that "both the war effort and the National Government would be effectively supported." Moreover, such preparation would enable the populace to overcome their lack of "knowledge and real understanding of basic national security considerations," which causes them to "accept . . . wild exaggerations and misinterpretations." The panel recommended an extensive grass-roots discussion program in an atmosphere of "calm deliberation with less emphasis on the symbols and images of disaster that so often characterize the emergency approach to attention getting," and pointed out that stress on " 'awareness' [of annihilation]" was harmful because it leads to "attitudes and behavior of the majority . . . attuned to the avoidance of nuclear war, no matter what the cost" and to "weaken public support of policies that involved any substantial risk of nuclear war." The report appealed to "our pioneer background and inheritance [which] predispose us to count hardships a challenge and fortify us against complacency."

The report abandoned scientific for visionary language in declaring the intent, by means of its grass-roots approach, "to draw inspiration from our forefathers and to point our children to the sources which make all American generations one and which raise hope for a new dynamics of the human race." By means of this "patriotic renewal and spiritual advance," nuclear disaster "might become the opportunity for resolute survivors"—so that we could "nerve ourselves to make the very best of the very worst." In actuality, once the words gave way to policy, there was little enthusiasm anywhere for such a grass-roots discussion program. There was a National Academy of Sciences report in 1962 (the Project Harbor study) which argued for an "invisible" civil defense program in order to avoid stirring up in the American population "latent pacifism and fear of war." But, as Vandercook points out, in commenting on the failure of the "human effects" panel's recommendations to be implemented, "It is perhaps impossible to finally convince people that the threat of annihilation is an 'opportunity' to 'make the very best of the very worst.' "

While I will make no attempt to list all of the lessons of that sadly revealing tale, let me note a few: the depth of political and social impulse

---

had been senior radiological monitor at the Bikini atomic-bomb tests of 1946. I can now understand a later conference he convened on nuclear threat, which I also attended, as an effort toward redemption. The important point here is that even people with outstanding human qualities could succumb to, and indeed further, that particular zeitgeist of nuclear normality.

from above (in this case the Eisenhower administration) to impose nuclear normality, even if the whole population must be trained to achieve that "normality"; the ultimate recourse to apocalyptic mysticism in the face of profound contradictions perhaps unconsciously perceived by the panel; the ultimate refusal of the American populace—any populace—to believe the false claim of protection from nuclear onslaught.

But the extent to which professionals collude in nuclear normality also has to be noted. For in that collusion—in projects of nuclear normality—lies the attempt to control discourse and attitudes at least in the nuclear-weapons sphere. Behind the collusion also lie narrow and technicized notions of professionalism, which allow for all too ready embrace of the role of agents of adaptation to *anything*—even arrangements for species annihilation. Psychology, psychiatry, social science, and medicine are most vulnerable to this kind of perversion because they tend to be given the power to define what is individually or socially *healthy* or ill. They can thereby lay claim, on behalf of the regime, to individual and collective reality—even in defending (as in the example here) the central illusions of their time. We can speak of a "medical-psychological-professional complex" called upon to impose a version of normality that is sought by leaders and by many in the society as well, even though that normality flies in the face of all evidence to the point of becoming an officially sanctioned national illusion.

A major function of the physicians' movement and related groups has been an exposure of the false nature of such "nuclear normality." That exposure was epitomized by the title of an important book by Philip Green (published in the early 1960s): *Deadly Logic.*[2] Putting the matter in proper psychological context, my related term is the "logic of madness." But whatever the term, our insistent claim is that the abnormality lies in the conditions for total self-annihilation, and the healthy alternative in changing those conditions and diminishing or eliminating the threat. I believe we have succeeded in pressing the discourse in this direction, as evidenced by the increasing acceptance of these issues by professional societies as proper subjects for evaluation and discussion. More important, there is much evidence that the American people and others throughout the world increasingly—if often still inchoately—reject the preposterous claim that a world of genocidal devices poised for total self-annihilation is healthy and normal. But the moral and psychological struggle over nuclear normalcy is far from over.

A major second-round reassertion of nuclear normalcy can be found in the intellectually and morally scandalous Harvard study *Living with Nuclear Weapons.* The study was published in 1983, by which time nuclear weapons had become ensconced both in their stockpiles and in our collective minds. That, the Harvard group tells us, is the order of things—so that (as we learn in the last paragraph of the book) "living with nuclear weapons is our only hope" and "there is no greater test of the human spirit." Committing oneself to more drastic nuclear disarmament is to this group a "form of atomic escapism," which in turn is labeled as "a dead end."[3] They stand majestically above such "either-or" thinking; and while they acknowledge that nuclear war would be terrible, they go to some lengths to insist upon the right of imagining, under certain circumstances, a moral use of nuclear weapons, and upon the necessity of living with some "risk of nuclear war." The tone of the book is one of calm authority; its goal (as stated by Derek Bok in the foreword) to "inform the people"; its stance that of a reasoned middle ground between "denying that nuclear dangers exist" and "finding refuge in simplistic, unexamined solutions."

But the book's sensibility is best revealed in its treatment of nuclear–holocaust-related humor. Stanley Kubrick is chastised for rendering Dr. Strangelove, originally "a serious book about how a nuclear war might begin," into "an absurd fantasy." Concerning the film's subtitle, "Or How I Learned to Stop Worrying and Love the Bomb," the righteously "realistic" comment is "One way to stop worrying was black humor." Tom Lehrer is put in the same category, his satirical lyrics dismissed as another form of denial and mere release of tension—that is, as an undesirable alternative to the healthier "search for a better understanding of the vast problems nuclear weaponry creates." But can these "realists" truly believe that Tom Lehrer was reassuring us when he sang, "We'll all go together when we go"? Or that Dr. Strangelove's subtitle about learning to stop worrying and love the bomb is to be understood literally?

In the last paragraph of this segment, the authors declare, "The goal then is to be realistic without being fatalistic; to treat the dangers soberly without being inhumane." A wonderful goal—except that, behind that alleged realism lies true madness, and the experimental madness of Dr. Strangelove and Tom Lehrer are—bless them—among our most precious cultural expressions of genuine sanity.*

We shall soon, unfortunately, arrive at a third wave of nuclear normalcy—the present wave associated with the Strategic Defense Initiative.

* I feel the right to a certain say in all this because the authors invoke a somewhat absurdist comment of my own on language to introduce their discussion of these examples of humor (Lehrer and Strangelove) as manifestations of denial: my mocking observation that the phrase "nuclear exchange" sounds "like something pretty good—almost like gift giving."

New Forms of Nuclear "Winning"

The large images I mentioned earlier—and above all, the scientific findings of nuclear winter—impinge on traditional concepts of "winning"—but not always in desirable or logical ways. One of the many reasons we need to get out of the habit of calling nuclear genocide war is that wars, by definition, are associated with winning or losing. Now, however, no mind is fully free of the kind of imagery of extinction which makes it clear that nobody wins a nuclear holocaust, that everybody loses, everybody dies. What results is a partial acknowledgment of this truth (statements from even nuclear hawks to the effect that "nobody can win a nuclear war"), and at the same time an aggressive resort to the far and dangerous reaches of compensatory fantasy. The principle of "winning" is embraced more fiercely, even as it becomes more removed, arcane, and bizarre. The fantasy continues to be fed by the fact that the very stockpiling of the weapons inevitably contains war-fighting options: that is, plans for fighting and winning a "limited nuclear war."

Now the imagery of winning fluctuates strangely among three different levels. There is first the idea of winning the arms race in a sense of bankrupting the Soviet Union (leaving out such things as mutual excess weaponry, the Soviet Union's determination to maintain "parity," and our own formidable budgetary deficiencies). Then there is reversion to talk of winning the actual "nuclear war" (whatever the dubious assumptions required in the nature of restraint by the nuclear adversaries). Finally there is the newest (also the oldest) arena, which we might call "winning the survival." Here the fantasy may take the most malignant form of all.

The vision created by the marriage of neo-Nazis and survivalists, as mentioned earlier, is one clear example: Armageddon is *required* for a special group of survivors to win the day for the Nazi dream. But while that vision exists only on a limited social fringe, the association of nuclear holocaust with a Biblical Armageddon does not. In a revealing exploration of the nuclear–weapons-related imagery in Amarillo, Texas, where (at the Pantax Corporation) all weapons are finally assembled, A. G. Mojtabai demonstrates how broadly "end-time" imagery penetrates the Christian imagination in that city. A Pentecostal preacher puts the matter most concretely when he declares Revelation to be "almost an exact description of thermonuclear blast," and adds that "if the Amarillo bomb dropped today, it wouldn't bother me one bit." All would happen *in a moment* . . . [quoting from 1 Cor. 15:52] *for the trumpet shall sound, and the dead shall be raised incorruptible, and we shall be changed.* Then "the whole world would come into a knowledge of Jesus Christ, and a complete understanding of his pattern of living, then, without doubt, we would have peace."[4] But beyond the Moral Majority and other fundamentalists, that tendency (according to Mojtabai) to view "nuclear belligerence . . . simply as implementation of God's own design for creation," and the tendency of people to "consider themselves instruments of Providence and . . . help the millennium along," that impulse "lurks everywhere, and deeply, in the habits of mind and heart of innumerable ordinary citizens who vote for those who help make policy."[5]

Dividing the world into a "locus of evil" and a parallel locus of good merely enhances the tendency. In the most literal of expressions of this theme, Mojtabai quotes a Pentecostal sermon: "We sit here and we're supposed to be quiet? When we're on the winning team! This isn't the Superbowl, man, this is a run for the glory world!"[6] We know such end-of-the-world imagery to be available from Christian and other religious doctrine, as a way of imagining a mode of survival—and not just acceptable survival but an ultimately desirable form associated with a "new heaven and a new earth." "Rapture" means ecstasy and more, being literally "transported" to heaven. Nuclear holocaust, then, becomes the agent of realizing the ultimate Christian victory over evil. More than that, these imaginary survivors (in a way that is logical in the very extremity of its absurdity) win the ultimate victory by annihilating death itself. One can but wonder at the terrible ingenuity of the human imagination.

Again, ironically, that misplaced ingenuity has to do with the power of the human impulse for survival. For we human beings are the creatures who must strive to maintain not only the continuity of life (on the order of the evolutionary function of other animals) but the *feeling* of life, the *sense* of vitality, the *experience* of surviving. So strong is that inclination that we will express it no matter what, sometimes in ways that could, if carried through, subvert the very possibility of actual survival. Relevant here is the increasing imagery of a new Adam and Eve, not just in the Biblical form but in a secular equivalent of a surviving man and woman who can, after nuclear holocaust, succeed in repopulating the earth—in the process improving greatly on its prior human populace. Winning the survival here is expressed in the not infrequent wish on the part of some nuclear strategists and many others that the Adam and Eve in question be American.

As nuclear winter takes hold in our psyches, images of winning are directed increasingly toward winning the survival. They move in the direction of a perversely mystical realm, indeed one of true nuclear escapism and worse. For they become the means by which nuclear threat combines with primal imagery of death and rebirth to form a *malignant myth of regeneration via nuclear holocaust*—that is, of regeneration where there is no regeneration, where there is no life at all. Here, too, Star Wars is very much at issue; and I can no longer postpone looking psychologically at that odd set of arrangements.

Star Wars: The Culmination

It was inevitable, given the trends of nuclear strategic thinking, that someone would come up with the concept of Star Wars.* And it was probably equally inevitable that somebody like me would seek to expose its contradictions. For all that I have said so far is prologue: Star Wars clearly constitutes the overarching, all-inclusive image fantasy of our nuclear age.

At the heart of the Strategic Defense Initiative is a denial, indeed a magical reversal, of what is in actuality the central truth of the nuclear age: *total, universal vulnerability.* Our psychological understanding of Star Wars begins and ends with its aggressively elaborate scheme for refusing and circumventing precisely that simple but devastating truth.

In earlier work, I stressed a series of illusions specific to the nuclear age (see chapter 10 and, for more detail, *Indefensible Weapons*): the illusion of limit and control (especially the claim of limited nuclear war); the illusion of foreknowledge (that knowing what to expect would help you); the illusion of preparation (the efficacy of evacuation plans and the like); the illusion of protection (the idea that shelters would save your life); the illusion of stoic behavior under nuclear attack (Boy Scout-like dedication to helping others and avoiding undue [by Herman Kahn's criteria] "hypochondriasis" in relation to fear of radiation effects); the illusion of recovery (the unseen hand that would rebuild annihilated cities and towns); and the illusion of rationality (in scenarios of nuclear buildup and warfighting). These illusions have by no means disappeared, but over time each has been sufficiently questioned and undermined to lose much of its distorting power—a tendency again accelerated by the impact of nuclear winter. Nuclear gallows humor concerning civil defense and its effectiveness for survival both re-

* Star Wars is the popular term for the Strategic Defense Initiative, an elaborate, space-based missile defense system, making use of laser beams (but requiring nuclear detonations) in order to form what is described as a "protective shield" against an adversary's weapons.

flected and intensified the general disbelief in these official illusions (see chapter 10).

But just as these nuclear illusions were beginning to lose their hold on many (by all evidence, the majority of Americans), along came Star Wars and replaced these separate deceptions with a single, encompassing "grand illusion"—an all-consuming expression of collective fantasy. While the prior, separate illusions had touched on—one may say, chipped away at—the unacceptable fundamental truth of universal vulnerability, the Star Wars "grand illusion" dissolves that truth more comprehensively. The deadly logic, the logic of madness, is more throughgoing, more complete.

There is a reciprocal relationship between the Star Wars "grand illusion" and the findings of nuclear winter: nuclear winter provides a grim cosmic truth; Star Wars, a reassuring cosmic falsehood. One cannot say that Star Wars is a direct response to nuclear winter, but they are part of the same apocalyptic currents of threat—the one honorable in its truths, the other corrupt in its illusion.

Star Wars is the ultimate technological fallacy. The entire program is based upon technicism, upon an absolute embrace of technology for warding off an ultimate threat to human existence. A *technology of protection* is now to counter a *technology of destruction,* and human beings become virtual bystanders in this cosmic confrontation. We are not surprised that, among the projections of the Strategic Defense Initiative, are scenarios in which the whole defensive system is automatically—that is technologically—activated, with no presidential (or, broadly speaking, human) order necessary. Technology now emerges as not just the "shield" we are told it is to be but as a realm from which we can draw magical, life-enhancing power.

In this way, technology is seen, to a new degree, as literally replacing human responsibility. In that sense, we may say that our very humanity is sacrificed on the altar of technology worship. Here one must distinguish between small kernels of truth in the Strategic Defense Initiative: its actual possibilities for destroying *some* missiles, for preventing a certain percentage of them from reaching their targets. It is the overall technological mission of *total* protection that is newly radical in both its illusion and its dehumanization.

More than that, Star Wars, under the guise of being a "nuclear shield," actually has the effect of a guarantee that the nuclear-arms race will continue. Deployment of the system would create an *endless* psychological action-reaction sequence to that effect (You build a big shield; I need better nuclear weapons to penetrate it, and perhaps a shield of my own; you need better weapons for my shield, and an improvement on yours, etc.).

Critics of prior versions had begun to expose the danger of such action-reaction sequences. And, in that sense, Star Wars is nothing short of a rescue operation for global nuclear terror.

That degree of misplaced mysticism can only take the form of a crusade. Star Wars is put forward as a *scientific* and *technological crusade.* There is much talk of scientific frontiers, and there are constant comparisons with such successful past technological-scientific crusades as the creation of atomic bombs at Los Alamos during the Second World War and the early American commitment, in its space program, to place men on the moon. But Star Wars is also a *moral* crusade—in fact something of an ultimate moral crusade in its claim that it, and it alone, has the means of doing away with the nuclear demon. Recall President Reagan's speech introducing Star Wars in: "The human spirit must be capable of rising above dealing with other nations and human beings by threatening their existence." And a little later: "I call upon the scientific community who gave us nuclear weapons to turn their great talents to the cause of mankind and world peace: to give us the means of rendering these nuclear weapons impotent and obsolete."

By use of the rhetoric of moral crusade, and probably believing in his own rhetoric, the President (as E. P. Thompson commented) "comforted a lot of people, and made them feel patriotic and altruistic about spending billions more dollars on military ventures."[7] Another critic, this one from within the administration, was even less complimentary about the Star Wars moral crusade: "This is the President's program. We can't tell the President he's got a nutty idea."[8] To which I feel compelled to add: Yes, we can and must tell him he's got a nutty idea—for his own sake, ours, and the earth's. The Star Wars moral crusade inevitably draws upon the expanding international revulsion toward nuclear weapons. Proponents have suddenly discovered that it is "immoral" to threaten to destroy millions of people with these weapons, that they are indeed a "scourge." These phrases ring strangely in the ears of anti-nuclear activists: are they not, after all, *our* words?

It is common knowledge that early enthusiasm for Star Wars drew precisely upon such sentiments previously associated with the nuclear-freeze movement. Have the arms race proponents been converted? Are they now with us in moral judgments? The answer to these questions is hardly affirmative, but not simply negative either. Rather, it is yes and no: yes, in the sense that they share with us some of the truths of nuclear winter and can, via Star Wars, permit themselves previously suppressed moral judgments about nuclear destructiveness. But the negative side to the answer lies in their uninterrupted commitment to nuclear weapons just the same. It is as if we in the peace movement have half-succeeded with them, in a way that is both dangerous and hopeful. The danger lies in extreme impulses to cover over those moments of insight about nuclear vulnerability with ever more energetic efforts on behalf of Star Wars (and therefore of the arms race). The hope lies in pressing the half-conversion into a fuller one—not in the sense of people changing completely so much as of their opening themselves more fully to the truth of nuclear-age vulnerability.

I have suggested that Star Wars contributes to specific forms of nuclear normality and the image of winning, and we need to look at just how that works. The claim of logic, sanity, and rationality is almost self-evident. What could be more "reasonable" than to render the nuclear scourge "impotent and obsolete"? Moreover, the very technicism of Star Wars gives its version of nuclear normalcy greater potential impact: one is invited, in effect, to sit back and relax in the comfort of the nuclear shield. In this new self-righteous claim to normalcy, the insanity lies in prior nuclear systems (which even bear that acronym—MAD, or Mutually Assured Destruction), and, after all, what is more sane and normal than to want to be shielded and protected?

The image of winning, though the opposite of the Star Wars claim, is nonetheless close to the surface. Clearly inferred is the idea that *our* superior Star Wars defensive shield (if we have the will to make it superior) will keep us strong, stronger than the enemy, better able to defend ourselves and to "prevail." The inference is strengthened by the first-strike imagery immediately associated with Star Wars: the defense readily seen by a nuclear adversary as part of a first-strike plan (since one would be protected against retaliation)—and therefore as an incentive for that adversary to mount its own nuclear strike prior to the other's planned first strike. For once one denies or suppresses the central truth of nuclear vulnerability, one sets in motion imagery of winning. And in this case the denial of vulnerability gives rise to a grandiose system that, as we shall see, has crucial nuclear components—to a new nuclear triumphalism. That triumphalism operates at the three levels mentioned earlier. Now we will surely triumph economically, given the unprecedented costs of this weapons system, and still at the level of the arms race we will also triumph in the superior Strategic Defense Initiative technology we are capable of building. We can triumph in nuclear holocaust itself because we will be better defended (Star Wars advocates slip back and forth between a vision of *total* defense and one of partial effectiveness), but there can be little doubt about the assumed contribution of Star Wars to something on the order of victory. Finally, Star Wars, at least by implication, will enable us to have more American Adams and Eves (if not the single couple itself), will contribute to the "regeneration" of American values and people. Star Wars reasserts prior imagery of *winning* but goes further in invoking a more mystical tone of *triumph.*

No additional contradiction about Star Wars should surprise us. Still, there is considerable irony in the fact that this futuristic expression of ultimate technicism contains a deeply nostalgic dimension. The vision of the Strategic Defense Initiative harkens back to the security of a pre-nuclear past, to an age when Americans were granted what historians call "free security" by the two great oceans that surround us. The nostalgia, of course, is for a past sense of relative invulnerability—for a time of less extreme, one might say, softer, technologies. Itself a child of the technology of annihilation, Star Wars expresses a longing for a time when technologies were not associated in our minds with that imagery of doomsday.

That nostalgia is fed by manipulation—by what nuclear strategists themselves refer to as "perception." Used in that way, perception can mean impressions that are contrary to actuality but cultivated by those making policy because they consider such impressions to be desirable. That is the way in which the word was used by a high Pentagon official to Steven Kull as part of the latter's valuable interview study of the mind-sets of nuclear strategists:

> The origins of SDI—that was purely perception. Pure vision of the President. Even the Department of Defense didn't want to have anything to do with it. This is a President who is well attuned to the American viscera. Somewhere in the American viscera we don't want to believe that some son of a bitch on the other side can destroy us. He's offering us that wonderful defense in the sky. It has nothing to do with military planning. Anyone who takes a serious look at this knows that the Reagan version is unattainable. It's just this gut reaction that comes from the deepest recesses of the American viscera that Reagan is attuned to.[9]

Great talent has gone into the call for Star Wars, but it is the talent of the populist ideologist, as E. P. Thompson characterizes Reagan, a man indeed attuned to the American viscera in resisting the truth that we, too—this country, Americans—can, like everyone else, be completely annihilated. That kind of talent can be a formidable enemy of truth, precisely because of its psychological power to mobilize untruth—in others, of course, but also in oneself.

Ultimately, Star Wars is a cosmology—a matter for theologians as much as for psychologists or political theorists. As one studies diagrams and descriptions of its layers and manifestations "out there" (as close to what we call heaven as human beings or their artifacts have ever been), as one follows the blips and beeps of the booster phase, the phase of mid-course interception, and the terminal defense phase, one gets the sense of nothing less than a theological nightmare. It is the kind of constellation one might imagine encountering in connection with the troubled sleep of a sensitive theologian worried about fellow human beings straying from their Creator and becoming subject to new forms of idolatry. Idolatry is sometimes described as "the worship of a physical object, usually an artifact, as god." It can also be the worship of phantoms, images, things—of false gods, and includes the deification of forms or appearances that are (as one definition has it) "visible but without substance." Idolatry tends to include "immoderate attachment . . . or veneration . . . that approaches that toward the divine power."[10] In the case of Star Wars, the new idolatry is of completely unprecedented dimensions in scope and consequences and emerges from a national call articulated by none other than the head of state. Given that endorsement, along with its pervasive wishfulness, no wonder that so many people can find Star Wars to be at some level persuasive, comforting, or even inspiring, whatever their nagging feelings that the whole thing may be a fraud.

In short, Star Wars is all things to all men and women. Surely nothing in national life is free of its potential influence—theological, psychological, military, political, social, economic, and educational. No wonder so many are tempted by its combination of money, career advantage, and (at least at times for some) idealism. Above all, Star Wars is notable for the extremity of its dualities: it stirs deep longings for peace and security even as it powerfully perpetuates the arms race and the most dangerous consequences of that race. It also represents two antagonistic sides of the mind. While one must be careful not to overpersonalize what is clearly a mass phenomenon, Ronald Reagan, in addition to being its most vocal and committed proponent, illustrates that mental dichotomy very well. I have heard two different versions of a survivor mission taken on by President Reagan, following his death encounter at the hands of a would-be assassin. (That kind of survivor mission has to do with the sense, whether in religious or secular terms, that one has survived for a purpose one must then carry through.) One such purpose I have heard described seems incontestable: his sense that he must restore American greatness and defeat the Soviet threat. But the other survivor mission I have heard described has to do with a man leaving the highest attainable office at an advanced age, so that his only remaining constituencies become God and history—and who wishes to achieve his peace with both as a *man* of peace, as one who helped stave off the dreaded nuclear event. My point is that it is possible to hold to both missions—the combination rather precisely consistent with the fundamental Star Wars contradiction. The capacity to tolerate that contradiction, in Reagan and many others, may well be increased by a kind of end-time backup: should others fail to embrace one's Star Wars vision, should peace efforts meet with insurmountable difficulties—or should there be an escalation of Manichean judgments concerning Soviet evil and American virtue—should that dreaded event for any reason draw closer—well, that may simply be an expression of Providence, something preordained and perhaps even necessary.

If the human mind is ingenious in its illusory capacity, it has also the capacity to dispel illusion, to reject specifically the Star Wars "grand illusion." But there are impediments to that life-enhancing course.

Doubling and the New Nuclearism

How can specific individual strategists and policy makers continue the nuclear buildup in the face of *their* knowledge of nuclear-winter truths and Star Wars falsehoods? There is no single answer, but my work with Nazi doctors has provided an important clue for understanding the psychological behavior of people who have become associated with actual or potential mass killing. Doubling involves the formation of a relatively autonomous second self, which becomes involved in the killing activities or projections (see chapter 14). I must immediately make clear that I am not equating nuclear strategists (or anyone else) with Nazi doctors; rather I am applying a *principle,* a psychological mechanism, which, like any such mechanism, can occur in different people in a great variety of situations. We may thus speak of a "nuclear weapons self" as existing somewhat separately from the strategist's ordinary self; as being a part-self that functions as an entire or inclusive self (helps one to adapt to the working world and subculture of nuclear strategists); helps the strategist to avoid death anxiety; and, above all, protects one from feelings of guilt—not by eliminating conscience but by what I call a "transfer of conscience" to one's nuclear-weapons commitment.

Again Kull supplies us with ample evidence for this pattern in strategists. Much of it revolves around their manipulation of "perception theory"—their assumptions of how others perceive nuclear-weapons situations as opposed to the frequently antithetical truth of what the weapons actually do. But there has to be an inner division to maintain steady involvement in this duplicity. One strategic thinker at the Rand Corporation spoke frankly to Kull of the disparity between the actuality of nuclear overkill on the one hand and alleged perceptions of nuclear weapons as providing added strength on the other—and when caught up in the contradiction, added, "Well, you have to distinguish between what you think and what you think as a policy analyst."[11] That is, as a thinking human being, this man knew that the United States and the Soviet Union each had more nuclear weapons than needed; but as a policy analyst, he took the position that it was necessary to promulgate to the American people the false perception that more were needed. This man displays not really a "split" but a comprehensive second self necessary to the daily work and overall life pattern of a nuclear strategist.

For the pattern is greatly promoted by group process—by what psychologist Irving Janis has called "groupthink," the shared, unexamined suppositions required by individuals if they are to remain functional and "credible" members of a group. Crucial to doubling is shared ideology, so that even in strategists who claim to be pragmatic, or who are technicists in their mind set, there can be fundamental underlying imagery of pervasive Soviet evil and contrasting American good. Assumptions of male strength, or *macho,* can enter into this ideology, as attested by the frequent reference of strategists to "nuclear chicken" (see page 6). In my view, the key ideological element is the continuing attachment to the weapons themselves: the ideology of nuclearism, within which the weapons are depended upon, clung to, for strength, protection, and threat, whatever the evidence that they do only the last, and that they themselves are the instruments of genocide.

Star Wars greatly magnifies this institutional nuclearism by its vast call for societal participation. In the Nazi Holocaust, as Raul Hilberg has demonstrated, virtually every major bureaucracy became implicated. By establishing that kind of bureaucratic net in regard to nuclear weapons, Star Wars renders nuclearism a *societal phenomenon.* Hence the enormous impetus to the doubling process in strategists, to the formation of a *comprehensive nuclear-weapons self.* That second self becomes widely "baptized," in the term used originally by Pierre Janet, in describing how a new self or element of self, when recognized and addressed, becomes a lasting entity. Star Wars also eases the transfer of conscience—the claim to idealism on the part of nuclear strategists—the focus on one's *duty* or *moral requirement,* to build both the weapons and the "defensive shield." As one such strategist told Kull, "I'm a child of the '60s—an idealist trying to make the world a better place."[12] (For Nazi doctors, the transfer of conscience could enable them to view Auschwitz killing also as one's duty, however unpleasant, as one's moral obligation to country, race, and immediate military group.) Those ideological prods can of course be reinforced by lures of money, prestige, and influence, all of which contribute to the doubling process.

Policy makers and strategists, psychologically speaking, epitomize attitudes and patterns rampant throughout society. Strategists in that sense, by means of the nuclear-weapons self, do what Erik Erikson called the "dirty work" of the larger group. But the process is by no means passive. Their doubling enables them to become not only the bearers of societal illusion but the active agents of ever-expanding falsification. By means of doubling, they internalize that illusion and falsification—that is, make it part of a functioning self.

Star Wars provided a new impetus for this combination of doubling and nuclearism. The Star Wars technological fix has the ostensible purpose of *replacing* nuclear weapons. Yet Star Wars includes a significant nuclear component of its own, and the claim is made that this component must be extensively tested if Star Wars is to realize its goals. That is, the nuclear component of a system whose purpose is to render nuclear weapons obsolete prevents arrangements that might bring about cessation of the testing or building of nuclear weapons. Such a claim requires not only doubling but a form of nuclearism that is as powerful as it is hidden. A more accurate reading of the syllogism is: we need to deepen our reliance on nuclear weapons by including them in our defensive constellation, which in turn sets up arrangements that guarantee our uninterrupted development of the weapons themselves. The true "defensive shield" is the blocking out of truth and potential genocide. Star Wars may be said to be a rescue operation for nuclearism and its special forms of doubling; and these two unhealthy psychological patterns reinforce, in turn, Star Wars deceptions.

The bizarre alliance of survivalists and Nazis is a manifestation of the new nuclearism: the buildup and use of the weapons are welcomed as creating apocalyptic opportunity. But Nazi influence on nuclearism long predates this alliance. During the Second World War, early Nazi brutality in the bombing of undefended cities led to Allied retaliation in kind: the policy of saturation bombing of civilian populations eventuated in the atomic bombings of Hiroshima and Nagasaki. In that sense, the Nazis helped initiate a continuous cycle of brutality and genocide, the interruption of which is the goal of the anti-nuclear movement. That sequence suggests we should take another look at the concept of "appeasement" and the imagery of "Munich." That concept and imagery signify a failure in courage and imagination on the part of Western democracies in their inability to respond appropriately to threat and evil. The equivalent to "Munich appeasement" today is not, as is frequently claimed, a "soft" attitude toward the Soviet Union, but is rather the failure to take appropriate moral and political action in the face of the greatest threat and potential evil of our time: nuclear holocaust. Genuine courage and imagination, as opposed to appeasement, consist of renouncing nuclearism and mobilizing international efforts on behalf of human continuity. On several levels, then, nuclearism and Nazism are malignant bedfellows, readily sustained by various forms of doubling, and necessary for us to identify, to confront, and to renounce. We can begin to find the wisdom to do that, and to mobilize and sustain our moral imagination, by confronting the idea of *nothingness* (discussed in chapter 12).

The Species Self

Are we in the process of carving out a new sense of self that might contribute to our survival as a species? It does not look much that way, but perhaps one is being thrust upon us. If we return to the principle that we live on images, that the self is affected by powerful social and historical currents, then we must assume that important things are happening to the contemporary self. We cannot be without some awareness of the threat of the nuclear end—an awareness that lives in the self with an odd mixture of vagueness and amorphousness on the one hand and a quality of deadly absoluteness on the other. We know the self to live most of the time in the realm of everyday concerns—concerns that can be formidable in their ordinariness. Nuclear threat becomes inextricably bound up with these everyday concerns. One may therefore say that nothing the self manifests—no specific tendencies or symptoms—can be attributed *solely* to nuclear threat, but also that nothing in the self's existence is completely free of that shadow. Notably in question (but still actively sought) are long-term enterprises, relationships that are concerned with a personal and collective future. There is evidence that, within this duality—the double life of normal existence on the one hand and imagery of extinction on the other—nuclear awareness is increasing. The trend is toward greater legitimacy in acknowledging that terrible shadow, in sharing one's perceptions of it with others.

Inevitably, that process leads also to increased recognition of the principle of *shared fate.* I have long held that this principle should be the cornerstone for our approach to the Soviets, individually and collectively. One can simply say to one's Soviet counterpart, whether person to person or government to government: "If you die, I die." "If I survive, you survive." Now, with the help of the findings that forecast nuclear winter, we extend the arena of shared fate to every inch of every human life on the earth. Insofar as that realization takes hold, it contributes to an individual sense of a more inclusive self, of broader human identity. I can feel myself increasingly to be not just an American—as others can feel themselves to be not just Russians or Danes or Chinese or Nigerians—but a human being bound to all other human beings, and as that sense of self becomes integral to my psychological function, my attitudes and actions—my private life and public ethical and political commitments—become profoundly influenced by it.

We can then speak of the emergence of a *species self,* of a self-concept inseparable from all other human selves in sharing with them the ultimate questions of life and death. The species self permits a more inclusive human identity: I need not, speaking personally, negate my sense of myself as American, Jew, psychiatrist, professor, husband and father, and even avid tennis player and sometimes cartoonist—but all of these are joined with the broader self-definition, which in turn becomes an aspect of every immediate or "local" action (toward my family, students, friends) I undertake. That sense of species self also helps me to understand why I must continue to work closely with my Soviet medical colleagues even as I take a stand against Soviet victimization of heretics and Jews; I must take my stand against both American and Soviet nuclear-arms buildup and against actions by either country (the Soviets in Afghanistan, the Americans in Nicaragua or Libya) that threaten the peace and increase the danger of nuclear holocaust. Within that sense of species self, I must struggle to balance these commitments and make the best ethical and political choices I am able—with that species self keeping me mindful of the *human beings* involved in stands on survival and justice.

This broadening and deepening of an inclusive sense of human self is one of the most fundamental sources of hope available to us. The species self makes its claim on more and more people throughout the world. To be sure, it is fragile. We are experiencing only its beginnings, and it requires our constant conceptual and ethical cultivation. And clearly it is not without its formidable enemies, whether in Washington or Moscow or Manila, or Tripoli, or Pretoria, or Warsaw. But we sense that the psychological news is out: the species self is spreading, recognized, legitimate—and, as we know, desperately needed everywhere.

This inclusive sense of self does not provide any specific politics or religious convictions or organizational focus. It does not replace necessary risks and struggles, tough decisions and difficult actions. Nor, in itself, does it get rid of a single nuclear weapon or solve a single international dispute. But the species self infuses us with a special kind of inclusive human possibility. It tells us that a commitment to humanity—and the struggle against nuclear weapons is never anything less—is not only an idea but a psychological and political principle whose time has come.

10

The Nuclear Illusion

I associate this essay with the reawakening of the physicians' anti-nuclear movement that took place beginning about 1979. Helen Caldicott was a special voice in that reawakening—as were Herbert Abrams, Jack Geiger, Howard Hiatt, Bernard Lown, and Victor Sidel. It was during one of the first of the series of symposia, in Cambridge, Massachusetts, in early 1980, that Howard Hiatt used the now famous metaphor of "the final epidemic" for nuclear holocaust. The simple message of the doctor's movement—we cannot patch you up after a nuclear war—conveyed a basic truth that was authoritative and ready to be heard. Similarly, many doctors were ready for the movement. They were ready, that is, to find social expression for a healing ethos they had surely at one time possessed before it had become eroded by temptations of career, money, and (in another way) medical technology. For me, medical colleagues in the anti-nuclear movement have an added personal meaning in standing at the opposite pole to the Nazi doctors I have been studying.

This essay derives from a number of talks given mostly at occasions sponsored by Physicians for Social Responsibility (I have retained much of the spoken style), and then published in The Final Epidemic: Physicians and Scientists on Nuclear War[1] *and in a version stressing teaching and learning, in* Teachers College Record.[2] *The scandal I mention concerning the absence of the subject on campuses has, since I wrote the essay, been somewhat mitigated: teaching programs and research centers addressing nuclear threat have taken shape in a number of universities. But the creation of an intellectual and moral response to the threat, of a dimension that could be called appropriate, has hardly begun.*

IT IS A FACT of the greatest absurdity that we human beings threaten to exterminate ourselves with our own genocidal technology. One must never lose that sense of the absurdity, the madness, the insanity of it. Indeed, all work in nuclear areas has to combine a sense of that absurdity with a pragmatic, everyday struggle to do something about it. This struggle begins with our confronting the issue of what the bomb does to our minds and our mental ecology, and that includes the terrible question of the bomb's ability to impair our capacity to confront it.

In our universities, we have done virtually nothing to address the situation, to explore it as compassionate thinkers and scholars. This is an intellectual and moral scandal. A provost of a small eastern college who was also awakening to this idea recently wrote to me on just that score. He said: "I have a minor nightmare that in the year 2050 there will be [survivors] looking in disbelief at our 1980 and 1981 catalogues. It's as if, living on the edge of the cliff, the Academy seemed not to care." Now there are many reasons for that attitude, but I think they are all bound up with a single basic matter. We are accustomed to teaching as a form of transmitting and recasting knowledge. And in the service of that aim we compose various narratives and interpretations of knowledge. But we have no experience teaching a narrative about the potential extinction of ourselves as teachers and students, of our universities and schools, of our libraries and laboratories. So our pedagogical impulse instinctively and understandably shies away from such a narrative. Yet it does so at a terrible cost, including a betrayal of our mission as teachers. In this essay, I will sketch some of the dilemmas out of which our teaching emerges, and also some of the possibilities for learning from our present nuclear predicament.

Today, many of us, perhaps even all of us, share a kind of confusion: not just confusion about identity or the ordinary issues of selfhood that we all have to face, but doubts about *being* itself, about collective human existence. In that sense, teaching and learning in the nuclear age contain, or at least touch, an element of despair. Yet it is also true that such despair, if confronted—a big if—can be a powerful source of the finest teaching and learning. This is a strange moment in our nuclear situation. The danger of nuclear war is greater, perhaps, than it ever has been—as anybody close to the weapons situation more or less attests. The reason has to do with nuclear saber rattling on our part and sometimes on that of the Soviet Union. It has to do with the proliferation of nuclear weapons within the two nuclear superpowers. There is proliferation in other countries as well, but it is impossible to restrict international proliferation if we do not first restrict it where it is greatest. Then there is the tense political climate and the threat and counterthreat that constantly emanate from these two camps, along with a massive tendency toward something like expectation of nuclear war.

Each of us, looking at friends or inside oneself, can see a pattern something like this: I let the bad news—the danger—in because I cannot keep that actuality out for too long. Then I feel anxious, and one of the sources of anxiety is the inner question of whether I do anything about that anxiety. The psychological temptation, all too widespread, is to move toward the ostensibly safe ground of resignation or even cynicism: the stance I call "waiting for the bomb." One expects it, declares it inevitable—and, in that very process, contributes to its occurrence. The most sophisticated expression of this kind of pattern is found in universities. In a recent informal exchange at a faculty luncheon at a university I was visiting, one teacher expressed the view that one need not concern oneself with nuclear threat. As he put it, "Well, look, what's so special about the human species? There's nothing in evolution that says a species has to last forever; other species have come and gone. So maybe the way to look at it is that our species may have come to the end of its reign, or the end of its story." The philosophical detachment with which he spoke conveyed the ultimate "above the battle" position—in plainer language, the ultimate moral cop-out.

Still, it is also true that at this time there is a partial breakdown in collective denial and numbing. People have begun to doubt the rationalizations put forward by their political and military leaders. People throughout the world have become more fearful, and appropriately so, of the threat of nuclear war. This growing concern has even become apparent in public debates and presentations of the major television networks in this country. Yet our leaders call for more denial, for more numbing. They seek to control not just the weapons but our *perceptions* of the weapons. They do not want us to address this issue. In that way, our leaders call forth a medieval worldview in addressing postmodern technological-genocidal issues, and call it an American renaissance. There are struggles in all this between knowledge and refusal of knowledge, a direct issue for us as teachers and students; and between confrontation and denial, between feeling and numbing. Our task as teachers and students could be expressed in a very simple question: Can we overcome the impediments to, and the unprecedented demands on, our imaginations in order to explore what is real, to look carefully at nuclear reality? And that is using *real* and *reality* very differently from the way in which some of our ostensible realists (who turn out to be wild romanticists—and dangerous ones at that) employ those words. We need a very different agenda if we are to teach or learn anything of importance, and if we are to act.

Here I want to emphasize that I do not mean that teaching and learning are to substitute for action, but that they can constitute a form of action that leads to further action. In my involvement in the doctors' movement to prevent nuclear war, I have tried to think about the healing imagination. Of the various issues and arguments we have put forward, the most important concerns whether a physician should step out of the one-to-one office or client situation with a patient in order to move into this difficult realm of addressing nuclear war. And we, of course, insist that this is the central issue for us as healers, and we hold to that in our doctors' movement. The same situation applies to teachers: whether they can move from standard classroom habits toward this larger question. Perhaps this situation is epitomized by Dick Gregory's reply to someone at an anti-nuclear rally who asked him, "What are you doing here? Why don't you just limit your efforts to Black Power?" "Hell," Gregory replied, "if I go to a Black Power rally in the morning and they drop a bomb at noon, won't be no Black Power rally in the evening to go to." There is a lot of wisdom in that, and it is the same for us as teachers.

I have also, I must confess, been much influenced in thinking about these questions by recent work I have been doing on Nazi doctors and the European Holocaust (see chapters 6, 7, and 14). It is a very different situation, but one can draw certain lessons from the Nazi extremity, and especially the Nazi doctors. One important lesson is that the Nazi doctors that I interviewed were all ordinary people. They teach us that it is possible for ordinary men and women who are not inherently demonic to engage in demonic pursuits—for healers to become killers. And it can be said that among the Nazis, teachers and other professionals with pride in their professions, lent themselves to mass murder. The majority of teachers in the universities in Nazi Germany did not actively take part in mass murder, but they accommodated themselves and went along, or sat back and did nothing to prevent it.

I want to address three central issues. First, I want to convey something about Hiroshima and its neglect. Second, I want to consider the impact of the existence of nuclear weapons on us—even without their being used again. And third, I want to point to some hopeful developments, toward a change in consciousness.

In chapter 2, I described the experience of people in Hiroshima: how, from the moment of exposure to this first "tiny" bomb, people experienced lifelong death anxiety. At the end of my study *Death in Life*,[3] I spoke of Hiroshima and Nagasaki as a last chance—as nuclear catastrophes from which we can still learn, from which we can derive the knowledge that could contribute to holding back, perhaps preventing, even more massive extermination. Yet where is Hiroshima being taught? Where are these images—given to us from Hiroshima at such tragic cost to the victims—seized upon, studied, learned from? Not in too many places. But Hiroshima is a passionate narrative from which we must learn.

If Hiroshima were taught in relation to our present predicament, it would help us recognize not only the contrasting dimensions of our present nuclear threat (as also suggested in chapter 2), but the illusions and falsehoods promulgated in connection with that threat. Consider first the claim that psychological preparation is useful for actual nuclear disaster. Here one has to ask a question. Will foreknowledge help? In any future nuclear disaster, will knowledge of what might happen help people in the disaster? If you are in danger of tornado or flood, you imagine in advance what may happen and prepare yourself for how to avoid the worst effects: such foreknowledge helps enormously in terms of providing physical aid to others and coping psychologically with the danger. But not quite so for nuclear weapons. Full knowledge about the effects of radiation and the weapons' massive destructive power would hardly help.

A second illusion is that civil defense will protect us from nuclear disaster—not true at all. A third is that medical help will restore survivors. This is the falsehood that we in the doctors' movement are vigorously contesting. We say that we will not be around to patch you up after nuclear war. We will be dead and you will be dead, and if any of us are around, nobody in the band of survivors living in Stone Age circumstances will be in a situation where healing is possible.

Those are three central illusions one has to address in teaching and learning. At the heart of the constellation of falsehood is the illusion of limit and control. It is a simple truth that once the weapons are used, they are uncontrollable: there is no limit to their destructiveness; and there are enough literally to destroy life on earth, human and most animal.

Much of our teaching and learning must involve questioning false assumptions about nuclear war. The concept of limited nuclear war is not new; it began with the very development of the weapons. Some of the earliest discussions of limited war were written about decades ago by Edward Teller and Herman Kahn. Teller, for instance, in his extraordinarily misleading book *The Legacy of Hiroshima*, wrote: "Rational behavior consists of the courage to use nuclear weapons where tactically indicated"—still our present policy with so-called limited nuclear war. It then follows, in Teller's argument, that "being prepared to survive an all out nuclear attack is what we should strive for."[4] I must say to Teller that this kind of rational behavior—notice the use of the word *rational,* as he defines it—is nothing more than the logic of madness, and deadly madness at that.

Similarly, Herman Kahn in his book on thermonuclear war calls for a reasonable or "non-hypochondriacal" response to nuclear war and says that we should be prepared to experience nuclear war with some equanimity, that we will not be exposed to much more risk than we are in peacetime. He goes on to say that in order to prevent—"undo" is his word—the fear of radiation in a nuclear attack, each person should be supplied with an individual Geiger counter-like radiation meter to record his or her radiation level. Kahn explains, "If somebody is complaining of feeling weak or not feeling too well, you look at his meter and say 'You've only received 10 roentgens—why are you vomiting? Pull yourself together and get to work.' "[5] Here we must, as teachers and scholars, tell Herman Kahn and others like him that nuclear weapons make either corpses or at best hypochondriacs of us all, that this wishful scenario of nuclear recovery has little to do with the way people behave, and that his psychological assumptions here are as faulty as his moral ones. So whether we are psychological professionals or scientists or humanists, it is our task to expose and combat these false assumptions, to take note of the bootlegging of psychological and physical assumptions about nuclear war and about the way in which people would behave.

In 1945, a new image came into the world, an image of extinguishing ourselves as a species by our own hand, with our own technology. This "imagery of extinction" derived primarily from the atomic bombing of Hiroshima and Nagasaki and from the Nazi Holocaust in Europe. Since the Second World War that image has combined with images of possible future holocausts and with apocalyptic imagery involving such things as the possible destruction of our environment (because our environment is all too susceptible to our technology of destruction) and the drying up of resources such as food and energy.

But what happens to us when confronted with this imagery of extinction? What impact do these weapons, even if not used, have on us? As I mentioned earlier, addressing these matters requires us to change or question our basic assumptions. I myself have changed the way I look at psychological experience because of my 1962 Hiroshima study, and have evolved a different model or paradigm of symbolization of life and death. I think that all teachers and scholars acknowledge that their ideas and concepts derive, to some degree, from the historical situation in which we live because we are agents and children of history. Yet if these concepts are to have any power, we must struggle toward something like universality, some generalizing possibility beyond the historical moment. In this sense, I think our ideas about nuclear weapons, and the entire constellation of physical, psychological, and social experience associated with them, can teach us a great deal about everyday life, about psychology, history, and humanistic endeavor in our contemporary moment.

If one begins to ask how the very existence of these weapons and this imagery of extinction have affected us, I would say something like this: We need first of all a model of psychological behavior that looks not only at the nitty-gritty everyday experience, what I call "proximate experience," but also at larger or "ultimate experience"—at the connections of the self beyond the self. I take this to be an ordinary human requirement of feeling connected to those who have gone before and those who will go on after our finite life span. That need is not always conscious, but it is there. Ordinarily this imagery of larger connectedness, what I call the "symbolization of immortality" (see chapter 1), is expressed in the five general modes: the biological (or biosocial), the theological, the creative, the natural, and the experience of transcendence. The presence of nuclear weapons makes us begin to doubt all these modes, because, from the age of five or so, we are exposed to imagery of extinction. Who in our culture can be sure of living on through our children or our works when we can imagine the possibility of the extermination of everything in nuclear holocaust? Even eternal nature is susceptible to our pollution and our weapons. That is one reason we desperately embrace the experience of transcendence in a direct way. This experience, traditionally made available to cultures, has been too much denied in advanced industrial societies, but now it is seized upon with desperation, often through drugs or in the search for altered states of consciousness.

The issue here is the radical sense of futurelessness discussed earlier, and we need a sense of a human future if we are to function in our everyday lives right now. Hence the projections of space colonies as a substitute for a destroyed earth, or of new religions, or of a new return to nature. In other words, in each of these modes we see some desperate effort to break out of what we take to be an interruption of a continuous process that we require. Indeed, everything that happens to us is in some degree affected by our nuclear age, although nothing can be explained totally by nuclear weapons. We still go through struggles with people we love, we have ambitions that we seek to achieve, we have conflicts that bedevil us, but every issue arises within the context of this larger image of threatened extinction. Here again is where teaching and learning and genuine scholarship could do much to illuminate our collective nuclear-age situation.

There are also direct political problems of great importance for us to begin to look at, and to study and teach. For instance, nuclear threat infuses ordinary political and diplomatic actions with potentially ultimate consequences, a situation that is bound to affect, however inchoately, those most closely involved. Jonathan Schell, in his *The Time of Illusion*,[6] proposes an interesting theory connecting the Watergate experience with the contradiction concerning the "credibility" of nuclear deterrence. Since the threat of retaliation is never quite credible, American presidents (Schell argues) tend to become touchy, and then paranoid, in relation to virtually *any* questioning of their credibility or of their policies. Whether or not one accepts his argument, Schell's questions about the way in which nuclear weapons imagery affects our politics and behavior have to be addressed (see also pages 70–73).

Difficult issues of secrecy and security are also raised by nuclear weapons. Much of McCarthyism and earlier witch hunts had to do with the struggle over secrecy—with the illusion that one can keep the secret of mass destructive capability from one's ostensible enemy. The concept of national security and the illusions around it are similar. I would say the beginning theme here should be the reverse of what is generally said: More weapons do not bring more security; they bring less security to everybody, especially to those who hold them. We will not have a relevant politics in this country until some political leaders have the courage to act boldly on that truth. And we have to start including it in our teaching and learning. We still have the freedom to do this in the universities. We can teach and learn along lines that we choose. We have to use that freedom.

An important study was done by Michael Carey, a former assistant of mine and a freelance writer with a background in psychology and history. This study confirms on a direct empirical level some of the psychological issues raised by imagery of extinction. Carey interviewed people of his generation when they were in their late twenties or early thirties about the nuclear air-raid drills held, in the 1950s, in schools throughout the United States.[7] Carey has collected an extensive library of records and photographs, some of which have been published in a series of articles in the *Bulletin of the Atomic Scientists.* I am sure that many of us can recall those quaint experiences, in which the general tone was: There is the big, bad atomic bomb, but with American know-how and cooperation we can defeat it. The way to defeat it was to not look out the window—so that your eyes wouldn't get hurt—and to take some paper and put it over your head as protection against radiation fallout; if that didn't work, hide under your desk. Of course, the kids were too smart to believe that, but were confused.

Carey demonstrates that many were overwhelmed with anxiety. A pattern of fear, nightmares, and terror evolved early on, followed by a kind of suppression or numbing toward the whole experience. The effects would often emerge later: recurrence of nightmares and anxiety in response to talk of nuclear danger, or even to Carey's research, as well as to some traumatic experience.

From Carey's work and other evidence, certain thematic processes of the greatest importance become apparent. One is the confusion, even equation, of ordinary death with grotesque massive annihilation. This happens just as a child is learning the terrible truth that death is final; you cannot go to sleep and wake up again as a child wants at first to believe. At this time he or she is also inundated with imagery of extinction, or meaningless death, in which children, adults, and old people all die together, without reason. As the idea of dying with dignity becomes a cruel joke, the already difficult matter of coming to terms with one's own mortality is made still more difficult, and we have hardly begun to address the psychological consequences. That is why I called a recent book *The Broken Connection.*[8] The threat to the connection between living and dying, between the idea of death and the continuity of life, is a major issue for us today.

A second theme is that nothing can be depended on. There are pervasive doubts about the enduring nature of anything. We do not have faith that anything will last, and this lack of faith has contributed to the development of a new ephemeralism. This can be seen in some of the shifts in attitudes toward work, for instance—the hippie attitude in the late 1960s or early 1970s that work is meaningless, giving way to a seeming reversal, in which everybody wants to be a business tycoon or a doctor or a lawyer or find some other safe job haven. I think that both attitudes are part of the same social process in which, whatever the shifting economic currents, we are uncertain about what lasts, what work has meaning.

A third perception that can be drawn directly from Carey's work is the theme of craziness. Certainly there is craziness in the situation mentioned at the beginning of his essay of two great world powers poised to drop their bombs and thereby annihilate each other and the rest of the world. That is crazy in a collective sense. It does not require individual psychosis. The people promoting these arrangements are clinically sane—and one must remember that. There is also craziness in the remedies suggested to children by the authorities during the drills. There was a perception of that kind of craziness in the great explosion of absurdity and mockery that occurred, sometimes very brilliantly and appropriately, during the uprisings of the 1960s and 1970s (see chapter 1). To the manifold sources of collectively perceived absurdity, the bomb contributes a pervasive sense of the final madness.

A fourth theme found in Carey's work and in other parts of the culture is a less healthy one. It has to do with an identification with the all-powerful weapon itself. In some, that identification takes the form of wanting to witness its awesome power, wanting to see it used, and can connect with the various forms of Armageddonism we have discussed (see introduction and chapters 9 and 11).

Finally, there is a theme that is perhaps the overriding theme for all of us, since these themes are not solely the possession of those who went through the nuclear drills. This fifth theme is the double life we live in the nuclear age. On the one hand, we know that a series of bombs could be dropped that, within moments, would destroy us—all of us and everything we have known, loved, or touched—and on the other hand, we go about our lives with business as usual, as though no such threat existed. To some extent we have to do that; we have to get through the day and take care of our daily tasks. But we routinize and mute our situation at great peril. Ours is not so much an age of anxiety as an age of numbing. Our fundamental impairment lies in the gap between knowledge and feeling.

The entire issue of feeling and not feeling in relation to historical and personal events needs to be addressed in our teaching. Such teaching might help not only students, but many in the culture at large—including, perhaps, even some of our political leaders—to break out of various manifestations of nuclear numbing.

The worst kind of development, and perhaps the most obscene dimension of the nuclear age, is nuclear fundamentalism, which includes the worship, literally the deification, of the very agents of our potential destruction (see also chapters 1 and 15). In this phenomenon of nuclearism the weapons become deities that are all the more influential for being unacknowledged as such. If this sounds extreme, one need only examine some of the literature on the reactions of people who have watched a nuclear test, and of atomic scientists upon receiving the news of the nuclear explosions on the two Japanese cities (see chapter 12). In at least a few cases that "conversion in the desert" was to the devil religion of nuclearism. Nuclearism can be manifest in the use of the weapons to win diplomatic games that cannot be won. Nuclearism then becomes a means of invoking technology, now associated with ultimate power, to substitute for the necessary human arrangements. Here again I have to invoke Edward Teller and his strange observation in *The Legacy of Hiroshima*[9] that radiation from test fallout might indeed be beneficial to human beings (see chapter 12, pages 162–63). What I want to suggest is that nuclearism can dangerously distort a mind as accomplished as Teller's and produce lethal nonsense. The sense that the all-destructive deity must also be able to create is one of the reasons we are so loath to give up nuclear energy for ostensibly peaceful purposes, whatever the evidence of its danger. Nuclearism is not limited to the United States or to the Soviet Union: all countries that seek a bomb are drawn to this, the most grotesque form of spiritual corruption in our time. We have to continue to explore its varied expressions, and to combat it.

Despite all these troubling psychological aspects, something constructive and life enhancing is taking place. I would characterize the situation as both desperate and hopeful. John Dunne, the contemporary Notre Dame theologian, asks: "What story are we in?" What he means is, What happens to us and what do we become? It is a story of the human imagination, and one thinks of Yeats's words, "Oh Lord, let something remain."

At the heart of the story and the struggle is our quest for awareness. What is awareness? One meaning of it is being cognizant of danger, being wary. The other side of it, however, the more recent meaning, is insight, understanding, illumination that takes one beyond what is given. That is what we must seek; that is what is involved in imagining a future. Threats and confrontations involving the Soviet Union and the United States have awakened people to danger. Another way of looking at it is that the numbing process, collectively maintained, has itself become worn and under duress. At moments something close to a groundswell of nuclear concern has emerged from our culture. But it has not been sustained—and, in any case, why has it taken so long? Nuclear awareness includes, first, tension bordering on anxiety leading to the questioning of existing arrangements; and then a more structured sense of predicament and purpose—the formed awareness necessary for sustained advocacy and action. Again, where are the teachers and students who should be explorers and committed creators of that awareness?

There is a significant individual step that each of us must take, the movement from that destructive and self-destructive stance of resignation and cynicism toward one of confronting the problem, feeling responsible to it, joining with others in taking a stand. That step is a significant personal watershed; awareness includes self-awareness. It requires a cultivation of hope, perhaps even of various forms of secular faith. One has to imagine a human future without nuclear war and then bring expressions of human power, authentic and vital, to that imagination.

In the doctors' movement we have found that people are hungry for truth. They experience the threat and want to achieve some grasp, some mastery, of their predicament. Even from pure professional self-interest, we ignore these issues at our peril. If we numb ourselves to the forces that threaten the existence of our civilization and our species, how can we call ourselves students of humankind? How can we call ourselves teachers or mentors?

Strangely enough, or perhaps not so strangely, confronting these grim issues of death and holocaust has the effect of putting us more in touch with what we most value in life—with love and sensuality and life projects that have satisfaction and meaning for us. So my call—our call—is not for a death trip, but quite the opposite. It is for the personal and professional and intellectual efforts that we need to make on behalf of the wondrous and fragile entity that we call human life.

11

Beyond the Nuclear End

> The first promise of the atomic age is that it can make some of our nightmares come true. The capacity painfully acquired by normal men to distinguish between sleep, delusion, hallucination, and the objective reality of waking life has for the first time in human history been seriously weakened.
>
> —EDWARD GLOVER, 1946

My work in Hiroshima left me with a sense of the psychologist's task of re-examining imagery of the end of the world. I have done that in various ways, beginning with my explorations in The Broken Connection. *But I find myself increasingly queasy about the task because the idea of that end has, over recent years, taken shape in our minds as something closer to literal possibility. Not surprisingly, there has been a recent tendency toward addressing the subject at academic meetings and conferences, and I have presented different aspects of this material at a seminar series at the Massachusetts Institute of Technology entitled "Visions of Apocalypse: End or Rebirth," a Jungian exploration of the same subject held at a magnificent Rhode Island villa, and a large conference at the New School for Social Research on the significance of mythology for contemporary life. I developed the more specific nuclear applicability of the general issue for a volume on the psychological dimensions of nuclear winter.*[1] *Now I see the subject as still another neglected dimension of psychological thought, one that newly joins extreme mental aberration (such as schizophrenia) with contemporary imaginative need—and also with the mind's potential for extending its reach.*

THE DEVELOPMENT of nuclear weapons in the mid-1940s, symbolized by the visual image of an overwhelming mushroom cloud, evoked a broader conceptual image: the extermination of our species by means of our own technology. The image, of course, is not totally new. Versions of it have been held by visionaries—H. G. Wells is an outstanding example—at least from the time of the Industrial Revolution. To that image, nuclear winter gives concrete substance: using just a small portion of our nuclear stockpiles, we may so impair our habitat, the earth, that it no longer can sustain human and other forms of life. Never has the human imagination been called upon to encompass a concept quite like that.

The element of self-extermination must be differentiated from older religious images of Armageddon, "Last Judgment," or the "end of the world." Terrifying as these may be, they are part of a worldview or cosmology that envisions the apocalyptic conclusion to human history as a redemptive event. Human beings are acted upon by a higher power who destroys only for spiritual purposes, such as achieving the "kingdom of God"—a far cry from our destruction of ourselves with our own tools, and to no discernible purpose.

Several special features mark this contemporary end-of-the-world imagery. There is first the suggestion of biological extinction. Second, the image is related to specific external events of recent history, Hiroshima and Nagasaki as well as the Nazi death camps. And third, unlike earlier imagery of world destruction—even that associated with such events as the plagues of the Middle Ages—the danger comes from the designs and imperatives of human technology. Our "end" is in considerable measure perceived as a form of self-destruct. We therefore see in it little justification, only absurdity. If some people view nuclear holocaust as inevitable, they do so with resignation or hopelessness—as opposed to the meaningful inevitability of an eschatology or the submission to irresistible forces of nature.

This potential self-destruction has bearing on issues of widespread guilt as well as psychic numbing, our diminished capacity to feel. We are compelled to imagine ourselves as both executioner and victim, the two roles Camus warned us never to assume. We numb ourselves both toward destruction itself and toward our guilt as potential perpetrators of that destruction. Traditionally, guilt is contained within an eschatology: if humanity is guilty, it must be punished, it must be destroyed in order to be re-created in purer form. Within our present context, however, one perceives the threat of a literal, absolute end, without benefit of a belief system that gives form, acceptance, or solace to that idea.

Given the temptation of despair, our need is simply stated. We must confront the image that haunts us, making use of whatever models we can locate. Only then can we achieve those changes in consciousness that must accompany (if not precede) changes in public policy on behalf of a human future.

Hiroshima and the End of the World

We recall (pages 32–33) the images of Hiroshima survivors that, not only would they die individually, but "the world is ending"; that they were undergoing "the collapse of the earth, which was said to take place at the end of the world," and that "all people . . . were dead"; and that "this was the end of Hiroshima—of Japan—of humankind." The sense of world collapse could also be expressed symbolically, as in the immediate thought of a devoutly Buddhist domestic worker: "There is no God, no Buddha."[2]

Some survivors called forth humor, inevitably gallows humor, as a way of mocking their own helplessness and the absurdity of total destruction. A professional cremator, for instance, though severely burned, managed to make his way back to his home (adjoining the crematorium) and felt relieved because "I thought I would die soon, and it would be convenient to have the crematorium close by."[3]

Many recollections convey the dreamlike grotesqueness of the scene of the dead and the dying, and the numbed wandering of the living. All this was sensitively rendered by Dr. Michihiko Hachiya in his classic *Hiroshima Diary:*

> Those who were able walked silently toward the suburbs in the distant hills, their spirits broken, their initiative gone. When asked whence they had come, they pointed to the city and said "that way": and when asked where they were going, pointed away from the city and said "this way." They were so broken and confused that they moved and behaved like automatons.
>
> Their reactions had astonished outsiders who reported with amazement the spectacle of long files of people holding stolidly to a narrow, rough path when close by was a smooth easy road going in the same direction. The outsiders could not grasp the fact that they were witnessing the exodus of a people who walked in the realm of dreams.[4]

People characterized those they saw in such strange states (near-naked, bleeding, faces disfigured and bloated from burns, arms held awkwardly away from the body to prevent friction with other burned areas), and by implication themselves, as being "like so many beggars," or "like . . . red Jizō* standing on the sides of the road." Above all, there was so great a sense of silence as to suggest the absence of all life. As a woman writer remembered: "It was quiet around us. . . . In fact there was a fearful silence which made one feel that all people and all trees and vegetation were dead."[5] Similarly, Dr. Hachiya was struck by the "uncanny stillness" permeating his hospital: "One thing was common to everyone I saw—complete silence. . . . Why was everyone so quiet? . . . It was as though I walked through a gloomy, silent motion picture."[6]

These Hiroshima memories, then, combine explicit end-of-the-world imagery with a grotesque dreamlike aura of a nonnatural situation, a form of existence in which life was so permeated by death as to become virtually indistinguishable from it.

Schizophrenia and the End of the World

The second set of quotations I want to present are from a gifted man's account of his disturbed mental state. Daniel Paul Schreber, a distinguished German judge, could hardly have realized, in 1903, when he published his *Memoirs of My Nervous Illness* a decade or so before, that he was providing psychoanalytic psychiatry with a landmark "case." From these memoirs Freud constructed a concept of schizophrenia, especially paranoid schizophrenia, that has informed, haunted, and confused psychiatric work on psychosis ever since.

Schreber was preoccupied with the idea of a "world catastrophe," which he thought at times necessary for the re-creation of the species, and for the possibility of his (Schreber's) giving birth to children in the manner of a woman. In one passage he describes some of this delusional system in connection with observations on the stars and mysterious cosmic events:

> When later I regularly visited the garden and again saw—my memory does not fully deceive me—two suns in the sky at the same time, one of which was our earthly sun. The other was said to be the Cassiopeian group of stars

* A Buddhist deity, whose images in natural stone can be found along roads and paths.

> drawn together into a single sun. From the sum total of my recollections, my impression gained hold of me that the period in question, which according to human calculations stretched over three to four months, had covered an immensely long period. It was as if single nights had a duration of centuries. So that within that time the most profound alterations in the whole of mankind, and the earth itself, and the whole solar system might very well have taken place. It was repeatedly mentioned in visions that the work of the past 1400 years had been lost.

When Schreber says "repeatedly mentioned" he refers to his "visions" or hallucinations. He interprets the figure of 1,400 years to be an indication of "the duration of time that the earth has been populated," and remembers hearing another figure, about 200 or 212 years, for the time still "allotted to the earth."

> During the latter part of my stay in Flechsig's Asylum [Professor Flechsig was the director] I thought this period had already expired and therefore I was the last real human being left, and that the few human shapes I saw apart from myself—Professor Flechsig, some attendants, occasional more or less strange-looking-patients, were only "fleeting-improvised-men" created by miracle. I pondered over such possibilities as that the whole of Flechsig's Asylum or perhaps the city of Leipzig with it had been "dug out" and moved to some other celestial body, all of them possibilities which questions asked by the voices who talked to me seemed to hint at, as for instance whether Leipzig was still standing, etc. I regarded the starry sky largely, if not wholly, extinguished.

Here the world catastrophe is accompanied by re-creation, with Schreber himself at the center of it. Thus he goes on to speak of seeing "beyond the walls of the Asylum only a narrow strip of land," so strange and different that "at times one spoke of a holy landscape."

> I lived for years in doubt as to whether I was really still on earth or whether on some other celestial body. . . . In the soul-language during [that] time . . . I was called *"the seer of spirits,"* that is, a man who sees, and is in communication with, spirits or departed souls.[7]

These quotations convey the kind of end-of-the-world imagery that occurs in acute and chronic forms of psychosis, usually paranoid schizophrenic psychosis. The psychotic dies *with* the world, in that his sense of inner disintegration includes self and world. But by rendering himself at the same time the only survivor, he expresses the paranoid struggle with power and vitality, and a distorted paranoid vision of regeneration. These schizophrenic end-of-the-world images seem to be in sharp contrast with those experienced in Hiroshima: the one an expression of delusion and inner disorder, the other of actuality and externally imposed destruction. But the distinction is far from absolute. In Hiroshima, for instance, the overwhelming *external* event stimulates an immediate and corresponding internal experience, something like internal breakdown or overwhelming psychological trauma. And although we generally think of schizophrenia as a strictly *internal* derangement, it, too, is subject to external influences and to the struggle for some kind of meaning structure. Hence the content, style, and impact of the condition upon others—the dialogue or non-dialogue between schizophrenic people and society—all this varies enormously with historical time and place. Correspondingly, the end-of-the-world imagery of schizophrenia is strongly affected by historical and technological context.

My own work on schizophrenia and other psychiatric syndromes carries these relationships a bit further. I have stressed three significant areas: death imagery and the simulation of death (inner deadness); the nature of the perceived threat; and the relationship to meaning. Concerning the nature of the threat in schizophrenia, Freud focused on homoerotic impulses and the fear of homosexuality, particularly in paranoid schizophrenia. More recent work, along lines we have begun to discuss, points instead to the threat to existence, to the fear of being annihilated, as central to schizophrenia. This does not mean that sexual confusion and fear of homosexuality are unimportant. But I would argue that they are an aspect of a more general category, rather than themselves the central threat as perceived in schizophrenia.

Ida Macalpine and Richard A. Hunter, who produced the first full English translation of the Schreber *Memoirs,* also provided a valuable reinterpretation of that case. They took major issue with Freud's view, and stressed instead issues of death and life-continuity. They understood Schreber's psychosis as "a reactivation of unconscious, archaic procreation fantasies concerning life, death, immortality, rebirth, creation, including self-impregnation, and accompanied by absolute ambisexuality expressed in doubt and uncertainty about his sex." And they go on to say that "homosexual anxieties are secondary to the primary fantasy of having to be transformed into a woman to be able to procreate." Hence, "Schreber's system centered on creation and the origin of life, whether by God or the sun, sexually or parthenogenetically."

They focused on Schreber's own experience of what he called "soul murder," a theme "of which Freud could make nothing," but one which may well have been "the center of [Schreber's] psychosis." Schreber's own elaboration of "soul murder" makes it clear that he was thinking along lines of death and life-continuity:

> The idea is widespread in the folklore and poetry of all peoples that it is somehow possible to take possession of another person's soul in order to prolong one's life at another soul's expense, or to secure some other advantages which outlast death.[8]

Macalpine and Hunter tell us that not only was the self being annihilated in soul murder, but so was all possibility of human connection. They saw this as an explanation for Schreber's end-of-the-world fantasy, as well as his delusion that he was immortal ("A person without a soul, i.e. life substance, cannot die"). That fantasy in turn could enable Schreber to imagine himself as "sole survivor to renew mankind." The perception of annihilation remains central.

Similarly, recent work by Searles emphasizes the difficulty schizophrenic persons have in consistently experiencing themselves "as being *alive.*" Many do not seem to fear death because "so long as one feels dead anyway . . . one has, subjectively, nothing to lose through death." Yet there can be an accompanying near-total inability to accept the finiteness of life (hence the grandiose delusions of omnipotence and immortality) because of the sense of never having really lived.[9] Behind both experiential deadness and literalized immortality is something close to Schreber's "soul murder," that is, the perpetual dread of annihilation.

The perceived threat of annihilation begins early in life and may even have a significant genetic component. This perception then becomes totalized, so that for many schizophrenics these early experiences become the whole of life experience. At an immediate level, the schizophrenic feels flooded with a death anxiety that he both embraces and struggles against. At the ultimate level, his absence of connection beyond the self, the sense of being cut off from the chain of being, from larger human relationships, leaves him with the feeling that life is counterfeit, and that biological death is uneventful because psychic death is everywhere. Here a form of pseudo-immortality exists as contrasted with a more viable, symbolized sense of immortality, a broader human continuity. This combination of radically impaired meaning and constant threat of annihilation is at the heart of the schizophrenic's imagery of the end of the world. By understanding that *process* in schizophrenia, we can learn about and begin to interpret our own end-of-the-world imagery regarding nuclear holocaust. For the external threat of contemporary nuclear weapons approaches the terrain of schizophrenia.

End-of-the-world imagery is a fundamental expression of the far reaches of the human mind, and can be understood as a delicate cutting edge in the balance or imbalance between the struggle against disintegration on the one hand, and the struggle toward renewal and restitution on the other.

Nuclear Winter, Millennialism, and Renewal

To claim, as I have, that schizophrenia has relevance for all end-of-the-world imagery requires a psychological model or paradigm, which will enable us to find common ground among the various end-of-the-world images I discuss in this essay. The paradigm presumes both a proximate or immediate level of experience and an ultimate level close to what the theologian Paul Tillich has called "ultimate concern" (see chapter 1). That is, the schizophrenic not only fears annihilation, but—as the psychoanalyst Harold F. Searles and others point out—fears (and to some extent welcomes) being severed from the great stream of human existence. There can be an element of ecstasy in the schizophrenic perception of the end of the world, along with its terror. Indeed, this very fear of being historically annihilated needs much additional psychological attention.

What is involved here is an evolutionary triad. To become human one takes on simultaneously: first, the knowledge that one dies; second, the symbolizing function that I take to be the fundamental form of human mentation, requiring the internal re-creation of all that we perceive; and third, the creation of culture, which is by no means merely a vehicle for denying death (as many psychoanalytic thinkers, from Freud to Norman O. Brown, have claimed) but is integral to the human cultural animal, and probably necessary for the development of the kind of brain we have come to possess.

When the image of nuclear winter threatens our symbolization of immortality, then it threatens a level of psychic experience that defines our humanity. When it threatens our proximate level of experience, it undermines and instills with fear and doubt our sense of moving safely through ordinary steps in human life.

Yet the idea of nuclear winter serves us well in these imaginative struggles. In concretizing the idea of the "end," nuclear winter clarifies our existential situation and helps us to liberate ourselves from illusion (see chapter 9). In reaching proximate and ultimate dimensions of our minds in its message of annihilation, nuclear winter divests us of all hope in association with fighting a nuclear war, and places hope precisely where it belongs: only in prevention.

Nuclear winter also prods our imaginations in the direction of nothingness—a direction we must explore to grasp our predicament. Here, a brief return to Hiroshima is useful.

A history professor I interviewed in Hiroshima told me of witnessing the bomb's destruction from the outskirts of the city: "I climbed Hijiyama Hill and looked down. I saw that Hiroshima had disappeared . . . I was shocked by the sight . . . what I felt then and still feel now I just can't explain with words. . . . Hiroshima didn't exist. That was mainly what I saw. Hiroshima just didn't exist."[10] When asked how he thought Hiroshima should be commemorated, he said that there should be a wide area around the hypocenter in which there is absolutely *nothing;* and that on 6 August, the commemoration day, no one should stir, all homes and stores should be closed. Hiroshima would then become a "city of the dead" and people would learn the simple truth that such a weapon has the power to convert everything into nothing.

A number of traditions of thought and experience stress concepts of nothingness. In religious practice, there is the *nirvana* in Buddhism and Hinduism, and specific forms of Zen Buddhist meditation, as well as various forms of Christian mysticism. Secular expressions of nothing or "non-being" occur in different expressions of existential philosophy, notably Martin Heidegger, and have been depicted novelistically by Sartre. But all of these traditional quests for nothingness reflect the human imagination at work on behalf of itself. Nothingness clears the mind of impurities, permits fusion with a deity, frees one from the endless burden of reincarnation, or in its very contrast with true being, provides a means for the self to achieve freedom and identity. That is, there is always *something* on behalf of which nothingness has value.

Nuclear nothingness has no such redeeming virtue. It is just that—*literal* nothingness, an end to human existence and to the existence of most other animal species and to plant species as well. The mind not only rebels against such a stark image but has no experience with which to conjure it up. Human language and imagination, adaptive functions that they are, tend to be bound to the flow of life, and of continuing human events. We can and often do imagine interruptions of this flow, and we frequently experience various forms of inner deadness. But that kind of imagination and experience takes place within a context of larger flow and ongoing events, a context of expectation that life will somehow resume or continue.

Freud touched on this mental struggle in his famous statement that we cannot image our own death but are only present as spectators. But (though Freud did not say this) we do regularly imagine a human world that continues without us as individuals (which is why we take out life insurance, prepare wills, and in other ways provide for people and projects that will outlive us). In that post-self world, the self's influences and contributions, however modest, continue to reverberate. That is very different from there being no human world at all—and precious little world of anything else. The latter is what defies our imaginative capacity—so much so that literal nothingness may be a contradiction in terms.

Yet nothingness can be suggested, approached. There is a photograph by Bernard Hoffman on the cover of *Last Aid,* an essay collection of the International Physicians for the Prevention of Nuclear War, depicting a lone cyclist pedaling through the Hiroshima rubble, through nothing but rubble—nothing standing.

When I visited Auschwitz recently, in connection with research on Nazi doctors, I saw many exhibits there that spared little in revealing what human beings can do to other human beings. But the two exhibits that had the strongest impact on me were two rooms: one that was simply full of shoes, many of them baby shoes; and another full of suitcases of the rectangular old-fashioned kind with the addresses of people on them. Such exhibits require the viewer to do the psychological work of imagining the missing people. It is their absence—the element of nothingness—that captures the imagination. This form of nothingness, then, can serve to mobilize us to reject the elimination of human beings and to maintain the flow of life. Nothingness is thus part of our imaginative wisdom, helping us toward the only honorable path: prevention.

But the threat of extinction and nothingness can provoke problematic responses as well, millennial imagery called forth clinically or theologically in the name of regeneration. In schizophrenia and other clinical syndromes, Freud understood symptoms to express attempts at what he called "restitution" of the disordered self to a healthier state. That principle has particular relevance to imagery of the end of the world, and the Schreber case shows how that imagery can be bound up with the idea of the world being purified and reconstituted. In millennial imagery associated with religious thought, the element of revitalization and moral cleansing—the vision of a new and better existence—is even more prominent, and considerably more functional. Theological tradition can provide form, coherence, and shared spiritual experience, in contrast to the isolated delusional system of the individual schizophrenic person.

Ultimately, we may say that millennial ideas of all kinds are associated with an even larger category of mythological imagery of death and rebirth. They represent later theological invocations and refinements of that earlier, fundamental category. We miss the significance of millennial imagery if we see in it *only* the threat of deadness or the absence of meaning; but we also misunderstand it if we do not recognize in it precisely that threat and absence. In other words, millennial imagery includes something on the order of death equivalents—of threatened annihilation—and at the same time, in its various symbolizations, something on the order of renewal and revitalization.

In schizophrenia that imagery of revitalization is radically literalized. With desymbolization there is an inability to carry out the specific human task of constant creation and re-creation of images and forms, or what I call the formative-symbolizing function. What is called the "thought disorder" of schizophrenia involves a fundamental impairment to this function, the replacement of symbolic flow with static literalization.

An important question for religious millennial imagery is the extent to which it is experienced in literalized, as opposed to more formative or symbolized, ways. When a millennial vision becomes so literalized that it is associated with a prediction of the actual end of the world on a particular day on the basis of Biblical images or mathematical calculation applied to such images or whatever, we become aware of a disquieting border area of theology and psychopathology. Fundamentalist groups that invoke Biblical imagery to welcome nuclear holocaust also literalize and thereby renounce the regenerative dimensions of millennial imagery. The imagery of such groups may recall the schizophrenic person's paradoxical avoidance of annihilation by imagining a dead universe in which he or she is the last survivor. There is a sense in which the phenomenon I have been calling "nuclearism" is a technocratic cultural analogue of such debased millennialism.

Confronting end-of-the-world imagery can dramatically expose the dangers of nuclearism, and mobilize life-enhancing behavior. Eugene Rabinowitz provides a good example of just this possibility for renewal when he writes about the circumstances in which he and other nuclear scientists drafted one of the earliest petitions against the use of a nuclear weapon:

> In the summer of 1945, some of us walked the streets of Chicago vividly imagining the sky suddenly lit up by a giant fireball, the steel skeleton of skyscrapers bending into grotesque shapes and their masonry raining into the

> streets below, until a great cloud of dust rose and settled onto the crumbling city.[11]

This image of the "end of the world" inspired him to urge his colleagues to return quickly to their work on the "Franck Report," which he, James Franck, Leo Szilard, and other physicists in Chicago were instrumental in creating. To be sure, the report's recommendation that the atomic weapon not be used on a human population without warning was not heeded, but it has become a central document in our contemporary struggle to imagine the end of the world in order to preserve the world.

Similar efforts of restitution, which restore symbols of human continuity to our numbed imaginations, are needed by the rest of us as well. Just as we know that we must imagine our own death in order to live more fully, so must we now imagine the end of the world in order to take steps to maintain human existence.

12

Prophetic Survivors

While working on Hiroshima, I read all I could find on the experience of nuclear scientists in making the bomb—a genuinely tragic role. What complicated their situation was the clear sense of an evil out there (mostly the Nazis, but also Japanese fascism) that had to be dealt with, and of a war that had to be won. Hence, the ultimate irony of the most murderous weapon to date being constructed within a utopian community.

Yet the efforts on the part of those same nuclear scientists to reverse, if not undo, the very process they helped initiate also takes on primal—and, as the title of this essay suggests, prophetic—dimensions. Since my writing of the piece, additional ironies have emerged. Martin Sherwin's historical research demonstrated that even Leo Szilard, perhaps the most inspiring figure in the scientists' anti-bomb movement, was not free of nuclearism: beyond his having taken steps to initiate work on the bomb, he subsequently became impatient with the slow progress in producing it because he feared, at least for a while, that unless atomic bombs were used in the war and their destructive power demonstrated, the American public would not be ready to make the sacrifices necessary to keep the peace.

But what the essay mostly demonstrates is the prophetic potential of survivors—in this case of nuclear scientists "surviving" the effects of the weapon they themselves had produced. In the sequence of the scientists' deepening insight, insight that began with Los Alamos and

Hiroshima, there is a special kind of human power, a kind we have insufficiently drawn upon.

THE AWE experienced by scientists witnessing the first test explosion, on 16 July 1945, is revealed in statements they made soon afterward or in recollections of what they felt at that time. Some of these have become well known: for example, "The sun can't hold a candle to it"; "I am become death, the shatterer of worlds"; and "This was the nearest thing to doomsday one can possibly imagine." There were also more irreverent statements: "Now we're all sons of bitches," or, "What a thing we've made!" This last statement is the most simple, and in many ways the most profound of all.

Now I am in no way suggesting that scientists who made these statements became converts to nuclearism, but rather that they were expressing their response to an awesome situation, to a shaking of the foundations, to an end-of-the-world experience of their own. Even after that, of course, the majority of scientists continued with their work, maintaining a certain amount of psychic numbing or, in some cases, seeking to remove themselves from the problem by dissociating their efforts from military purposes. But significant minorities of them either went on to embrace the weapon or, more frequently, to devote a good part of their subsequent lives to warning the public, on the basis of their own hard-won knowledge, about what this weapon really could do. The sense of awe one experienced when close to the weapon, or when possessing it, was by no means limited to some scientists or scientific commentators; one could find it in military and political leaders, some of whom, as Gar Alperovitz has shown, came to rely on the weapon to do things (achieve political goals) that they could *not* do.[1]

The general impact of the bomb was vividly expressed in an article in the New York *Herald Tribune* that appeared immediately after the presidential announcement of the dropping of the bomb on Hiroshima. The article described the bomb as "a weird, incredible and somehow disturbing force." Its author went on to say that "one forgets the effect on Japan and on the course of the war and one senses the foundations of one's own universe trembling."[2] This is very close to the language of William James in his description of religious experience, particularly conversion.

One could give many examples of people who became enmeshed with the bomb and fell into the pattern of nuclearism. The science writer William

Lawrence, who was given the task of becoming the bomb's more or less official nontechnical historian, conveyed his awe in the language he employed in describing the first test explosion: "On that moment hung eternity. Time stood still. Space contracted to a pinpoint. It was as if the earth had opened and the sky had split. One felt as if one had been privileged to witness the Birth of the World."[3] Years later, when describing another test explosion, that of the first airborne hydrogen bomb, taking place in the Northern Pacific, the same writer told how "for nearly an hour after the fireball had faded I watched incredulously the great many-colored cloud that had been born in the gigantic pillar of fire." He spoke of the "rising sun to the east of it" and of his imagining that New York, Chicago, Washington, Paris, London, Rome, Moscow—all the major cities of the world—were being destroyed by such a weapon. But then he went on to say, "This great, iridescent cloud and its mushroom top, I found myself thinking as I watched, is actually a protective umbrella that will forever shield mankind everywhere against the threat of annihilation in an atomic war." And he admonished "those who would have us stop our testing in the Pacific" by assuring them that

> these tests, and others of improved models to come, serve as an effective substitute for war. History will record, I am sure, that World War III was fought and won on the Pacific proving grounds in the Marshall Islands, without the loss of a single life, or without the slightest damage to any inhabited locality anywhere in the world.[4]

Among nuclear scientists themselves, Edward Teller has moved farthest into nuclearism. Again I speak of an individual in order to illustrate a general phenomenon. And Teller's book *The Legacy of Hiroshima* (see chapter 10, page 145ff.) is a very striking document to someone like myself who has had a rather different view of Hiroshima and derives from that city a very different legacy. Teller objects vehemently to other scientists' moral repugnance, after Hiroshima, toward the idea of making nuclear weapons. And, on the basis of nonexistent evidence, he makes the claim that a respected authority would have joined the cause of nuclearism: "I cannot rid myself of the thought that President Roosevelt may have planned to use the existence of the atomic bomb, after the war, as a powerful driving force toward world government." He describes elsewhere the spirit of adventure and spontaneity surrounding the overall discussion of thermonuclear problems.[5] These are very real feelings; and we must recognize that there can be a kind of heroic, perhaps Promethean, quality in work on nuclear weapons—and, at least at times, a sense of being on a scientific frontier.

Teller goes on to argue that too much fuss is made about these weapons and the possible damage they might do, especially with regard to fallout. After all, he tells us, "Radiation from test fallout is very small. Its effect on human beings is so little that if it exists at all, it cannot be measured. Radiation from fallout may be slightly harmful to humans. It may be slightly beneficial. It might have no effect at all."[6] An incredible but "balanced" view of fallout—perhaps good, perhaps bad, perhaps neither good nor bad—which must be viewed as the kind of lapse in logic that comes from embrace of the deity. Similarly, Teller and others have so minimized both the potential damage and the permanence of the damage as to make one wonder whether Hiroshima, brought about by a weapon one-thousandth the strength of its present successors, really occurred. Are we to believe Dr. Teller when he tells us, "This much is certain: Properly defended, we can survive a nuclear attack; we can dig out of the ruins; we can recover from the catastrophe"?[7]

What happens, it seems to me, is that the nuclear scientist—indeed, the public which in some final analysis serves as the culture he or she influences—lives out survival processes similar to those I observed in interviews with those in and near Hiroshima during the holocaust.

The first of the four themes in the nuclear scientists' efforts to control the bomb is *establishing a responsible international order of scientist keepers of the secret.* As early as 1935, Leo Szilard had the idea, which he discussed with other colleagues, that scientists should cease publication of papers and articles bearing on the possibility of atomic weapons, especially those that might conceivably be of use to the Nazis or to German military technicians, who were already very much on the scene.

It is interesting to follow not only Leo Szilard but also Werner Heisenberg, the distinguished German physicist, in this regard. Heisenberg much later said, in retrospect, that during the summer of 1939 the prevention of the construction of the atomic bomb would have required the mutual agreement of only twelve people. And Carl Frederick von Weizsäcker, his German colleague, said, "Perhaps we ought to have been an international order with disciplinary power over its members."[8]

Paradoxes were imposed by events; and Szilard, who was among the most perceptive and humane of all the scientific prophets, became the driving force in creating the atomic bomb, through initiating the famous Einstein letter to President Roosevelt. And Heisenberg and Weizsäcker, brilliant partakers of the free and beautiful scientific atmosphere at Göttingen and Copenhagen, were enlisted by the Nazis for work on the German atomic bomb. Though it was later claimed that they and other German scientists resisted actually producing the bomb, there is little evidence to suggest anything more than administrative shortsightedness on the part of the Nazi hierarchy and perhaps a certain lack of inspiration among the otherwise cooperative scientists.

But what I want to emphasize is the idea, however impossible to carry out, of scientists attempting to assume the prophetic form of an international order of "keepers of the secret." The attempt was frustrated by various political, personal, and scientific pressures. (For example, when Szilard tried desperately to persuade the physicist Frédéric Joliot-Curie, who was doing significant work in France at that time, to cease publishing, he met with little response. Despite Szilard's letters, telegrams, and emissaries, Joliot-Curie was stubborn because of his commitment to his research institute, then desperately in need of funds. He felt that the institute had to turn out publications in order to attract those funds.) Indeed, the only reason physicists could even consider making themselves into such a prophetic order was the international predominance of three academic centers—Göttingen, Copenhagen, and Cambridge—at which a relatively small number of nuclear scientists from all over the world came together in exclusive fraternity, knowing one another quite well and creating a kind of subculture within which they could, even after leaving the three centers, remain in active communication.

While no such concentration of scientists or scientific knowledge exists any longer, something of the vision may be said to linger on. For there is a new impulse toward international communities, certainly of scientists, but also of youth, intellectuals in general, humanists, peace groups, and so on. Exclusivity is no longer desirable or possible; and these groups, at least ideally, seek to transcend national prejudices and to express their sense of continuity or symbolic immortality through universalist forms of commitment.

A second theme among nuclear scientists can be called *experiencing both disease and cure*. This theme is expressed in the tragic life trajectory of Robert Oppenheimer—his first falling (or plunging) into nuclearism, and then extricating himself from that position. It was Oppenheimer's tragedy to find realization in the creation of the bomb. A man of protean brilliance, a great synthesizer who knew everything rather than one particular thing (in Isaiah Berlin's terms, a fox rather than a hedgehog), Oppenheimer made no original discoveries in physics commensurate with his genius. His creative moment—his psychohistorical breakthrough—came at Los Alamos. As Philip Stern later wrote, "It was as if the man and the job had been created with the other in mind."[9]

Most people who worked with Oppenheimer revered him. He was a generous and a humane leader, and it was through his extraordinary leadership that the phenomenon of psychic numbing toward the bomb could so thoroughly imbue the Los Alamos community. There were many reasons that scientists did not think, could not allow themselves to think, about what the weapon they were working on would do.

The project had been initiated because of the fear of a German bomb; and until the time of the German surrender, the scientists were terrified that the Germans would produce the weapon first—all the more so since many were themselves refugees from Nazism. No wonder nuclear scientists in America responded with moral fervor to the call to produce the weapon! They saw themselves as contributing not only to winning the struggle against evil but to shortening the war as well, which they knew the weapon they were working on could help to do. As Alice K. Smith wrote, after discussing their state of mind with them later, "They all agree that they were frantically busy and extremely security conscious and suggest that there was even some half-conscious closing of the mind to anything beyond the fact that they were trying desperately to produce a device which would end the war."[10] That says it very well.

To maintain the sense of accomplishment, of doing an important job, the object being made had to be "detoxified" by the terms used for it. The bomb was thus spoken of as "the gadget," "the device," "the gimmick," "the thing," "the beast," "X-1," or simply "It." Anyone who has gone to medical school recognizes this tendency. It is the way we deal with corpses. Psychic numbing of this kind permitted the bomb to be made.

More than that, there existed a kind of utopian community at Los Alamos. People felt it to be a very special kind of place. As one later said, "We felt that the fence which was around Los Alamos, around our enclosure, kept the rest of the world from us, not us from them."[11] Oppenheimer spurred people on to their very greatest efforts, and there was a general sense of higher purpose, of transcendent mission.

It was significant, however, that when Germany surrendered, the work became more rather than less intense. And Oppenheimer himself resisted attempts, when they finally did occur, to question the idea of using the bomb. This idea, it must be said, tended not to arise in Los Alamos, where the bomb was actually assembled and where the main preoccupation, until the very end, was whether the gadget would work. Rather, the question arose in Chicago, where other scientists working on the same project had completed their tasks much earlier; a few of them, with a bit of time on their hands and with geographical as well as psychological distance separating them from the last stages of producing the bomb, were able to resensitize themselves to its human consequences.

When the beginning movement against the bomb spread hesitantly from Chicago to Los Alamos, Oppenheimer tried to still the small voices of protest. He said, first, that if the bomb could be completed and tested by civilian scientists, that would keep it from becoming a secret restricted to the military; and, second, that scientists were ill equipped to consider such matters. Others knew better, and these things were being dealt with at a higher level. This was the point of view he expressed to Edward Teller, who, prodded by Leo Szilard and others in Chicago, tried to raise the question of whether some method of demonstration—some policy other than dropping the bomb on a populated city—might be used.* Nor did Oppenheimer in any way favor that kind of alternative when he served as chairman of an official scientific advisory subcommittee on the use of the bomb. Oppenheimer, perhaps inevitably for a man in his position, had his own form of nuclearistic identification with the bomb: the "higher purpose," the bomb itself, became a way (in the words of Nuel Pharr Davis) "to shake mankind free from parochialism and war."[13]

After the war, Oppenheimer apparently became much more ambivalent about these matters; but he still worked actively on nuclear-weapons programs, on the assumption that he could contribute from within to their control, nationally and internationally. Yet he surprised many of his colleagues when he supported the May-Johnson Act, which proposed placing the bomb under full military control; disdained the scientists' crusade (successful, as it turned out) against the bill; and took a generally hard line on disarmament negotiations with the Soviet Union.

Only around 1949, when the hydrogen bomb began to approach reality, did Oppenheimer make a significant reversal and begin to raise fundamental criticisms about the direction of the nuclear-weapons program. He still worked on the hydrogen bomb, as a spokesman for smaller, more diversified nuclear weapons as opposed to the Air Force's "big bomb" policy. But he began to have profound doubts; and his expression of these doubts took him, and the country, to the heart of the problem of nuclearism. He said, "What concerns me is really not the technical problem . . . but that this thing appears to have caught the imagination, both of the Congressional and military people, as the answer to the problem posed by the Russians' advance"; and he expressed the fear that Americans would "become committed to it as the way to save the country and the peace." He went on to say, "Our atomic bomb will not do all things," and, "The least we can conclude is that our twenty-thousandth bomb . . . will not in any deep strategic sense offset their two-thousandth."[14]

* Martin Sherwin, however, has produced letters suggesting that "Teller's views were never in conflict with Oppenheimer's on this matter,"[12] whatever Teller's later claims to the contrary.

While he was immersed in nuclearism, Oppenheimer was a national hero; when he painfully extricated himself from that condition and underwent his nuclear backsliding, he was crucified and became something of a "divine victim." He was more dangerous to proponents of nuclearism, especially within the Air Force, than other scientists who were more critical from the beginning.

But can we any longer afford this kind of trajectory of immersion into the disease and then struggle for cure? Clearly we have come to the point where we must understand nuclearism and reject it.

The third theme is one more traditionally associated with prophecy: the *apocalyptic imagination* mentioned earlier. Involved in this theme is the capacity to imagine the end of the world, to imagine the effects at the other end of the weapon *before* they occur. Outstanding examples of physicists who have expressed this theme are Leo Szilard, James Franck, Eugene Rabinowitch, and, before them, Niels Bohr. The apocalyptic imagination was an old story among biblical prophets; what was new for the nuclear physicists was a technology that rendered the imagined apocalypse an imminent likelihood. The apocalyptic imagination became a necessary means of perceiving reality. A few of them were able to help narrow the gap between technology and imagination by calling forth a combination of their professional intimacy with this new technology and their individual sensitivities to death anxiety.

When Robert Oppenheimer made his famous post-Hiroshima statement, "The physicists have known sin," he was describing a special form of survivorhood—of death guilt and death anxiety related not only to having constructed a murderous instrument but to having believed in that instrument—lived in nuclearism—as well. Oppenheimer articulated what others, notably Szilard and Rabinowitch, acted upon more quickly. The post–Second World War scientists' crusade against nuclear weapons was a way of finding significance in their own death immersion by disseminating what Alice Smith has aptly described as a form of "spiritual revelation." From this survivor quest came not only the crusade against the May-Johnson bill but the Federation of American Scientists, the *Bulletin of the Atomic Scientists,* and the Council for a Livable World.

The crusade had actually begun before Hiroshima, with the deliberations in Chicago mentioned earlier, and with the anticipatory vision of the "giant fireball" described by Eugene Rabinowitch (chapter 11, page 158) that led to the moving and still significant Franck Report. What this sequence exemplifies is a combination of apocalyptic imagination with pragmatic, day-to-day effort, a combination that came to mark the approach of this group of scientists.

But perhaps Leo Szilard, most strikingly of all, expressed the anticipatory apocalyptic imagination. A perpetual survivor who lived through a wide variety of European upheavals, Szilard possessed what one commentator described as a "special gift for deducing future events from present facts," and a "vivid imagination . . . [that] outstripped events."[15] We may say that early psychological inclinations combined with a series of witnessed upheavals and survivals to create an exquisite sensitivity to abrupt and potentially catastrophic shifts in the overall human environment. The pattern led Szilard to flee Hungary and Germany, to attempt to get scientists to withhold nuclear publications that might lead to a bomb, to initiate the atomic bomb project in America, and thereafter to assume an early, energetic, and permanent form of leadership—intellectual, ethical, and political—in the struggle against nuclear weapons.

Szilard revealed himself in the parables he wrote. One essay, "My Trial as a War Criminal,"[16] has him brought to international justice for his part in Hiroshima, his defense that he had circulated an anti-bomb petition being made to no avail because, as the prosecutor points out, he followed advice and circulated the petition through proper channels, where it could be effectively quashed, instead of obeying his own impulse to act more radically and less legally. The essay was written whimsically and stressed everyone's culpability, but Szilard did deeply regret this failure; and his profound sense of guilt in relation to the overall atomic-bomb experience undoubtedly served as a driving force for his subsequent actions.

In his more famous parable "The Voice of the Dolphins,"[17] Szilard tells an amusing tale of brilliant scientific accomplishments by dolphins, checked by Russian and American scientists at the "Vienna Institute," of insights that can later be extended to political problems and enable politicians of the world to effect arrangements for universal disarmament and lasting peace. What Szilard was really pleading for in this parable was the application of free *human* imagination (the kind of imagination he knew to exist in science at its best—for which the dolphins served in the parable as a kind of "front") to present apocalyptic dilemmas. Yet even anticipatory apocalyptic imagination, though essential, has not been enough.

The fourth and most recent prophetic theme among scientists has been that of *a reasoned critique and reconstruction of our entire science-dominated cosmology.* This represents a turning inward and outward on the part of at least a significant minority of young scientists in search of a widening zone of ethical responsibility.

Of great symbolic significance in this regard was the March 4th Movement of 1969, outwardly a day of research stoppage* but symbolically a

* What came to be called the March 4th Movement began as a coalition of graduate students and faculty at the Massachusetts Institute of Technology, focusing first on the Vietnam

turning point marking concern with more fundamental issues: issues about the nature of science, what it does in and to society, what an individual scientist does and the consequences of his or her work. The questioning has been extended to ways of thinking in science and the social consequences of those modes of thought. I stress the critique from within. For when scientists themselves "reject the old credo that 'Research means progress and progress is good,' "—declaring, "Reliance on such simplistic ethical codes has led to mistaken or even perverted uses of scientific talents," and, "Misuse of scientific and technical knowledge presents a major threat to the existence of mankind"—then we are witnessing a direct expression of "ultimate concern" among those who sense that human history can be extinguished by the very "things" that result from their creative work.

The March 4th Movement was perhaps less a prophetic vision than the struggle for one. Although the movement no longer exists, similar radical questions continue to be asked.* But it can be seen as a part of a general critique of society by the young, a worldwide quest for revitalization, or for what I have called a "new history." It is part of an attempt to redirect an entire cultural tradition, going back hundreds or even thousands of years, and to head off a scientifically caused "end" by creating, within science and every other intellectual tradition, a new beginning, a new form of human connection. In separating science from scientism and technology from technocism, this new group of prophetic survivors seeks to liberate scientists from their present, closed priesthood—in which they continue to collude, however indirectly or secretly, with the nuclear deity—so that they can reconstitute themselves into an open brotherhood and sisterhood committed to the survival and growth of human beings.

I have been describing a continuous struggle for a prophetic direction among scientists in relation to the threat of nuclear weapons. It is, of course, just one of the major struggles for transformation now taking place within world society, and I focus on nuclear scientists only to illustrate the dilemmas and possibilities affecting all others who enter into that struggle. For the control of nuclear and other ultimate weapons is an enterprise upon which all other enterprises must rest. A prophet's quest for spiritual regeneration has always been bound to the technology of the time. We have come a long way from that biblical prophet who, in exhorting us to turn

---

War but increasingly on the broader uses and abuses of science and technology. On 4 March 1969, at major universities throughout the United States, scientific research and classes were suspended, and "teach-ins" were held instead.

* Indeed, the March 4th Movement gave rise to two groups dedicated to confronting these critical questions about science and technology, particularly in relation to weapons: the Union of Concerned Scientists, and Science for the People.

the other cheek, spoke not only in metaphorical but in literal terms, of face-to-face encounters. Today we have no choice but to confront the death anxiety and the threat of holocaust hanging over us. Our task is to take the imaginative plunge into this subterranean or apocalyptic realm in order to be able to re-emerge with greater awareness of our plight, with broader wisdom, and with a stronger capacity to act.

PART III

REFLECTIONS

Let me begin again as a speck
of dust caught in the night winds
sweeping out to sea. . . .
A tiny wise child who this time will love
his life because it is like no other.

—PHILIP LEVINE

. . . that newest of natural
phenomena—Mind—still faces
the mystery of all things young,
the secret of vital potentiality.

—SUSANNE K. LANGER

13

Dreaming Well: Frontiers of Form

If we do not dream, then the day is not very good.

—Zinacantec Indian saying

I am dreaming and I would
act well, for good deeds
are not lost, even in dreams.

—PEDRO CALDERÓN

This essay was originally given at a large symposium on dreams sponsored by the department of human development and health sciences of the University of California, Los Angeles, and the Southern California Psychoanalytic Society and Institute. I had long been making use of dreams of research subjects in all of my studies, while also recording dreams of my own. I had begun (in both The Life of the Self *and* The Broken Connection) *to outline a theoretical perspective I wished to develop, and wanted to go about the matter more systematically.*

*Freud's discovery of ways in which dreams served as what he called a "*via regna *to the unconscious" made it necessary, I believe, for any new psychological thought to reassess the twists and turns of that* via regna. *In connection with my work, dreams are crucial to an understanding of what I call "formative process," and to the overall life-continuity paradigm. This essay has at least one particularly hopeful message: dreams of individual people in extreme circumstances can contribute to a process of forward-looking integration and moral questioning.*

SOME years ago, when embarking on a study of Nazi doctors, I had a talk with a friend who was both an authority on the Holocaust and himself an Auschwitz survivor. I complained to him about the horrors of the material I was uncovering, that it was affecting me a great deal, especially in my dreams—that I was having horrible dreams about concentration camps, dreams that involved not only me but also my wife and children. My friend looked at me with a combination of sympathy and toughness. "Good!" he said. "Now you can do the study." We smiled at each other in recognition. He was telling me that my dreaming about this terrible subject meant that it was entering my mind in some important way, that I was not remaining distant from it but permitting it, however involuntarily, to connect with my own internal images. He could confirm and approve, as a survivor, my coming from the outside, so to speak, and experiencing a survivor's dreams. And still further, he was implying that dreaming about these events was also necessary to my *intellectual*—broadly speaking, *creative*—function in the work.

Those dreams have by no means disappeared. But the dreaming function is never simple. In doing the work and getting even closer to the material (through interviews with both Nazi perpetrators and Auschwitz survivors), I not only have dreamed of camp and other expressions of Nazi cruelty but have also had much more pleasant dreams, as if to counteract the fearful ones, some of them highly erotic.

The principle revealed here—and the central theme of this chapter—may be expressed in an anthropologist's comment on the dream patterns of the Zinacantec Indians of southern Mexico: "Dogs dream and cats dream. Horses dream, and even pigs, say the Zinacantecs.* No one knows why; but there is no question in the mind of a Zinacantec why *men* dream. They dream to lead a full *life*. They dream to *save* their lives."[1]

Or to put the matter another way: dreams have a more central role in the human imagination than we have realized. They are formative events and ingenious renditions of "the state of the mind"—its conflicts and prospects. In many ways an advanced psychic domain, they are notably prospective: that is, in their symbolizations, they can bring qualities of ingenuity that suggest, more than other forms of waking thought, directions in which the self is seeking to move and often will move.

* Mesoamerican Indian group of southern Mexico and Guatemala.

I

Applying the paradigm of symbolization of life and death to dreams makes especially clear that it is not a thanatology but a psychology of life. Within this paradigm, there is a continuous struggle to evoke and preserve the sense of the self as alive, and to avoid the sense of the self as dead. In this way, motivation revolves around life and death imagery, often experienced, respectively, as form and formlessness. There is great stress upon the image as the link between nervous system and environment, but also as anticipatory in nature—that is, the image as what Eric Olson calls "schema for enactment"—an important concept in relationship to dreams.[2] Combined or elaborated images become "forms" (or constellations)—and the term *form* takes on the philosophical meaning of "the essence of something as opposed to its matter,"[3] rather than the seemingly opposite popular meaning of appearance as opposed to content or reality.

II

Can we, then, speak of a historical dream? If all dreams are formative in the sense I have been describing, the category of historical dreams becomes somewhat problematic. But I have used that concept, originally in connection with the following dream and its associations:

> A student leader (whom I shall call Sato) in his early twenties described to me the following dream: "A student [political] demonstration is taking place. A long line of students moves rapidly along. . . . Then at the end of the line there seems to be a festival float (*dashi*) which other students are pulling."
>
> Sato laughed uncomfortably as he told his dream, because he could begin to perceive (as he explained later) that it seemed to suggest a relationship between student political demonstrations and traditional shrine festivals. This embarrassed him because such political demonstrations, and the student movement that sponsored them (the *Zengakuren*, or All Japan Federation of Student Self-Governing Societies) had been for the past few years the central and most sacred part of his life—in fact, the only part that held meaning for him; while a shrine festival, symbolized by the large float, seemed to him

something quite frivolous, or worse. He was particularly struck, and dismayed, by the fact that *students* were pulling the float.

In his associations to the dream, he recalled the shrine festivals he had witnessed in the provincial city where he had attended high school; these he remembered as dreary, unanimated, motivated only by commercial considerations, and ultimately degenerate, stimulating in him feelings like those he sometimes experienced when face to face with very old people—a combination of revulsion, sympathy, and a sense of contamination.

But he contrasted these negative impressions of relatively recent shrine festivals with the romantic and beautiful atmosphere of great shrine festivals in the distant past, as described in many court novels he had read. And he also thought of smaller festivals held at harvest time in the rural area of central Japan where he was born and had spent his early childhood.

He spoke vividly of the sense of total relaxation that came over the entire village, of the bright decorations and gay atmosphere around the shrine, of the exciting horse races made up of local entrants, of big feasts with relatives, of masked dances (*kagura*) giving their renditions of the most ancient of recorded Japanese tales (from the *Kojiki*), of fascinating plays performed sometimes by traveling troupes (*ichiza*) and at times by young people from the village.

Sato emphasized that in his dream he was a bystander, standing apart from both the political demonstration and the festival-like activities. This stance he associated with his recent displacement from a position of leadership within the student movement (because of a factional struggle) and with his feeling that he had failed to live up to his obligations to colleagues and followers in the movement. One meaning he gave to the dream was his belief that the student movement, now in the hands of leaders whom he did not fully respect, might become weak and ineffectual, nothing more than a "festival."

But the dream suggested that Sato was a "bystander" in a more fundamental sense: that he was alienated from those very elements of his personal and cultural past that were at the core of his individual existence. These same elements—still the formative essence of his developing self, or self-process—had not only lost their vitality but had become symbols of decay. The dream was partly a longing for childhood innocence and happiness, but was also an effort at integration. Thus, in his nostalgic associations, Sato commented that if he really did ever see students pulling a *dashi* in that manner at the end of one of their demonstrations, "I would feel that the world was stabilized," by which he meant in a personal sense that if he could harmoniously blend the old things he carried within himself with the new things to which he aspired, *he* would be stabilized. Like so many young people in Japan, Sato outwardly condemns many of the symbols of his own cultural heritage, yet inwardly seeks to recover and restore those symbols so that they may once more be "beautiful" and psychologically functional.[4]

The symbolic sophistication of the dream lies in its ingenious blending of the militant urban political demonstration with the traditional, playful, rural festival. In that combination, too, was the prospective suggestion of the dream: namely, of a life direction in which he might somehow bring together psychologically precisely these two historical images and all they stood for. He was struggling along such lines when I lost contact with him.

I originally published the dream as an example of what I call psychohistorical dislocation, the loss of vital relationship to traditional cultural symbols—a pattern evident in Japan at the time, and hardly absent from our own lives. I wanted to demonstrate Sato's combination of personal and historical dislocation and, indeed, to show them to be inseparable from each other. In this sense, every dream is a historical dream, just as every individual life is bound up with its cultural history—one might even say with the whole of human history. But "historical" elements strike us most vividly in connection with contrast and change, and perhaps also when occurring in cultures and histories alien to our own.

Consider another such "historical dream"—this one from a gifted Japanese student majoring in American history but also devoted to the traditional art of karate. The dream occurred shortly after he had temporarily withdrawn from the karate group of his university, ostensibly because of the pressure of his academic work:

> I was studying *karate* with a certain teacher who is the head of one of the schools of *karate,* and is also a rightist boss. . . . I asked another student there, "Why does the *karate* spirit become associated with ultranationalism? Why are we asked to demonstrate *karate* in front of a shrine?" I said that *karate* should not be like this. Then the master said, "What was it that this youngster was trying to say?" . . . I didn't talk back to him then, but returned to my place and decided to practice more and become more skillful . . . so that I could defeat that master, a master such as that.

And then his associations, revealing the dream's place in his struggle to accommodate inwardly the historical and psychological currents with which he was struggling:

> Since I quit *karate,* it seems that there are *karate* problems even in my dreams. . . . My real master, fortunately, is a very understanding person of a high intellectual level, suitable, I believe, for our university. . . . And the master who appeared in the dream has no connection with me in actuality. . . . Recently I came across a book with a very silly article about a man who practiced *karate* during the Meiji era, telling about all sorts of silly things such as spying for rightists and bragging about eating snakes. . . . I was surprised that this kind of book is still sold in the postwar period. . . . Somehow, there seems to be the tendency in Japanese society that once the heat around our throats is gone, we forget about that heat. . . . I feel that studious people should express themselves about these problems. . . . We should continue to recognize Japanese culture, not just forget about it and praise only American culture and Americans. . . . But we should not become intoxicated in doing this and decide that fine things are to be found only in Japanese culture, and that Japanese culture must be separated from all others. . . . There are people who do *karate* or *jūdō*

> or the like without considering these spiritual disciplines. . . . They are only interested in breaking roof tiles [which one does with the side of one's hand in *karate* practice]. We, as young people, should be progressive and create our own society. . . . But too often we indulge ourselves in moods . . . especially a mood of helplessness. . . . Hope is not easily realized in any society . . . and this society is unsteady. . . . But desperation should not be the way of youth.

I understood this dream as the student's embarrassed confrontation with undesirable elements in traditional Japanese culture, and to some extent with equally undesirable parental authority in general—the "bad master" of karate. Though this young man cannot yet defeat or even talk back to this "bad master"—or absorb the tainted elements in his personal and historical past—he dedicates himself to improving his "skills." These skills relate to the cultural and psychological accommodation he tells us about, his defeat of the "bad master," to rescue and purify his own past. The dream contains both a suggestion and a refusal of despair. It reflects the classical psychohistorical task of the accommodationist: the struggle to combine disparate cultural elements into a meaningful psychological whole. And the prospective dimension of the dream lies in its propulsion toward new integration of old cultural elements—that is, its propulsion toward personal and historical change.[5]

III

Can we speak of historical dreams closer to home—as in the case of Vietnam veterans, for instance? Here I want to discuss dreams that took place in the small "rap groups" that I and other psychological professionals held with Vietnam veterans in New York City during the early 1970s (see chapter 5). Most of these veterans had come to oppose the war and were struggling with emotions they experienced both in Vietnam and upon their return. Any dream reported was responded to by other members of the small group and would become a fulcrum for collective insight—and for connecting their immediate situation with their Vietnam experience.

For instance, the men often discussed their images of dying in Vietnam—and, indeed, their rejection of that fate was in many cases the beginning not only of opposition to the war, but of additional personal transformation as well. In one such discussion in a rap group, a veteran recalled his feelings while in combat: "I wanted to die clean. It didn't matter if I died—but I just didn't want to die with mud on my boots, all filthy. Death wasn't so bad if you were clean." Another man strongly agreed, and told of a repetitive dream he used to have in Vietnam, always with the same terrifying conclusion: "I would end up shot, lying along the side of the road, dying in the mud."

There was intense response in the group, as one veteran after another told of similar fears. And in their associations it became clear that "dying in the mud" meant dying in filth or evil, without reason or purpose—without nobility or dignity of any kind.

Then the man who had said virtually nothing in the group for several weeks suddenly spoke up, and everyone listened with close attention as he blurted out a story:

> I heard of one helicopter pilot in Nam who was carrying a shit-house [portable toilet] on his helicopter. He crashed and was killed, and was buried under the whole shit-house and all the shit. I thought that if I was going to die in Vietnam, that's the way I would like to die. I didn't want to die a heroic death. That was the way to die in Vietnam.[6]

The group again responded with comments and associations having to do with filth and excrement alone providing the appropriate burial ground in Vietnam. I, in fact, heard no more telling evocation of what they had come to view as the war's absurdity and evil.

And from there they went on to contrast that filth, and the bleeding and bodily mutilations of men in Vietnam, with the "clean" deaths portrayed in various expressions of the American mass media. "In Flash Gordon no one ever bleeds" was the way one man put it. Here we may trace a sequence in a dream's prospective potential: the original dream in Vietnam provides a beginning, but still largely inchoate, insight about the futility and ugliness of dying in Vietnam. That dream is recalled a couple of years later in connection with the group's effort to deepen more general understanding of ways of dying and the nature of the Vietnam enterprise. The dream in turn evokes an image of ultimate filth—the helicopter pilot being killed and buried "under the whole shit-house and all the shit"—through which they can confront some of the most painful aspects of their Vietnam experience. That image, in turn, leads to a critique of a more general false American mass media romanticism, in which "no one ever bleeds." The dream was clearly the key event in the sequence—and the associations of others in the group maximized its prospective potential.

And a Vietnam veteran, Michael Casey, echoes this sentiment in a poem entitled "On Death," from a prize-winning collection appropriately entitled *Obscenities:*

Flies all over
It like made of wax
No jaw
Intestines poured
Out of the stomach
The penis in the air
It won't matter then to me but now
I don't want in death to be a
Public obscenity like this[7]

And the veterans brought to the group other related dreams, such as a fragment of one by a former marine: "I was alone in a garbage dump. There was nothing but garbage all around me. I made a fire by burning *Life* magazines and things like that."[8] The dreamer and the rest of the group associated not only to actual garbage piles in Vietnam but to the accumulation of dead and the ultimate "garbage" there—not just because they were dead but because of their grotesque, premature, and unacceptable deaths. Again, the group was groping toward the insight that, for Vietnam, "garbage was truth," as opposed to any more romantic claim to nobility or "victory." And that sentiment was again expressed by a stanza of poetry written by a Vietnam veteran:

The Holy Army trampled
In the sun of Christmas Day,
But when they passed, the garbagemen
Took all the dead away.[9]

Dreams, that is, can propel individuals and groups toward the most painful kinds of insight—and in that very function and in the ingenious imagery with which it is carried out, they can also resemble illuminating imagery of poetry.

Among these veterans, I encountered what I came to describe as an "animating relationship to guilt." Feelings of guilt, of self-condemnation, could be experienced and then converted into anxiety of responsibility—so that the initial guilt became a source of reflection, commitment to humane principles, and constructive personal change. During some of the group sessions, men would try to make inner contact with a sense of guilt they thought they should but could not feel. One such veteran kept insisting, "I just can't *feel* any guilt"[10]—despite an incident in which he saw a grenade he had placed blow a Vietnamese person apart so that pieces of the corpse flew fifty yards into the air—and that at the time he remembered "just laughing out loud." When others suggested that his laughter might have been a way of covering up his feelings, especially ones of guilt, he merely shrugged his shoulders inconclusively. But just a few minutes later, he reported a rapid series of disturbing recent dreams, including the following three:

> I was riding on some kind of vehicle—a bus, I think—down Fifth Avenue. Somehow it turned into a military truck—and the truck got bigger and bigger, until it reached an enormous size. I was a soldier on the truck—and . . . I fell off . . . and was killed.
>
> I was riding on a subway—underground—and somehow [along the course of the ride] I seemed to turn into a soldier in uniform. . . . There was a lot of confusion and then there was a battle with the police . . . in which I was killed.
>
> I was in Vietnam and off in the distance there was a firefight. One of the guys near me panicked and kept telling me he thought he heard something, . . . acting very scared. . . . I was so disgusted with him that I said, "Why don't you light a flare?" Anyone who's been in Vietnam knows that that was ridiculous, and that I was only kidding him—because it would be crazy to light a flare since that would locate where you were for the VC. But this guy didn't know any better, being new in Vietnam, so he actually lit the flare. . . . There was firing and he was killed. [The veteran explained that this last dream recreated an actual incident in Vietnam, in which he had actually advised a GI to light a flare as a kind of joke, which the GI did, but no harm had actually resulted.]

The group responded actively to these three dreams, emphasizing the dreamer's fear of the military and especially the sense of guilt: the idea that he had done something wrong and had to be punished or killed—that he was not finished with the military or the war and still had important psychological work to do in connection with both; and also the idea of the dream being a message from the underground (suggested concretely by the subway) which had to do with the question of guilt, contradicting his surface (conscious) insistence that he was not experiencing any. (These last two interpretations were essentially my own.) The dreamer responded by saying, "Maybe I don't *want* to feel guilty—maybe I'm afraid to"—perhaps because, as he explained, he was already burdened with violent impulses and feared that feeling guilty would make things much worse and somehow undermine his control over his violence. I had the clear impression that he was moving closer to a recognition of a sense of guilt, but not to the point, he insisted, of *feeling* guilt.

But then something else happened. His sequence of dreams triggered another struggle with guilt in a former Marine sergeant. The latter, a forceful man with an aura of masculine strength, expressed antagonism to the idea of guilt, insisting that "guilt is just plain useless"; that he had no reason to feel guilty; that he had no malice toward the nineteen people he killed and had killed them because "I saw my buddies dead." But as he went on, he spoke, in a tone of extraordinary pain and bitterness, of "one very big mistake" he had made in Vietnam, that of trusting someone unworthy of his trust to lead a patrol and of not having given sufficiently precise orders to this man, with the result that twelve of his best men were ambushed and killed in the most grotesque fashion—so that some could not even be found. And this former Marine added:

> You know, when you see dead men—whether they're round-eyes or gooks, they're all the same. Their faces are screwed up—they're all fucked up. . . . I don't know why it all happened—there was the damned fool war—and maybe I just wasn't old enough to have responsibility for so many men.

At that point this man got up and ran out of the room, explaining that he just wanted to be alone for a while; but it was clear to everyone that he was beginning to confront guilt feelings of the most disturbing kind. At just that point, the other veteran who had dreamed those three dreams spoke up, now in tremulous tones:

> You know, I'm shuddering. . . . I'm shaking all over . . . because what he said hit me hard. . . . Before . . . we talked about guilt . . . but I didn't feel too much. But now I really feel remorse. I feel very badly about what I did in Vietnam—and it's a terrible feeling.

This sequence had much to do with the group's continuing struggle with guilt and with the effort to form an animating—that is, a morally energizing—relationship to it. But what I want to stress here, once more, is the role of dreams as the pivotal psychic force in this shared effort. Dreams seemed to possess something on the order of mythic power, of special illumination, that in turn enabled the veterans—as individuals and as a group—to make their special psychic leaps into the most painful mental terrain.

Sometimes the sequence can move, so to speak, from dream to dream.

> A veteran appearing at a rap group for the first time told of a frightening recurrent dream, in which an NLF soldier would shoot and kill him. The figure in his dream was the same NLF soldier he had actually confronted in what

> was, literally, face-to-face combat: as each of them shot they could see one another clearly. The veteran was wounded in the leg, and, without quite making things clear, gave us the impression that the NVA soldier had been killed. The combat incident had occurred a year earlier, but the recurrent dream together with diffuse anxiety had been intensified by two kinds of experience—the veteran's increasing involvement in antiwar protest, and his having been surprised by a mugger near his home in Manhattan a short time before.
>
> In the midst of these associations to his dream one of the other men suddenly asked him, "Do you feel guilty about being alive?" He answered without hesitation: "Yes. You're supposed to be dead."

Right afterward, another veteran reported a brief but pointed dream of his own: "I was arguing with myself. Then there were two separate selves, and one of them finally shot the other, so that I shot myself." The dream, and a few associations to it, epitomized the survivor conflict: an inner split that is both guilty and deadly; a simultaneous transgression and retribution—the self murdering the self. It also suggests the classic literary and mythological theme of the double, in which one self can represent life (sometimes immortal life) and its replica death (or mortality). Above all, it is the starkest of images—at the same time concrete and metaphorical—of one as both victim and executioner (see chapter 14).

Here the two dreams in tandem brought the veterans to the very heart of their overwhelmingly painful, war-linked existential dilemma. It was after such a discussion that one man told of killing a Viet Cong soldier with a knife, and then added softly, "I felt sorry. I don't know why I felt sorry. John Wayne never felt sorry."

The dreams in these sequences are clearly formative and prospective, in their early illumination of evolving insight and action. At the same time they are historical dreams, in their intertwining of personal and social change having to do with the shifting currents of their historical era.

IV

In my final exploration of a particular dream sequence, I must move to a still more painful realm, that of the Nazi death camp, the source of three dreams of a particular Nazi doctor. In this case, the dreams, in their formative and historical characteristics, suggest a moral struggle and a direction of partial resolution.

I have interviewed one doctor, a man in his late sixties, for a total of about thirty hours—five full-day meetings over a little more than two years.[11] Dr. Ernst B.—not his real name—came from an academic family of some standing, was as a child and adolescent in considerable rebellion against his father and the latter's wish for his son to enter medicine, and succumbed to that wish only after his brief effort at becoming an artist ended in dismal failure. He developed a *modus vivendi* of being liked and being very adaptable in a variety of environments. Thus Ernst B. got along well with fellow students and with the Nazis who quickly came to dominate the faculty and student structures—his standing greatly enhanced when he became one of the winners of a contest sponsored by a Nazi science group to discover a local product to replace imported ones in bacterial culture media. Though not a strong ideologue, he was impressed with some aspects of the Nazis, and certainly did not hesitate to join the party when advised to do so for the benefit of his personal and professional future. There were many aspects to his being called into the Waffen SS and assigned to Auschwitz—he had himself experienced some patriotic fervor and requested a military appointment; but one reason was undoubtedly the regime's perception of his ideological reliability. In Auschwitz he continued his pattern of getting on with everyone—with his Nazi medical colleagues, and also with inmates, especially prisoner physicians with whom he came to have close contact. This latter I confirmed through interviews with survivor physicians in different parts of the world—and through his having been acquitted in an Auschwitz trial on the basis of testimony of former prisoner doctors, to whom he had been particularly kind in Auschwitz and, in a number of cases, whose lives he had saved. He got on, then, with his captors when he became a prisoner; and then with his patients when he returned to medical practice in southern Bavaria; and, for the most part, with me, during our interviews. But the whole process was not quite as smooth as it may sound.

Upon arriving in Auschwitz, which he claims to have previously known nothing about, Ernst B. was appalled and overwhelmed and had a strong impulse to leave (which would probably have been possible). But he was taken aside by his immediate superior, who turned out to be an old friend who had helped him in the past. This friend told Dr. B., in effect: "Yes, Auschwitz represents the 'Final Solution' of the Jewish people; what happens here is not pretty but there is nothing we can do about it; and I need you here for my unit [the Hygienic Institute, which was outside the ordinary hierarchy of camp medical officers], and if you stay it will strengthen us greatly and we will be able to keep our hands completely clean." Dr. B. stayed.

A few days after his arrival in Auschwitz he looked out a window early in the evening and saw prisoners returning from their work outside the camp, marching double-time six abreast, and thought he saw among them a former classmate from his old *Gymnasium* (secondary school), named Simon Cohen. Ernst B. ran outside to find him, but the prisoners had already disappeared into their blocks. For the next couple of days he went desperately about the camp trying to locate Simon Cohen—and in the process learned at first hand about the killing and working arrangements at Auschwitz and about the status of Jews as non-people. At one point he went running into the office area he was assigned to and asked the prisoner physician working there whether he knew a Simon Cohen in the camp. The answer came back cautiously that "tens, thousands of Jews . . . come through," that "many of them were named Cohen," and that it would be impossible to find any such person. The prisoner physician answered that way, as I confirmed in a later interview with him, because he believed that the attempt to find such a person was hopeless and could be harmful both to him and to Dr. B. himself. And even though the Nazi doctor seemed compassionate, the prisoner doctor might have been worried about the intention of a man in an SS uniform inquiring about a Jewish prisoner. In the course of his fruitless inquiries, Dr. B. saw more clearly the labyrinthine, murderous nature of Auschwitz.

Later he came to wonder whether he had really seen Cohen—or whether it had been an illusion or perhaps even a dream. In any case, he immediately began to have a series of dreams about the incident that were really one basic repetitive dream with many variations. In every dream Simon Cohen's face would appear:

> He was always a very attractive young man. And now [in the dream] he had really deteriorated. . . . And he looked at me with a reproachful, beseeching expression . . . sort of [saying], "It can't be possible that you stand there and I am . . . [like this] . . ." or more like a disappointed expression: "How can you belong to those people? That can't be you."[12]

In telling me about these dreams, Ernst B. further explained that he and Cohen had been special friends during the early 1930s (the dream had occurred in about May 1943), having in common their mutual lack of interest in schoolwork and enjoyment of drinking alcohol. They took long bicycle trips together during vacations and remained personally close despite living quite far from one another and despite the already extensive general anti-Semitism.

Dr. B. had the dream most frequently after drinking and associated it at the time with what he called the "especially bad situation" in which he found himself in Auschwitz and with "my problem: Is it right to stay, or would it be better to leave?" On the side of staying was his feeling that "I could do something good here, . . . something humane."

And, indeed, the dream could be understood as a call to residual inner humanity—just as he recalled feeling, at the time he thought he saw Simon Cohen among the prisoners, that "if I can find him, I can make some kind of human contact."

These specific dream images are important: the identification with the "beaten down" or macerated face of the victim, who as a close school friend and a central character in the dream represented an important part of Ernst B.'s own self-process. And the pleading, reproachful look, together with disbelief—in effect, "That can't be *you* standing among *them*"—this representing B.'s own sense of unreality in, and partial removal from, the overall Auschwitz situation. And perhaps the formative aspect in the dream lies exactly there—in its consistency with his subsequent capacity to divide himself to the extent that he was, so to speak, both: one of *them* (them being the Nazi victimizers) and *not* one of them (in the sense of standing apart from them sufficiently to be a consistent source of help to prisoners—so much so that a later historian of Auschwitz described him as "a human being in an SS uniform"). The dream is also, of course, replete with historical imagery—concerning Germans and Jews, and the historical transformations that turn friends into enemies.

One could argue, of course, that Ernst B.'s decision to remain in Auschwitz instead of leaving violated that prospective dream message of calling forth residual humanity. And one could support this argument by Dr. B.'s own insistence to me that, despite the extent to which he was appreciated and even admired by the inmates, he belonged, after all, to the group of Nazi doctors—to the Auschwitz camp structure. Toward the end of our interviews, he expressed for the first time a certain nostalgia for what he considered a few positive features of the Nazi era. He did not cease, that is, being one of "them."

But it is also true that, during his time in Auschwitz, he was unique in his consideration for inmates, especially those prisoner doctors who worked in his unit—taking personal risks to help them in such small (but, in Auschwitz, very big indeed) matters as enabling husbands and wives among prisoners to meet and carrying letters and messages from inmates to people on the outside. So, at least in that sense, the dream's prospective call to personal humanity was by no means totally ignored. And that call had its greatest effect when it was most needed—during his nineteen months at Auschwitz—after which it did not entirely disappear but became much more infrequent.

A second dream Ernst B. described to me also emerged from the Auschwitz situation—though he insisted he never had the actual dream in Auschwitz, but only years later upon returning to his home in Germany. It concerned a young Jewish laboratory assistant who had worked at the Hygienic Institute. In the dream he fled with her from Auschwitz to nearby mountains, where they joined a group of Polish Partisans (anti-Nazi underground fighters). That was the central theme of a recurrent dream that he had in a number of different versions. Dr. B. gave me the impression that he had a special relationship to this dream, a kind of proprietary affection. He introduced it to me, in response to my asking about dreams other than the one about Cohen, by saying, "Perhaps there is one other dream, . . . a purely, deeply psychological question perhaps. Maybe it is a key. I can't exactly explain it."

And when describing the dream's few details, he quickly added, "That is the only other Auschwitz dream that has remained. I'm sure that there was no erotic background to this. In fact, . . . to the contrary."

An erotic component is of course very much present, but in a particular way. In discussing the dream, Dr. B. explained that this Jewish laboratory assistant had a certain artistic talent, which SS men took advantage of by having her make drawings from photographs, which they (the SS men) would then try to sell or make some other use of. All that, he explained, was part of the prevailing corruption in Auschwitz: everyone there was likely to be corrupted in some way: everyone, as Ernst B. put it in the German idiom, had "dirt on his walking stick" (*Dreck am Stecken*). And everyone knew about everyone else's "dirt."

Although to Ernst B. the girl "seemed so young and so primitive," she had an uncanny ability to vary the style of each drawing according to what she perceived the taste of individual SS men: drawing "simple red-cheeked" pictures for simple SS men and more delicate, aesthetically sophisticated pictures for more sensitive SS officers like himself—and, in fact, she did draw for him what he considered a "beautiful picture" of his wife and young children from a photograph he provided. He became preoccupied with this seeming dichotomy in her, suspecting that "she just fooled around during the day and then took the whole thing to an artist in her block every evening": "I just couldn't believe that this girl would be able to do these kinds of things by herself"—adding that precisely that kind of suspicion was "in Auschwitz the normal reaction." Eventually he became convinced that she did indeed do all the drawings herself; though when he further observed her and spoke to her, he was "again and again surprised at how primitive she actually was," and concluded that "she was a primitive, naturally talented person." The mountains to which they flee in the dream were near the area from which she had come; and in one conversation they had when he spoke of his possibly taking a drive into that area, she warned him not to because there were likely to be too many partisans there.

He managed to take the picture with him from Auschwitz and to retain it despite his subsequent years of custody and trial. Upon returning to medical practice, he first hung it in his office and later in his bedroom. But he eventually, as he explained, "took it out of the room to get rid of the dream"—though the dream persisted after he had removed the picture. As we talked about all this, he had his wife bring in the picture, which he looked at affectionately; and when I asked whether he still valued it very much, he answered, "Yes, of course—I had it in Auschwitz the whole time, you understand. And later I kept it here." He added that now, with more detachment, he could say that it was "really a very nice picture but close to being *kitsch*"—a word that usually means "shoddy, pretentious, and without artistic merit." But Dr. B. qualified that judgment, and somewhat defended the picture, by adding, "Many good artistic things, including Goethe's *Faust*, always move close to kitsch."

And he went on to associate the picture further with "this emotion I had in Auschwitz . . . my bad feelings to my family"—what he had described as a "bad conscience" toward his wife for his having initiated the steps (asking for military duty) that led him to be assigned to Auschwitz—so that when he managed to get away from Auschwitz briefly to visit his wife, "I had a good feeling and a bad feeling. . . . I was of course very happy to be there but I . . . hoped to make things good again."

Ernst B. was right in seeing the dream as a special psychological key, as it contains virtually every conflict and contradiction he experienced in Auschwitz. At the heart of the dream, I believe, is a doubling, rather than a splitting, of the self (see chapter 14): that is, Dr. B had two virtually autonomous selves: the one, the older, relatively humane self of healer and family man; the other, the Auschwitz self (with its numbed adaptation and capacity to witness or participate in mass murder* and continuous brutality). Characteristically, the older, more humane self was reinforced by visits to his wife and family, but his guilt toward his wife suggests that he was less able than many former Nazi doctors to carry through successfully this doubling process. Indeed, the image of affectionate and compassionate flight with the young Jewish inmate is a way of reconnecting erotic feelings with human acts, all within the context of Auschwitz itself—and, in that sense, is a rejection of the doubling process and an assertion of at least prospective wholeness. But the dream also contains his profound

* Dr. B was able to avoid direct participation in Auschwitz murder and brutality (see chapter 6, pages 90–91).

doubts about himself, while in Auschwitz and before, concerning authenticity (his discussions of kitsch and of the "primitive"—the latter with a strong element of German and Nazi worship of what is ostensibly primitive and natural) and his concern about corruption and corruptibility (his own "dirt on his walking stick") in Auschwitz particularly. I believe one reason he values this picture so much is its association for him—via the dream and his perception of the Jewish girl—with a struggle toward authenticity and humanity. And that struggle is the dream's prospective thrust: his message is to "go over to the other side"—to the side of those who would kill the killers, to the side of love and life enhancement. And that prospective message has to do once more with extreme historical currents engulfing Germans, Jews, Poles, and in important ways all others.

I cannot say that Ernst B. has, in his postwar existence, fully embraced this prospective message—but he has gone much further than most former Nazi doctors in that direction.

Ernst B. told me of a third dream—really a merest fragment of a dream, not even a clear image. But it is nonetheless important to us.

When held for trial after the war, he learned that the authorities had in their possession what he called "a room full of files dealing with the routine work of the [Hygienic] Institute"—his own working place in Auschwitz. At the judge's request, he agreed to study the materials and from them make a scientific projection of the relationship between caloric intake permitted the prisoners, the work they did, and the length of average survival of those not subjected to the gas chambers. The impact of the experience was profound—so much so that he stuttered somewhat in conveying it and mentioning his dreams:

> That room with all those files and the computations that occupied me and all that, . . . I still dream of it sometimes, somehow. . . . Whenever I have a dream that is related somehow to Auschwitz, those papers will appear too.

He worked methodically, over months, with the files, which were remarkably detailed, and eventually demonstrated that the Auschwitz near-starvation diet created a general life expectancy of three months. He knew that these findings were not in themselves of the greatest importance, but rather that something else was:

> What is important is that for months I was alone in a room [a cell] with these files. . . . And through dealing with these papers I established a special contact with Auschwitz. . . . It was an absolute reflection [of what went on in Auschwitz]. All of a sudden I was in this room confronting the problem and the

> memory in a different way and not under pressure to suppress things in the face of these confrontations—so one could deal with these thoughts without constraint. And that was very good. . . . You are dealing with the experience all the time with these files, so you couldn't waste energy in trying to forget.

He contrasted his approach to Auschwitz with my own:

> It is a completely different route to the camp itself. You are starting out now by identifying these things (or approaching this subject) on a theoretical basis—and you have no practical experience. And I started out on the practical side and later came to the theoretical point of view.[13]

We may say that he, like most other former Nazis, has never been able to confront fully the directly human consequences of the Nazi project. But in undertaking this study, he could abstract those consequences—the deaths and the suffering—in ways that nonetheless brought them closer to his awareness. Of great importance was that he conducted the study as a physician and prepared from it what was essentially a medical-scientific paper. He could at least touch some of the Auschwitz cruelty and in the process reclaim more of his pre-Auschwitz self.

Significantly, he bracketed this overall experience with his earlier adaptation to Auschwitz—the transition into Auschwitz, during which he consciously sought to integrate himself with his colleagues and the overall camp structure. This was, so to speak, his transition out of Auschwitz, during which he was now reintegrating himself—under the reversed circumstances of being himself a prisoner—with the non-Auschwitz, the anti-Auschwitz world. The dream fragment of the papers and files represents the burden of having been part of Auschwitz—the prospective message here that of confronting the experience, evaluating it, putting it in terms of human beings, applying to it humane medical standards.

V

A few conclusions—or rather, visions or dreams of conclusions. Let me state three principles:

First, the dream is prospective; it prefigures psychological and frequently behavioral functions. More than that, it is propulsive—it helps propel one toward certain kinds of experience.

Second, the dream has an immediate or proximate psychological level, where it records and contributes to the self's struggles toward vitality—toward connection, integrity, and movement.

Third, the dream operates also at an ultimate level: it suggests conflicts and directions in the self's larger historical relationships, and in efforts to maintain or recast forms of symbolic immortality.

Thus, the dreams of Japanese youths propel them toward new ways of looking at the world, combining confusing elements in the direction of integration and vitality and ordering their larger relationships to a partly desired past and a projected historical future. The dreams of Vietnam veterans help propel them toward painful insights and hard-won individual change, toward a new vitality based on experiencing and moving beyond guilt, and an equally new worldview with shifting relations to American historical currents. And the dreams of the Nazi doctor prodded him toward earlier standards of compassion and integrity amid murder and corruption (the dreams also, it must be added, had the more dubious function of helping him to adapt to those Auschwitz conditions), and ultimately toward confronting what Auschwitz actually had been.

If a dream can do all this—encompassing a trinity of propulsive psychic power, renewed vitality, and questions about ultimate concerns—then it must have even greater power and significance than we had imagined. Indeed, my claim here is that the dream has a central, life-enhancing, evolutionary function.

Precisely such a function is suggested not only by the somewhat unusual array of dreams I have been discussing, but also by laboratory studies, by the recent work on sleep and dreaming. The so-called REM state—named for its most dramatic feature, the rapid eyeball movement—is the time during which most dreaming occurs and is sufficiently distinct from both wakefulness and other sleep as to have been called a "third state" of the mind. In addition to rapid eyeball movements, the REM state includes increased muscle movements (sometimes with sucking activity), disappearance of postural tone, various forms of irregularity of the cardiac and respiratory systems, increased brain activity as recorded by the electroencephalogram, and, in men, penile erections.

Can a newborn infant, in whom the REM state is certainly identifiable (or for that matter the guinea pig in utero), be said to dream? Here one is reminded of Samuel Beckett's question, "Who knows what the ostrich sees in the sand?" The most reasonable interpretation of REM data, I believe, is that the dreaming function follows pretty much the same sequence I have described in connection with other imagery: at first, an "inchoate image" or mere neurophysiological directions of the organism; then, the formation of pictorial and other sensory images; and, finally, more elaborate symbolization. This interpretation stresses the importance of that state for general nervous-system function—for the daily or nightly processing and reordering of information and emotional experience—and for the regular restoration of the nervous system. The human newborn, then, does not dream in the sense of experiencing the images and symbols we associate with dreams—but enters the world with actively functioning neurophysiology specific to the later psychic elaboration of the dream. As Howard Roffwarg and his associates have put it, "Whether or not 'dreaming' understood as subjective sensation exists in the newborn, 'dreaming' understood as physiological process certainly does."[14]

This same body of research suggests that the inborn REM state could well be a central step to the overall capacity for image formation—that process taking place, as the same research states in their more technical language, as a "neurophysiological setting for hallucinatory repetition of accumulated experience." The penile erection, whatever its relationship to specific imagery, would seem to reassert the centrality of sexual elements in dreams. And when sexual imagery is prominent, dreams reveal their special biological power in their capacity to produce orgasm quite readily by means of that sexual imagery alone—in contrast, say, to pornographic films, which are very unlikely to result in anything more than sexual arousal.

Here one can raise an interesting evolutionary question: Why should a species be provided with such an everyday—or every night—means of discharging its reproductive fluids in a nonreproductive setting? How can such an arrangement be squared with encouraging the productive act as means of preserving the species? The answer to that question, I believe, begins to get at fundamental functions of the dream, and of the human symbolizing process in general.

We must first assume that sex in humans, as Freud's discoveries make clear, had hallucinatory evolutionary functions far beyond that of direct reproduction. In our sex lives, we epitomize much of our immediate struggle for vitality—and much of our ultimate quest for transcendence. Indeed, I believe that sexual experience is our everyday path to transcendence (see chapter 1)—to the state of mind usually equated with "ecstasy" or with what Freud called the "oceanic feeling." More generally, that experience of transcendence reaffirms the self's sense of larger connectedness through other modes of symbolic immortality. My argument here is that the sexual element in dreams is central to their relationship to immediate vitality and to ultimate concerns. Sexual elements can also relate directly to the prospective or formative aspects of dreams—as we saw so well in the case of the Nazi doctor's dream of running off with the young Jewish woman prisoner. As with other elements of the dream, we have so emphasized the pastness of sexual imagery that we have greatly neglected its formative or prospective significance.

To further answer that evolutionary question, we need to return to the dream's special relationship to symbolization. Freud was surely right (and Erikson strongly concurred) in stressing that "the dream is fundamentally nothing more than a special *form* of our thinking, which is made possible by the conditions of the sleeping state"—and that "the dream work . . . is the only explanation of its singularity."[15] But exactly what that dream work—really dream "process"—consists of is much less certain. Here again, even the pastness in a dream—its old memory elements—can contribute to its experiential and prospective push toward new combinations and even resolutions. That very pastness, in fact, can, as a reservoir of formative possibilities, provide much of the energy for precisely those new combinations and resolutions. Nor can we be satisfied with the two central functions of Freud's dream work—condensation and displacement—but must see these functions as aspects of the dream's overall symbolizing power.

I am suggesting that the dream's indisputable biological rootedness is inseparable from its advanced symbolizing function. We can thus begin to view the dream less as a "cover-up" and more as an "opening-out" of the psychic domain that is both close to organicity and unique in imaginative reach. For dreams permit ephemeral experimentation with the freest play of images and the most radically absurd and innovative symbolizations. Dream work or dream process would seem to be nothing less than the anxious edge of the mind's explorations. And the dream's ingenious symbolizations are highly subversive to the psychological status quo. This is so because of the sensitivity of the dream process to the contradictions and vulnerabilities of existing psychic forms, which is what we mean when we say that dreams reveal inner conflicts. It is the reason dreams are so disturbing.

Just why the symbolizing function of dreams is freer and more innovative than that of adult waking life is difficult to say. There are probably neuropsychological reasons we do not fully understand, and which are not adequately explained by the traditional concept of repression. The relaxation of censorship in dreams may be related to in-built psychobiological elements of the symbolizing process bound up with REM sleep.

So that, to return once more to our evolutionary question, we may say that symbolization provided by dreams is no less biological—no less central to species preservation—than is the reproductive function itself. Or to put the matter another way, to carry out our reproductive function we need to have our symbolizing capacity in working order: we need the capacity to *feel* alive, and the sense of larger human connectedness. Sex in dreams is in the service of those capacities and is therefore, in an evolutionary sense, far from wasted.

It should be clear by now that symbolization here is by no means the same as the more "primitive" function to which Freud relegated it—namely, the form of one-to-one symbolism Freud thought "characteristic of unconscious ideation": the idea that a particular dream symbol stands for a particular person or thing—emperor and empress for parents, an elongated object for the male organ, a room for a woman, etc. Rather, we are talking about the *process* of symbolization—of construction, combination, and recreation of images and forms—which is the essence of dreaming no less than of other expressions of human mentation. Even when we encounter relatively consistent meanings for certain symbols, there is an ever-present possibility that those meanings will be joined or replaced by others in the continuous play of the formative process.

We can thus view dreams as providing a perpetual dialectic between the most "primitive" psychic fragments and the most "enlightened" frontier of the formative imagination. Within this dialogue the dream flashes its powerful and yet fluid symbolizations before us, ours for the using according to the mind's readiness and capacity.

The dream, then, is central to our evolutionary heritage. In it we find, most profoundly, both clue to and expression of the human capacity for good and evil—for holding visions, for prospective imagination. More than ever, we must dream well if we are to confront forces threatening to annihilate us, and if we are to further the wonderful, dangerous, and always visionary human adventure.

14

Doubling: The Faustian Bargain

Not only will you break through the paralysing difficulties of the time—you will break through time itself . . . and dare to be barbaric, twice barbaric indeed.

—THOMAS MANN

Any of us could be the man who encounters his double.

—FRIEDRICH DURRENMAT

I included this chapter from The Nazi Doctors *because I consider the phenomenon to be widespread and extremely dangerous. As I write this, I am beginning work, together with Eric Markusen, on a study, tentatively entitled* Reflections on Holocaust: Nazi and Nuclear, *that examines the lessons of the Holocaust for our nuclear-weapons dilemmas. As I have already suggested in this volume, patterns of doubling figure greatly in those reflections.*

In reading the chapter, one should keep in mind the other mechanisms suggested in chapter 6: the great importance for doubling of ideology, and also of patterns of numbing and derealization, of omnipotence-sadism and impotence, of machinations of professional identity, and of perverse quests for meaning. While I describe these in relation to Nazi doctors, they probably all apply—especially the centrality of ideology—for any kind of doubling associated with mass murder and genocide.

What I say here and in The Nazi Doctors *about doubling is my beginning effort to look at the self's vulnerability to evil, and ultimately at its capacities for overcoming that vulnerability in favor of ethical transformations.*

THE KEY to understanding how Nazi doctors came to do the work of Auschwitz is the psychological principle I call "doubling": the division of the self into two functioning wholes, so that a part-self acts as an entire self. An Auschwitz doctor could, through doubling, not only kill and contribute to killing but organize silently, on behalf of that evil project, an entire self-structure (or self-process) encompassing virtually all aspects of his behavior.

Doubling, then, was the psychological vehicle for the Nazi doctor's Faustian bargain with the diabolical environment in exchange for his contribution to the killing; he was offered various psychological and material benefits on behalf of privileged adaptation. Beyond Auschwitz was the larger Faustian temptation offered to German doctors in general: that of becoming the theorists and implementers of a cosmic scheme of racial cure by means of victimization and mass murder.

One is always ethically responsible for Faustian bargains—a responsibility in no way abrogated by the fact that much doubling takes place outside of awareness. In exploring doubling, I engage in psychological probing on behalf of illuminating evil. For the individual Nazi doctor in Auschwitz, doubling was likely to mean a choice for evil.

Generally speaking, doubling involves five characteristics. There is, first, a dialectic between two selves in terms of autonomy and connection. The individual Nazi doctor needed his Auschwitz self to function psychologically in an environment so antithetical to his previous ethical standards. At the same time, he needed his prior self in order to continue to see himself as humane physician, husband, father. The Auschwitz self had to be both autonomous and connected to the prior self that gave rise to it. Second, doubling follows a holistic principle. The Auschwitz self "succeeded" because it was inclusive and could connect with the entire Auschwitz environment: it rendered coherent, and gave form to, various themes and mechanisms, which I shall discuss shortly. Third, doubling has a life-death dimension: the Auschwitz self was perceived by the perpetrator as a form of psychological survival in a death-dominated environment; in other words, we have the paradox of a "killing self" being created on behalf of what one perceives as one's own healing or survival. Fourth, a major function of doubling, as in Auschwitz, is likely to be the avoidance of guilt: the second self tends to be the one performing the "dirty work." And, finally, doubling involves both an unconscious dimension—taking place, as stated, largely outside of awareness—and a significant change in moral consciousness. These five characteristics frame and pervade all else that goes on psychologically in doubling.

For instance, the holistic principle differentiates doubling from the traditional psychoanalytic concept of "splitting." This latter term has had several meanings but tends to suggest a sequestering off of a portion of the self so that the "split off" element ceases to respond to the environment (as in what I have been calling "psychic numbing") or else is in some way at odds with the remainder of the self. Splitting in this sense resembles what Pierre Janet, Freud's nineteenth-century contemporary, originally called "dissociation," and Freud himself tended to equate the two terms. But in regard to sustained forms of adaptation, there has been confusion about how to explain the autonomy of that separated "piece" of the self—confusion over (as one thoughtful commentator has put it) "What splits in splitting?"[1]*

"Splitting" or "dissociation" can thus denote something about Nazi doctors' suppression of feeling, or psychic numbing, in relation to their participation in murder.† But to chart their involvement in a continuous routine of killing, over a year or two or more, one needs an explanatory principle that draws upon the entire, functioning self. (The same principle applies in sustained psychiatric disturbance, and my stress on doubling is consistent with the increasing contemporary focus upon the holistic function of the self.)[8]

Doubling is part of the universal potential for what William James called the "divided self": that is, for opposing tendencies in the self. James quoted the nineteenth-century French writer Alphonse Daudet's despairing cry "Homo duplex, homo duplex!" in noting his "horrible duality"—as, in the face of his brother Henri's death, Daudet's "first self wept" while his "second self" sat back and somewhat mockingly staged the scene for an imagined theatrical performance.[9] To James and Daudet, the potential for doubling is part of being human, and the process is likely to take place in extremity, in relation to death.

But that "opposing self" can become dangerously unrestrained, as it did in the Nazi doctors. And when it becomes so, as Otto Rank discovered

* This writer seemed to react against the idea of a separated-off piece of the self when he ended the article by asking, "Why should we invent a special intrapsychic act of splitting to account for those phenomena as if some internal chopper were at work to produce them?"[2] Janet meant by "dissociation" the hysteric's tendency to "sacrifice" or "abandon" certain psychological functions, so that these become "dissociated" from the rest of the mind and give rise to "automatisms," or segmented-off symptom complexes.[3] Freud spoke, in his early work with Josef Breuer, of "splitting of consciousness," "splitting of the mind," and "splitting of personality" as important mechanisms in hysteria.[4] Edward Glover referred to the psychic components of splitting or dissociation as "ego nuclei."[5] And, beginning with the work of Melanie Klein, splitting has been associated with polarization of "all good" and "all bad" imagery within the self, a process that can be consistent with normal development but, where exaggerated, can become associated with severe personality disorders now spoken of as "borderline states."[6]

† Henry V. Dicks invokes this concept in his study of Nazi killers.[7]

in his extensive studies of the "double" in literature and folklore, that opposing self can become the usurper from within and replace the original self until it "speaks" for the entire person.[10] Rank's work also suggests that the potential for an opposing self, in effect the potential for evil, is necessary to the human psyche: the loss of one's shadow or soul or "double" means death.

In general psychological terms, the adaptive potential for doubling is integral to the human psyche and can, at times, be life saving: for a soldier in combat, for instance; or for a victim of brutality such as an Auschwitz inmate, who must also undergo a form of doubling in order to survive. Clearly, the "opposing self" can be life enhancing. But under certain conditions it can embrace evil with an extreme lack of restraint.

The Nazi doctor's situation resembles that of one of Rank's examples (taken from a 1913 German film, *The Student of Prague*): a student fencing champion accepts an evil magician's offer of great wealth and the chance for marriage with his beloved in return for anything the old magician wishes to take from the room; what he takes is the student's mirror image, a frequent representation of the double. That double eventually becomes a killer by making use of the student's fencing skills in a duel with his beloved's suitor, despite the fact that the student (his original self) has promised the woman's father that he will not engage in such a duel. This variation on the Faust legend parallels the Nazi doctor's "bargain" with Auschwitz and the regime: to do the killing, he offered an opposing self (the evolving Auschwitz self)—a self that, in violating his own prior moral standards, met with no effective resistance and in fact made use of his original skills (in this case, medical-scientific).[11]*

Rank stressed the death symbolism of the double as "symptomatic of the disintegration of the modern personality type." That disintegration leads to a need for "self-perpetuation in one's own image"[13]—what I would call a literalized form of immortality—as compared with "the perpetuation of the self in work reflecting one's personality" or a creative-symbolic form of immortality. Rank saw the Narcissus legend as depicting both the danger of the literalized mode and the necessity of the shift to the creative mode (as embodied by the "artist-hero").† But the Nazi movement en-

* Rank's viewing of *The Student of Prague*, during a revival in the mid-1920s, was the original stimulus for a lifelong preoccupation with the theme of the double. Rank noted that the screenplay's author, Hanns Heinz Ewers, had drawn heavily on E. T. A. Hoffmann's "Story of the Lost Reflection."[12]

† In his earlier work, Rank followed Freud in connecting the legend with the concept of "narcissism," of libido directed toward one's own self. But Rank gave the impression that he did so uneasily, always stressing the issue of death and immortality as lurking beneath the narcissism. In his later adaptation, he boldly embraced the death theme as the earlier and more fundamental one in the Narcissus legend and spoke somewhat disdainfully of "some

couraged its would-be artist-hero, the physician, to remain, like Narcissus, in thralldom to his own image. Here Mengele comes immediately to mind, his extreme narcissism in the service of his quest for omnipotence, and his exemplification to the point of caricature of the general situation of Nazi doctors in Auschwitz.[15]

The way in which doubling allowed Nazi doctors to avoid guilt was not by the elimination of conscience but by what can be called the *transfer of conscience.* The requirements of conscience were transferred to the Auschwitz self, which placed it within its own criteria for good (duty, loyalty to group, "improving" Auschwitz conditions, etc.), thereby freeing the original self from responsibility for actions there. Rank spoke similarly of guilt "which forces the hero no longer to accept the responsibility for certain actions of his ego, but place it upon another ego, a double, who is either personified by the devil himself or is created by making a diabolical pact":[16] that is, the Faustian bargain of Nazi doctors mentioned earlier. Rank spoke of a "powerful consciousness of guilt" as initiating the transfer;[17] but for most Nazi doctors, the doubling maneuver seemed to fend off that sense of guilt prior to its developing, or to its reaching conscious dimensions.

There is an inevitable connection between death and guilt. Rank equates the opposing self with a "form of evil which represents the perishable and mortal part of the personality."[18] The double is evil in that it represents one's own death. The Auschwitz self of the Nazi doctor similarly assumed the death issue for him but at the same time used its evil project as a way of staving off awareness of his own "perishable and mortal part." It does the "dirty work" for the entire self by rendering that work "proper" and in that way protects the entire self from awareness of its own guilt and its own death.

In doubling, one part of the self "disavows" another part. What is repudiated is not reality itself—the individual Nazi doctor was aware of what he was doing via the Auschwitz self—but the meaning of that reality. The Nazi doctor knew that he selected, but did not interpret selections as murder. One level of disavowal, then, was the Auschwitz self's altering of the meaning of murder; and on another, the repudiation by the original self of *anything* done by the Auschwitz self. From the moment of its formation, the Auschwitz self so violated the Nazi doctor's previous self-concept as to require more or less permanent disavowal. Indeed, disavowal was the life blood of the Auschwitz self.*

modern psychologists [who] claimed to have found a symbolization of their self-love principle" in it.[14] By then he had broken with Freud and established his own intellectual position.

* Michael Franz Basch speaks of an interference with the "union of affect with percept without, however, blocking the percept from consciousness."[19] In that sense, disavowal re-

Doubling, Splitting, and Evil

Doubling is an active psychological process, a means of *adaptation to extremity*. That is why I use the verb form, as opposed to the more usual noun form, "the double." The adaptation requires a dissolving of "psychic glue"[20] as an alternative to a radical breakdown of the self. In Auschwitz, the pattern was established under the duress of the individual doctor's transition period. At that time the Nazi doctor experienced his own death anxiety as well as such death equivalents as fear of disintegration, separation, and stasis. He needed a functional Auschwitz self to still his anxiety. And that Auschwitz self had to assume hegemony on an everyday basis, reducing expressions of the prior self to odd moments and to contacts with family and friends outside the camp. Nor did most Nazi doctors resist that usurpation as long as they remained in the camp. Rather they welcomed it as the only means of psychological function. If an environment is sufficiently extreme, and one chooses to remain in it, one may be able to do so *only* by means of doubling.

Yet doubling does not include the radical dissociation and sustained separateness characteristic of multiple or "dual personality." In the latter condition, the two selves are more profoundly distinct and autonomous, and tend either not to know about each other or else to see each other as alien. The pattern for dual or multiple personality, moreover, is thought to begin early in childhood, and to solidify and maintain itself more or less indefinitely. Yet in the development of multiple personality, there are likely to be such influences as intense psychic or physical trauma, an atmosphere of extreme ambivalence, and severe conflict and confusion over identifications[21]—all of which can also be instrumental in doubling. Also relevant to both conditions is Janet's principle that "once baptized"—that is, named or confirmed by someone in authority—a particular self is likely to become more clear and definite.[22] Though never as stable as a self in multiple personality, the Auschwitz self nonetheless underwent a similar baptism when the Nazi doctor conducted his first selections.

A recent writer has employed the metaphor of a tree to delineate the depth of "splitting" in schizophrenia and multiple personality—a metaphor that could be expanded to include doubling. In schizophrenia, the rent in the self is "like the crumbling and breaking of a tree that has deteriorated

---

sembles psychic numbing, as it alters the *valencing* or emotional charge of the symbolizing process.

generally, at least in some important course of the trunk, down toward or to the roots." In multiple personality, that rent is specific and limited, "as in an essentially sound tree that does not split very far down."[23] Doubling takes place still higher on a tree whose roots, trunk, and larger branches have previously experienced no impairment; of the two branches artificially separated, one grows fetid bark and leaves in a way that enables the other to maintain ordinary growth, and the two intertwine sufficiently to merge again should external conditions favor that merging.

Was the doubling of Nazi doctors an antisocial "character disorder"? Not in the classical sense, in that the process tended to be more a form of adaptation than a lifelong pattern. But doubling can include elements considered characteristic of "sociopathic" character impairment: these include a disorder of feeling (swings between numbing and rage), pathological avoidance of a sense of guilt, and resort to violence to overcome "masked depression" (related to repressed guilt and numbing) and maintain a sense of vitality.[24] Similarly, in both situations, destructive or even murderous behavior may cover over feared disintegration of the self.

The disorder in the type of doubling I have described is more focused and temporary and occurs as part of a larger institutional structure which encourages or even demands it. In that sense, Nazi doctors' behavior resembles that of certain terrorists—and members of the Mafia, of "death squads" organized by dictators, or even of delinquent gangs. In all these situations, profound ideological, family, ethnic, and sometimes age-specific ties help shape criminal behavior. Doubling may well be an important psychological mechanism for individuals living within any criminal subculture: the Mafia or "death squad" chief who coldly orders (or himself carries out) the murder of a rival while remaining a loving husband, father, and churchgoer. The doubling is adaptive to the extreme conditions created by the subculture, but additional influences, some of which can begin early in life, always contribute to the process.* That, too, was the case with the Nazi doctors.

In sum, doubling is the psychological means by which one invokes the evil potential of the self. That evil is neither inherent in the self nor foreign to it. To live out the doubling and call forth the evil is a moral choice for which one is responsible, whatever the level of consciousness involved.† By means of doubling, Nazi doctors made a Faustian choice for evil: in the process of doubling, in fact, lies an overall key to human evil.

* Robert W. Rieber uses the term "pseudopsychopathy" for what he describes as "selective joint criminal behavior" within the kinds of subculture mentioned here.[25]

† James S. Grotstein speaks of the development of "a separate being living within one that has been preconsciously split off and has an independent existence with independent

Varieties of Doubling

While individual Nazi doctors in Auschwitz doubled in different ways, all of them doubled. Ernst B., for instance (see chapter 6), limited his doubling; in avoiding selections, he was resisting a full-blown Auschwitz self. Yet his conscious desire to adapt to Auschwitz was an accession to at least a certain amount of doubling: it was he, after all, who said that "one could react like a normal human being in Auschwitz only for the first few hours"; after that, "you were caught and had to go along," which meant that you had to double. His own doubling was evident in his sympathy for Mengele and, at least to some extent, for the most extreme expressions of the Nazi ethos (the image of the Nazis as a "world blessing" and of Jews as the world's "fundamental evil"). And despite the limit to his doubling, he retains aspects of his Auschwitz self to this day in his way of judging Auschwitz behavior.

In contrast, Josef Mengele's embrace of the Auschwitz self gave the impression of a quick adaptive affinity, causing one to wonder whether he required any doubling at all. But doubling was indeed required in a man who befriended children to an unusual degree and then drove some of them personally to the gas chamber; or by a man so "collegial" in his relationship to prisoner doctors and so ruthlessly flamboyant in his conduct of selections. Whatever his affinity for Auschwitz, a man who could be pictured under ordinary conditions as "a slightly sadistic German professor" had to form a new self to become an energetic killer. The point about Mengele's doubling was that his prior self could be readily absorbed into the Auschwitz self; and his continuing allegiance to the Nazi ideology and project probably enabled his Auschwitz self, more than in the case of other Nazi doctors, to remain active over the years after the Second World War.

The doubling of Eduard Wirths, the chief Auschwitz doctor, was neither limited (like Dr. B.'s) nor harmonious (like Mengele's): it was both strong and conflicted. We see him as a "divided self" because both selves retained their power: the prior self enabling him to be humane and thoughtful with many individual prisoners; his Auschwitz self enabling him to function as an efficient Nazi bureaucrat in setting up and maintaining the structure of Auschwitz medicalized killing. Yet his doubling was the

---

motivation, separate agenda, etc.," and from which can emanate "evil, sadism, and destructiveness" or even "demoniacal possession." He calls this aspect of the self a "mind parasite" (after Colin Wilson) and attributes its development to those elements of the self that have been artificially suppressed and disavowed early in life.[26]

most successful of all from the standpoint of maintaining the Auschwitz institution and the Nazi project. Even his suicide was a mark of that success: while the Nazi defeat enabled him to equate his Auschwitz self more clearly with evil, he nonetheless retained responsibility to that Auschwitz self sufficiently to remain inwardly divided and unable to imagine any possibility of resolution and renewal—either legally, morally, or psychologically.

Within the Auschwitz structure, significant doubling included future goals and even a sense of hope. Styles of doubling varied because each Nazi doctor created his Auschwitz self out of his prior self, with its particular history, and with his own psychological mechanisms. But in all Nazi doctors, prior self and Auschwitz self were connected by the overall Nazi ethos and the general authority of the regime. Doubling was a shared theme among them.

Doubling and Institutions

Indeed, Auschwitz as an *institution*—as an atrocity-producing situation—ran on doubling. An atrocity-producing situation is one so structured externally (in this case, institutionally) that the average person entering it (in this case, as part of the German authority) will commit or become associated with atrocities. Always important to an atrocity-producing situation is its capacity to motivate individuals psychologically toward engaging in atrocity.[27]

In an institution as powerful as Auschwitz, the external environment could set the tone for much of an individual doctor's "internal environment." The demand for doubling was part of the environmental message immediately perceived by Nazi doctors, the implicit command to bring forth a self that could adapt to killing without one's feeling oneself a murderer. Doubling became not just an individual enterprise but a shared psychological process, the group norm, part of the Auschwitz "weather." And that group process was intensified by the general awareness that, whatever went on in other camps, Auschwitz was the great technical center of the Final Solution. One had to double in order that one's life and work there not be interfered with either by the corpses one helped to produce or by those "living dead" (the *Muselmänner*) all around one.

Inevitably, the Auschwitz pressure toward doubling extended to prisoner doctors, the most flagrant examples of whom were those few who came to work closely with the Nazis. Even those prisoner doctors who held strongly to their healing ethos, and underwent minimal doubling, inadvertently contributed to Nazi doctors' doubling simply by working with them, as they had to, and thereby in some degree confirmed a Nazi doctor's Auschwitz self.

Doubling undoubtedly occurred extensively in nonmedical Auschwitz personnel as well. Rudolf Höss, commandant of Auschwitz, told how noncommissioned officers regularly involved in selections "pour[ed] out their hearts" to him about the difficulty of their work (their prior self speaking)—but went on doing that work (their Auschwitz self directing behavior). Höss described the Auschwitz choices: "either to become cruel, to become heartless and no longer to respect human life [that is, to develop a highly functional Auschwitz self] or to be weak and to get to the point of a nervous breakdown [that is, to hold onto one's prior self, which in Auschwitz was nonfunctional]."[28] But in the Nazi doctor, the doubling was particularly stark in that a prior healing self gave rise to a killing self that should have been, but functionally was not, in direct opposition to it. And as in any atrocity-producing situation, Nazi doctors found themselves in a psychological climate where they were virtually certain to choose evil: they were propelled, that is, toward murder.

Doubling—Nazi and Medical

Beyond Auschwitz, there was much in the Nazi movement that promoted doubling. The overall Nazi project, replete with cruelty, required constant doubling in the service of carrying out that cruelty. The doubling could take the form of a gradual process of "slippery slope" compromises: the slow emergence of a functional "Nazi self" via a series of destructive actions, at first agreed to grudgingly, followed by a sequence of assigned tasks each more incriminating, if not more murderous, than the previous ones.

Doubling could also be more dramatic, infused with transcendence, the sense (described by a French fascist who joined the SS) of being someone entering a religious order "who must now divest himself of his past," and of being "reborn into a new European race."[29] That new Nazi self could take on a sense of mystical fusion with the German *Volk*, with "destiny," and with immortalizing powers. Always there was the combination noted earlier of idealism and terror, imagery of destruction and renewal, so that "gods . . . appear as both destroyers and culture-heroes, just as the Führer could appear as front comrade and master builder."[30] Heinrich Himmler, especially in his speeches to his SS leaders within their "oath-bound community,"[31] called for the kind of doubling necessary to engage in what he considered to be heroic cruelty, especially in the killing of Jews.

The degree of doubling was not necessarily equivalent to Nazi Party membership; thus, the German playwright Rolf Hochhuth could claim that "the great divide was between Nazis [meaning those with well-developed Nazi selves] and decent people, not between Party members and other Germans."[32] But probably never has a political movement demanded doubling with the intensity and scale of the Nazis.

Doctors as a group may be more susceptible to doubling than others. For example, a former Nazi doctor claimed that the anatomist's insensitivity toward skeletons and corpses accounted for his friend August Hirt's grotesque "anthropological" collection of Jewish skulls (see chapter 6). While hardly a satisfactory explanation, this doctor was referring to a genuine pattern not just of numbing but of medical doubling. That doubling usually begins with the student's encounter with the corpse he or she must dissect, often enough on the first day of medical school. One feels it necessary to develop a "medical self," which enables one not only to be relatively inured to death but to function reasonably efficiently in relation to the many-sided demands of the work. The ideal doctor, to be sure, remains warm and humane by keeping that doubling to a minimum. But few doctors meet that ideal standard. Since studies have suggested that a psychological motivation for entering the medical profession can be the overcoming of an unusually great fear of death, it is possible that this fear in doctors propels them in the direction of doubling when encountering deadly environments. Doctors drawn to the Nazi movement in general, and to SS or concentration-camp medicine in particular, were likely to be those with the greatest previous medical doubling. But even doctors without outstanding Nazi sympathies could well have had a certain experience with doubling and a proclivity for its further manifestations.

Certainly the tendency toward doubling was particularly strong among *Nazi* doctors. Given the heroic vision held out to them—as cultivators of the genes and as physicians to the *Volk*, and as militarized healers combining the life-death power of shaman and general—any cruelty they might perpetrate was all too readily drowned in hubris. And their medical hubris was furthered by their role in the sterilization and "euthanasia" projects within a vision of curing the ills of the Nordic race and the German people.

Doctors who ended up undergoing the extreme doubling necessitated by the "euthanasia" killing centers and the death camps were probably unusually susceptible to doubling. There was, of course, an element of chance in where one was sent, but doctors assigned either to the killing centers or to the death camps tended to be strongly committed to Nazi ideology. They may well have also had greater schizoid tendencies, or been particularly prone to numbing and omnipotence-sadism, all of which also enhance doubling. Since, even under extreme conditions, people have a way of finding and staying in situations they connect with psychologically, we can suspect a certain degree of self-selection there too. In these ways, previous psychological characteristics of a doctor's self had considerable significance—but a significance in respect to tendency or susceptibility, and no more. Considerable doubling occurred in people of the most varied psychological characteristics.

We thus find ourselves returning to the recognition that most of what Nazi doctors did would be within the potential capability—at least under certain conditions—of most doctors and of most people. But once embarked on doubling in Auschwitz, a Nazi doctor did indeed separate himself from other physicians and from other human beings. Doubling was the mechanism by which a doctor, in his actions, moved from the ordinary to the demonic.

Doubling as German?

Is there something especially German in doubling? Germany, after all, is the land of the *Doppelgänger,* the double as formalized in literature and humor. Otto Rank, while tracing the theme back to Greek mythology and drama, stresses its special prominence in German literary and philosophical romanticism, and refers to the "inner split personality, characteristic of the romantic type."[33] That characterization, not only in literature but in political and social thought, is consistent with such images as the "torn condition" (*Zerrissenheit*), or "cleavage," and the "passages and galleries" of the German soul.[34] Nietzsche asserted that duality in a personal way by depicting himself as both "the antichrist" and "the crucified"; and similar principles of "duality-in-unity" can be traced to earlier German writers and poets such as Hölderlin, Heine, and Kleist.[35]

Indeed, Goethe's treatment of the Faust legend is a story of German doubling:

> Two souls, alas, reside within my breast
> And each withdraws from and repels its brother.[36]

And the original Faust, that doctor of magic, bears more than a passing resemblance to his Nazi countrymen in Auschwitz. In Goethe's hands, Faust is inwardly divided into a prior self responsible to worldly commitments, including those of love, and a second self characterized by hubris in its quest for the supernatural power of "the higher ancestral places."* In a still earlier version of the legend, Faust acknowledges the hegemony of his evil self by telling a would-be spiritual rescuer, "I have gone further than you think and have pledged myself to the devil with my own blood, to be his in eternity, body and soul."[38] Here his attitude resembles the Auschwitz self's fidelity to evil. And Thomas Mann's specific application of the Faust legend to the Nazi historical experience captures, through a musician protagonist, the diabolical quest of the Auschwitz self for unlimited "creative power": the promise of absolute breakthrough, of conquering time and therefore death; if the new self will "dare to be barbaric, twice barbaric indeed."[39]†

Within German psychological and cultural experience, the theme of doubling is powerful and persistent. Moreover, German vulnerability to doubling was undoubtedly intensified by the historical dislocations and fragmentations of cultural symbols following the First World War. Who can deny the Germanic "feel" of so much of the doubling process, as best described by a brilliant product of German culture, Otto Rank?

Yet the first great poet to take up the Faust theme was not Goethe but

* The passage concerning the "two souls" continues:

> One with tenacious organs holds in love
> And clinging lust the world within its embraces.
> The other strongly sweeps this dust above
> Into the higher ancestral places.

The historian of German literature Ronald Gray finds patterns of "polarity and synthesis" in various spheres of German culture: Luther's concept of a God who "works by contraries," the Hegelian principle of thesis and antithesis, and the Marxist dialectic emerging from Hegel. In all of these, there is the "fusion of opposites," the rending of the individual as well as the collective self, and the passionate quest for unity.[37] One could almost say that the German apocalyptic tradition—the Wagnerian "twilight of the gods" and the general theme of the death-haunted collective end—may be the "torn condition" extended into the realm of larger human connectedness and disconnectedness.

† Mann also captures the continuity in doubling by speaking of the "implicit Satanism" in German psychology, and by having the devil make clear to the Faust figure that "we lay upon you nothing new . . . [but] only ingeniously strengthen and exaggerate all that you already are."[40]

the English playwright Christopher Marlowe. And there has been a series of celebrated English and American expressions of the general theme of the double, running through Edgar Allan Poe's "William Wilson," Robert Louis Stevenson's *The Strange Case of Dr. Jekyll and Mr. Hyde,* Oscar Wilde's *Picture of Dorian Gray,* and the comic strip *Superman.* Indeed, the theme penetrates the work of writers of all nationalities: for instance, Guy de Maupassant's *Le Horla* and Dostoevski's novel *The Double.*[41]

Clearly, the Nazis took hold of a universal phenomenon, if one given special emphasis by their own culture and history. But they could not have brought about widespread doubling without the existence of certain additional psychological patterns that dominated Auschwitz behavior. These internalized expressions of the environment of the death camp came to characterize the Auschwitz self, and have significance beyond that place and time.

15

Cults: Religious Totalism and Civil Liberties

With the emergence, during the early 1970s, of fundamentalist religious cults, I was at first no more than an interested spectator. My interest was related to a more general concern with "ideological totalism"—all-or-none belief systems—and their individual-psychological expressions. Then others began to invoke my work in connection with the cult phenomenon. I began to hear that chapter 22 of my book Thought Reform and Psychology of Totalism[1] *was being used for various forms of "deprogramming" of cult recruits, and then that the same chapter was being studied by cult leaders, ostensibly for the purpose of dissociating their groups from the patterns I described.*

I began to be consulted by parents of young people who had joined cults, and also by such young people who had left cults but retained various conflicts; and others who were ambivalent about whether to stay in, or return to, specific cults. I also began to receive two very different kinds of pressure: from anti-cult groups (consisting of parents as well as former cult members) to denounce all cults as nothing but "brainwashing"; and from civil libertarians, to denounce the misuse of my work by "deprogrammers" who were violating the rights of young people. I felt the work had to stand on its own but that I had some responsibility to state my views on its applicability to the whole issue. An invitation to speak at a general conference on the subject of "The Law and the New Religious Movements" at the Graduate Theological Union at Berkeley, California, seemed a useful occasion to do so, and this essay was the result. (Here, too, I have retained some of the spoken style.) While I tried to sort out various psychological, historical, and moral-professional strands, I must add now that the whole subject is much more excruciating than the essay may suggest—excruciating for parents who experience their children's cult involvement as the most fundamental of rejections; for the young recruits themselves as they struggle with the powerful conflicts mobilized by cults; and for American society in ways that need to be looked at more closely.

TWO MAIN IMAGES inform one's moral and psychological perspective on cults: totalism, or what I would also call fundamentalism; and civil liberties, the concern that has been continuously raised in connection with cult members.

Totalism and civil liberties are both issues that concern me deeply. Although my work is directed more toward totalism, the issue of civil liberties is central to me. I have fought for causes that are not always popular, and understand how important civil liberties are. There is, however, an immediate problem here: in the name of defending civil liberties, there is often an impulse to glorify the object of one's defense. Certainly it could be said that some of the cults have done nasty things, but civil liberties are as necessary for people who do nasty things as for those who do nice things. We need to make such distinctions; within the American tradition of civil liberties, it is possible to dislike certain cults without making them illegal.

I think anyone talking about the cults does best to identify where he or she lives, intellectually and morally. My own sense of the problem has been much influenced by my first study on Chinese thought reform, which left me with something like an allergy toward totalism. I happen to think totalism is a very dangerous process in our society—all the more in connection with what I would describe as a worldwide epidemic of fundamentalism in its political, religious, or combined forms. Within that worldwide epidemic I would place many cults in this country and many religious and political groups on all sides in the Middle East and throughout the world. There are reasons for this epidemic, and I will address them later.

As one deeply concerned about nuclear threat and problems of totalistic attitudes regarding nuclear weapons, I would stress that fundamentalism now—including some of the cults—presents a particular danger, because fundamentalists can relate their theology to a nuclear-weapons Armageddon—and even welcome it.

During my study of Chinese thought reform in the mid-1950s, I evolved generalizing principles, not simply to condemn the Chinese Communists, but to bring a critical perspective to the process itself. My way of being even-handed was to bring the subject home into more familiar patterns or environments in which one could identify themes of ideological totalism. That is why I developed chapter 22, along with other chapters that examined totalistic practices in such things as McCarthyism in American politics, and in training and educational programs. I have since continued to examine ideological totalism: in work with Vietnam veterans, who demonstrated quick and sometimes moving transformations in rejecting war-related totalism; and more recently in a study of the psychology of Nazi doctors. Some of the issues studied come back to haunt and inform one. Certainly the issue of totalism is alive for my direct work, as it is for the work of many other people. In terms of my psychohistorical approach to this issue, I have tried to evolve shared themes in certain groups in relation to particular historical currents and events.

The shared themes I have laid out in my work on the concept of ideological totalism apply in some cult situations. Of course, one person's cult is another's religion—the word *cult* is itself somewhat pejorative. Many people prefer the term *new religions,* and I have no objection to that usage. I tend to speak of cults in terms of a cluster of groups that, for the sake of definition, have certain characteristics: First, a charismatic leader who, as in the case of Jim Jones and the People's Temple (see chapter 16), increasingly becomes the object of worship. Spiritual ideas of a more general kind are likely to give way to worship of the person of the leader. Second, a series of processes that can be associated with what has been called "coercive persuasion" or "thought reform."* A third characteristic of what I am calling cults has to do with the tendency toward manipulation from above (by the leader of the ruling coterie), with exploitation—economic, sexual, or other—of often genuine seekers who bring idealism from below (as ordinary supplicants or recruits).[2] In considering whether these characteristics apply, each group—each environment—must be judged on its own.

* I do not use the word *brainwashing* because it has no precise meaning and has been associated with much confusion. But that does not mean that we should shy away from recognizing the existence of coercive persuasion or thought reform, of systematic application of the totalistic patterns described later in this essay. It must also be added that thought reform, and totalism in general, are not necessarily illegal, however we may deplore them.

I wish to examine first the characteristics of ideological totalism and their applicability in some of these cult situations; next, some larger historical considerations; and finally, some issues of young adulthood. In addition, I will discuss the importance of intense experience, what I call the "experience of transcendence" (a dimension left out in much discussion about cults), and of nuclear weapons and their possible influence.

Ideological Totalism

The phenomenology I used when writing about ideological totalism in the past still seems useful to me, even though I wrote that book in 1960. The first characteristic process is "milieu control," which is essentially the control of communication within an environment. If the control is extremely intense, it becomes an internalized control—an attempt to manage an individual's inner communication. This can never be fully achieved, but it can go rather far. It is what sometimes has been called a "God's-eye view"—a conviction that reality is the group's exclusive possession. Clearly this kind of process creates conflicts in respect to individual autonomy: if sought or realized in such an environment, autonomy becomes a threat to milieu control. Milieu control within cults tends to be maintained and expressed in several ways: group process, isolation from other people, psychological pressure, geographical distance or unavailability of transportation, and sometimes physical pressure. There is often a sequence of events, such as seminars, lectures, and group encounters, which become increasingly intense and increasingly isolated, making it extremely difficult—both physically and psychologically—for one to leave.

These cults differ from patterns of totalism in other societies. For instance, the centers that were used for reform in China were more or less in keeping with the ethos of the society as it was evolving at the time: and therefore when one was leaving them or moving in and out of them, one would still find reinforcements from without. Cults, in contrast, tend to become islands of totalism within a larger society that is on the whole antagonistic to these islands. This situation can create a dynamic of its own; and insofar as milieu control is to be maintained, the requirements are magnified by that structural situation. Cult leaders must often deepen their control and manage the environment more systematically, and sometimes with greater intensity, in order to maintain that island of totalism within the antagonistic outer world.

The imposition of intense milieu control is closely connected to the process of change. (This partly explains why there can be a sudden lifting of the cult identity when a young person who has been in a cult for some time is abruptly exposed to outside, alternative influences.) One can almost observe the process in some young people who undergo a dramatic change from their prior identity, whatever it was, to an intense embrace of a cult's belief system and group structure. I consider this a form of doubling (see chapter 14): a second self is formed that lives side by side with the prior self, somewhat autonomously from it. Obviously there must be some connecting element to integrate oneself with the other—otherwise, the overall person could not function; but the autonomy of each is impressive. When the milieu control is lifted by removing, by whatever means, the recruit from the totalistic environment, something of the earlier self reasserts itself. This leavetaking may occur voluntarily or through force (or simply, as in at least one court case, by the cult member moving across to the other side of the table, away from the other members). The two selves can exist simultaneously and confusedly for a considerable time, and it may be that the transition periods are the most intense and psychologically painful as well as the most potentially harmful.

A second general characteristic of totalistic environments is what I call "mystical manipulation" or "planned spontaneity." It is a systematic process that is planned and managed from above (by the leadership) but appears to have arisen spontaneously within the environment. The process need not feel like manipulation, which raises important philosophical questions. Some aspects—such as fasting, chanting, and limited sleep—have a certain tradition and have been practiced by religious groups over the centuries. There is a cult pattern now in which a particular "chosen" human being is seen as a savior or a source of salvation. Mystical manipulation can take on a special quality in these cults because the leaders become mediators for God. The God-centered principles can be put forcibly and claimed exclusively, so that the cult and its beliefs become the only true path to salvation. This can give intensity to the mystical manipulation and justify those involved with promulgating it and, in many cases, those who are its recipients from below.

Insofar as there is a specific individual, a leader, who becomes the center of the mystical manipulation (or the person in whose name it is done), there is a twofold process at work. The leader can sometimes be more real than an abstract god and therefore attractive to cult members. On the other hand, that person can also be a source of disillusionment. If one believes, as has been charged, that Sun Myung Moon (founder of the Unification Church, whose members are consequently referred to frequently as "Moonies") has associations with the Korean Central Intelligence Agency and this information is made available to people in the Unification Church, their relationship to the church can be threatened by disillusionment toward a leader. It is never quite that simple a pattern of cause and effect—but I am suggesting that this style of leadership has both advantages and disadvantages in terms of cult loyalty.

While mystical manipulation leads (in cult members) to what I have called the psychology of the pawn, it can also include a legitimation of deception (of outsiders)—the "heavenly deception" of the Unification Church, although there are analogous patterns in other cult environments. If one has not seen the light, and is not in the realm of the cult, one is in the realm of evil and therefore can be justifiably deceived for the higher purpose. For instance, when members of certain cults have collected funds, it has sometimes been considered right for them to deny their affiliation when asked. Young people have been at centers of a particular cult for some time without being told that these were indeed run by it. The totalistic ideology can and often does justify such deception.

The next two characteristics of totalism, the "demand for purity" and the "cult of confession," are familiar. The demand for purity can create a Manichean quality in cults, as in some other religious and political groups. Such a demand calls for radical separation of pure and impure, of good and evil, within an environment and within oneself. Absolute purification is a continuing process. It is often institutionalized; and, as a source of stimulation of guilt and shame, it ties in with the confession process. Ideological movements, at whatever level of intensity, take hold of an individual's guilt and shame mechanisms to achieve intense influence over the changes he or she undergoes. This is done within a confession process that has its own structure. Sessions in which one confesses to one's sins are accompanied by patterns of criticism and self-criticism, generally transpiring within small groups and with an active and dynamic thrust toward personal change.

One could say more about the ambiguity and complexity of this process, and Camus has observed that "authors of confessions write especially to avoid confession, to tell nothing of what they know."[3] Camus may have exaggerated, but he is correct in suggesting that confessions contain varying mixtures of revelation and concealment. A young person confessing to various sins of pre-cultic or pre-institutional existence can both believe in those sins and be covering over other ideas and feelings that he or she is either unaware of or reluctant to discuss. In some cases, these sins include a continuing identification with one's prior existence if such identification has not been successfully dishonored by the confession process. Repetitious confession, then, is often an expression of extreme arrogance in the name of apparent humility. Again Camus: "I practice the profession of penitence, to be able to end up as a judge," and, "the more I accuse myself, the more I have a right to judge you."[4] That is a central theme in any continual confessional process, particularly where it is required in an enclosed group process.

The next three patterns I describe in regard to ideological totalism are the "sacred science," the "loading of the language," and the principle of "doctrine over person." The phrases are almost self-explanatory. I would emphasize especially sacred science, for in our age something must be scientific as well as spiritual to have a substantial effect on people. Sacred science can offer considerable security to young people because it greatly simplifies the world. The Unification Church is a good example, but not the only one, of a contemporary need to combine a sacred set of dogmatic principles with a claim to a science embodying the truth about human behavior and human psychology. In the case of the Unification Church, this claim to a comprehensive human science is furthered by inviting prominent scholars (who are paid unusually high honoraria) to large symposia that stress unification of thought; participants express their views freely but nonetheless contribute to the desired aura of intellectual legitimacy.

The term "loading the language" refers to a literalization of language—and to words or images becoming God. A greatly simplified language may seem cliché-ridden but can have enormous appeal and psychological power in its very simplification. Because every issue in one's life—and these are often complicated young lives—can be reduced to a single set of principles that have an inner coherence, one can claim the experience of truth and feel it. Answers are available. Lionel Trilling has called this the "language of non-thought" because there is a cliché and a simple slogan to which the most complex and otherwise difficult questions can be reduced.

The pattern of doctrine over person occurs when there is a conflict between what one feels oneself experiencing and what the doctrine or dogma says one should experience. The internalized message in totalistic environments is that one must find the truth of the dogma and subject one's experience to that truth. Often the experience of contradiction, or the admission of that experience, can be immediately associated with guilt; or else (in order to hold one to the doctrine) condemned by others in a way that leads quickly to that guilty association. One is made to feel that doubts are reflections of one's own evil. Yet doubts can arise; and when conflicts become intense, people can leave (see pages 217–18). This is the most frequent difficulty of many of the cults: membership may present more of a problem than money.

Finally, the eighth, and perhaps the most general and significant of these characteristics, is what I call the "dispensing of existence." This principle is usually metaphorical. But if one has an absolute or totalistic vision of truth, then those who have not seen the light—have not embraced that truth, are in some way in the shadows—are bound up with evil, tainted, and do not have the right to exist. There is a "being versus nothingness" dichotomy at work here. Impediments to legitimate being must be pushed away or destroyed. One placed in the second category of not having the right to exist can experience psychologically a tremendous fear of inner extinction or collapse. However, when one is accepted, there can be great satisfaction of feeling oneself a part of the élite. Under more malignant conditions, the dispensing of existence, the absence of the right to exist, can be literalized; people can be put to death because of their alleged doctrinal shortcomings, as has happened in all too many places, including the Soviet Union and Nazi Germany. In the People's Temple mass suicide-murder in Guyana, a single cult leader could preside over the literal dispensing of existence—or, more precisely, nonexistence—by means of a suicidal mystique he himself had made a central theme in the group's ideology. (Subsequent reports based on the results of autopsies reveal that there were probably as many murders as suicides.) The totalistic impulse to draw a sharp line between those who have the right to live and those who do not—though occurring in varying degrees—can become a deadly approach to resolving human problems. And all such approaches involving totalism or fundamentalism are doubly dangerous in a nuclear age.

I should say that, despite these patterns, none of these processes is airtight. One of my purposes in writing about them is to counter the frequent tendency in the culture to deny that such things exist; another purpose is to demystify them, to see them as comprehensible in terms of our understanding of human behavior.

The Historical Dimension

I want to stress the enormous significance of what I call "historical" or "psychohistorical dislocation" (see chapter 1, page 18) in contemporary life. Such dislocation derives from absence or partial loss of the symbolic structures that have tended to organize and provide ritual transitions in the life cycle, as well as common cultural belief systems—whether concerning religion, authority, governance, marriage, family, or death. Many of these classical symbolizations, having lost their internal coherence, become burdensome.

In that sense, cults provide substitute symbols that have intensity and meaning for many young people. When one talks about totalism, one can never take it out of history: one has to relate it to, and examine it within, a specific historical context.

I would stress in this historical spirit that many of the cults are both radical and reactionary. They are radical in that they raise rude issues about middle-class family life and general values in American society: issues concerning hypocritical approaches to spirituality, liberalism, pluralism, materialism, and overall moral advocacy. In this sense, the cults show some continuity with movements of the 1960s and early 1970s. The apparent radicalism can make them appealing to young people and accounts for part, although by no means all, of others' resistance to cults. The cults also tend to be reactionary in the sense of returning to premodern structures of authority and sometimes going so far that they can be accused of establishing patterns of internal fascism in their organizational structure. Their assault on autonomy and self-definition can also be reactionary: in it they condemn, violate, and reject a liberating dimension of Western history that has evolved, with great struggle, pain, and conflict, from the time of the Renaissance. Again, I emphasize that one has to consider a particular cult situation to evaluate these tendencies fairly.

Another relevant historical tendency is the pattern I have referred to as the "protean style" (see chapter 1), the continuous psychological experimentation with the self and the capacity to undergo relatively easy shifts in ideas, people, and ways of life—as well as to hold seemingly contradictory images in one's mind about all of these. I have associated the protean style with historical dislocation as well as the mass-media revolution. Yet the constricted style the cults embody is a fleeing from experimentation, often on the part of the same young people. The constricted self seeks a straight and narrow psychological process in life, partly to escape the confusion of our protean world and its multiple, intrusive images. I have suggested that, despite the very real contrasts in the protean and constricted styles, they are related products of the dislocations and confusions in the sense of self during particular historical moments. Groups and individuals can embrace the one and then the other: for instance, the shift from the so-called hippie ethos of the 1960s and 1970s, concerning work and its meaninglessness to the present so-called Yuppie preoccupation with safe jobs and comfortable incomes. Allowing for oversimplifications promulgated by the media, and changing economic conditions, one may say that this sequence itself is part of a shared theme of historically influenced struggles concerning the sense of self. For some people, experimentation with a cult is part of the protean search. They go in, try it, experience something, but stop short of conversion, and leave. But it may be difficult to leave, and partial converts can be in great conflict about leaving. The conflict is over whether, how much, and in what way one wants, or does not want, to extricate oneself, along with how to cope with the pressures that are applied by cult members and leaders to persuade one to stay.

The imagery of extinction I have discussed in various essays in this volume is also very much a historical factor, as is its influence on patterns of fundamentalism throughout the world. The term *fundamentalism* derives from an early twentieth-century American Protestant movement seeking to stem the liberal theological tide and to restate what were considered to be the fundamental doctrines of the Christian faith (see also chapters 1 and 10). In terms of the paradigm of symbolization of life and death, the ultimate threat involves that of human continuity itself: the uncertainty of living on in one's children or works, in spiritual principles or in nature. Cults seize upon this impairment to the symbolization of immortality, and quickly provide immortalizing symbols of their own. Central to the cult environment is the continuous opportunity for the experience of transcendence—the mode of symbolic immortality so much sought in our society in the face of its general suppression in advanced industrial society, and of doubts about the other modes.

One of the most significant functions of a cult is to provide an initiation rite, a group process and community, in the transition to early adult life, the stage of the life cycle of most cult recruits. Such a process fills the need for ritual and symbolic structures not provided by the larger culture. Attempts by the larger culture to make such provision are seen as hypocritical or confused, and often for good reason. In the very transition, the cults provide "high" or transcendent states, and these are described with great intensity by those who have experienced them. These "high" states are particularly important to young people and to the working out of adolescent and young adult struggles. The cults can be a psychologically attractive medium for the movement of young people from individual and family ties to a collective historical dimension, as one forms an adult identity and becomes associated with various idea structures or ideologies.

From my perspective, then, cults are not primarily a psychiatric problem, but a social and historical issue. Of course they raise psychological concerns of great importance, and there is a place for psychologists and psychiatrists in understanding these processes (as I have tried to do in certain limited ways) and in treating people when they need it. I think that psychological professionals can do the most good in the area of education. I myself feel critical of much of the totalistic inclination in many cults, but I do not think that pattern is best addressed legally. It is best addressed educationally. There have been repercussions already from increased knowledge about cults. That is one reason that many cults have had increasing difficulty in obtaining members. Patterns of deception become less easy to maintain and perhaps less present. People can be better aware of what becoming a member of a cult involves, and make more of a personal decision about whether they wish to join one.

Not all moral questions are soluble legally or psychiatrically, nor should they be. I think psychiatrists and theologians have in common the need for a certain restraint here, to avoid playing God and to reject the notion that we have anything like a complete solution that comes from our points of view or our particular disciplines. When helping a young person confused about a cult situation, at whatever level he or she may be involved, it is important to maintain a genuine personal therapeutic contract so that one is not working for the cult or for the parents. Totalism begets totalism—and there can be notable totalism in so-called deprogramming. What is called deprogramming includes a continuum from intense dialogue on the one hand to physical coercion and kidnaping, with thought-reform-like techniques, on the other. My own position, which I have stated many times and have conveyed to parents and others who have consulted me, is that I am against coercion at either end of the cult process.

Having said all this, I know that there remain painful moral dilemmas. Where laws are violated—through fraud or specific harm done to recruits—legal intervention is clearly indicated. But what of situations of a kind I have seen in which young people involved in intense cult situations have become virtually automatized, their behavior rote, their language little but cliché, and yet express a certain satisfaction or even happiness in that state? We do well to continue to seek ways of combining social commitment to individual autonomy with avoidance of coercion and violence.

I will close with some words of ancient Chinese Taoist wisdom, which I used as an epigraph for another book: "Only simple and quiet things will ripen of themselves. For a whirlwind does not last the whole morning. Nor does the thundershower last the whole day. Who is their author? The heaven and earth. Yet even they cannot make such violent things last. How much more true this must be of the rash endeavors of men."

16

Suicide: The Quest for a Future

I prepared this essay for an annual workshop on suicide sponsored by the department of psychiatry of the Cambridge Hospital at Harvard Medical School. (For the material on Mishima, I am grateful to Shuichi Kato and Michael Reich, my co-authors of Six Lives/Six Deaths: Portraits from Modern Japan.)[1] *I wanted to apply the life-continuity paradigm in a way that would place suicide in a social and historical context, including that of contemporary nuclear threat. The association of suicide and nuclear threat has to be, at best, tentative, but the principles I put forward here could provide a basis for further explorations. The atrocities and unmanageable deaths of the twentieth century make especially evident that a careful, reflective study of the overall question of suicide could provide insight into virtually every significant psychological, cultural, and historical question. This essay is a brief probe in that direction.*

NUCLEAR WEAPONS have given us a new capacity for relatively quick and efficient species suicide. Yet however global our outlook, we have to return to individual self-destruction for a proper moral and experiental perspective. It is, after all, the person, the individual human being, who must concern us. At the same time we must recognize that each individual suicide, or prospective suicide, has a larger context that directly affects the seemingly paradoxical quest I speak of in my title "The Quest for a Future." With that recognition we ask in turn, How is that context affected by serious doubts about whether a society or a civilization or a species has a future? How do those doubts influence decisions about suicide and its relationship to that quest for an individual future? Answers to such questions are at best elusive, but we learn a great deal in seeking them.

My discussion can be divided into three parts. In the first portion, I want to suggest some general principles about suicide that may slightly clarify what is probably the most confused and confusing psychological literature that we have. Second, I want to suggest three basic psychic components of suicide. And third, I want to illustrate the operation of its principles and components in a celebrated public suicide, that of the Japanese novelist Yukio Mishima in 1970.[2] Finally I will return to the larger theme of collective human suicide.

General Principles

The first larger principle is that suicide is not a psychiatric problem per se. The psychiatric profession cannot claim to be the exclusive authority on, or guardian against, suicide. Yet, as a touchstone for its sensitivity and humanity, any psychiatry can be judged by its approach to suicide.

Second, there is a back-and-forth swing, a polarity between the traditional Judeo-Christian horror and condemnation of suicide and a critical view of this stance in the form of affirmation of suicide and even romantic idealization. As psychiatric physicians and at the same time advocates of human rights, we need to find our way between the principle of autonomy in suicide and our concern about human life and commitment to its perpetuation.

The third theme I wish to stress, one that is not popular right now, is what I call the "unitary principle" in suicide. Recent study of differentiating details in suicide has stressed its varied forms, and rightly so. I would insist, however, that there is common ground in suicide, no matter who carries it out, as a violent statement about human connection, broken or maintained. Whatever the differences between the suicide of Socrates as an affirmative act of a healthy mature man and the suicide of the most regressed schizophrenic person, each is an absolute act of the killing of the self. That is why Karl Menninger could describe suicide as "a peculiar form of death which entails three elements: the element of dying, the element of killing, and the element of being killed," while he stressed that "the death penalty is self-inflicted." Menninger also spoke of ordinary forms of suicide as "prototypes of acute, generalized, total self-destruction."[3] Any suicide under any circumstances harkens back to this principle of "generalized, total self-destruction" as a broad human capability.

The fourth principle concerning suicide is its universality. It is difficult to find a culture, or a mythology, in which suicide does not play a significant role. One must in fact assume that individual suicide is in some way compatible with the perpetuation of the human species. We may say that when man discovered death, began to symbolize, and created culture—when man became man—he realized that he could kill others and kill himself. More simply, in learning that we die, we learn that we can inflict our own death. Kurt Eissler states that "the potentiality of such an action rests in every person," and "in every analysis we have to grapple with suicidal tendencies in the patient."[4] One could say that to be human is to be exposed to the possibility of killing oneself.

A fifth principle is the paradoxical attitude toward suicide on the part of cultures and religions. James George Frazer speaks of the "dread and fear" of the spirits of those who have taken their own lives, spirits or ghosts considered dangerous because of being rendered restless and homeless by the deviant and unacceptable form of death that produced them.[5] Yet Gregory Zilboorg, after an extensive survey of primitive suicide, concluded that the majority of primitive cultures "idealize . . . rather than condemn . . . suicide."[6] The problem lies in the either/or assumption that a particular culture prohibits or else honors suicide. All cultures do both.[7] The Greeks accepted certain forms of suicide as appropriate to particular situations (again that of Socrates, but also of Jocasta, mother of Oedipus),[8] yet also had the custom of cutting off the right hand of a suicide and burying it apart from his or her body as a means of disarming a dangerous ghost.[9] There is a similar impulse in the medieval custom of putting a stake into the corpse of the suicide and burying him or her at the crossroads. Indeed, in various expressions of Christian doctrine, suicide is rendered a crime without possibility of repentance, or even a form of murder in which man becomes "his own assassin."[10] Yet Christianity, from its beginnings, reveres a particular form of suicide, that of martyrdom, as an ultimate spiritual principle and even a life goal.

There is a similar dichotomy in non-Christian Japanese tradition. We often think of the Japanese as idealizing suicide, as in the ritual act of *hara-kiri* or *seppuku,* in which one ends one's life voluntarily in order to reassert eternal cultural principles. But behind ritual suicides there could be considerable pressure, even coercion. Moreover, no such ennobling act was expected of ordinary people, who were in fact subject to prohibitions against suicide.

Reverend Tuke, the seventeenth-century English preacher, captured this overall duality of suicide by contrasting two forms, "the one lawful and honest" (that of martyrs, modeled on Jesus himself) and the other "dishonest and unlawful" (in which human beings without divine sanction take it upon themselves to end their own lives).[11] The general principle here is that all cultures have a place for suicide, but bring to it a mixture of awe, terror, and prohibition. The fear lies in the threat suicide poses to existing definitions and rules concerning human connection. But for the same reason, cultures, religions, governments, and political movements embrace certain forms of suicide when it can be performed specifically on behalf of their immortalizing principles. Everything depends upon which way the winds of immortality are blowing.

Involved in all of this is, of course, a form of death management that cultures take on. The designation of who may or should kill himself or herself, and under what circumstances, is the essence of a group's relationship to, and control over, life and death. One could say much about war and suicide, and about terrorism and suicide—the designation of suicide missions of one form or another for the ostensible purpose of maintaining the life of the larger group. Even nuclear holocaust could be seen by some—at whatever level of consciousness and illusion—as some such "life-enhancing" suicide mission.

The sixth principle involves another dialectic: the suicide wants both to die and to live, desiring literally to bring his or her life to an end but wishing also to assert a form of vitality in the act of self-destruction. There is fundamental truth to the insight, beginning with Freud, that one may kill oneself to deny the fact of death. But when Freud insists that the suicide wishes to kill an "internalized object" rather than the self, I would modify that assumption by insisting that it is that "object"-dominated *self*—the self still suffering from unresolved relationships and experiences—that the suicidal person does indeed seek to kill.[12] Yet the vitality sought in suicide, I maintain, goes beyond a "cry for help" and is more on the order of a demand for unending recognition and life power.

Elements of Suicide

The paradigm of symbolization of life and death (see chapter 1) is, I believe, particularly crucial for understanding suicide. In this paradigm, the stress is not on this symbol or that but on continuous symbolization, on the constant creation and re-creation of images and forms—that is, on a formative process. The self becomes both the overall coordinator of symbolization and the inclusive symbol of one's own organism. We distinguish proximate and ultimate levels—death equivalents and symbolic immortality, respectively—only for intellectual convenience. In actuality they merge in a struggle for vitality and larger connectedness, a struggle in no way limited to the time of anticipated dying but going on through all of one's life.

With suicide, there are psychological questions about death equivalents—about separation, stasis, and the fear of disintegration—and about death itself. It is amazing how often death can be left out of our concepts of suicide. But, then, death can be left out of almost anything. Though death has recently become a popular subject, people still have great difficulty thinking about it rigorously in relation to psychological theory—a failure we may look upon as our conceptual denial of death. That conceptual denial bedevils our thought in general; in the case of suicide it becomes ludicrous. Yet suicide is concerned not only with death but with the quest for life continuity. Indeed, suicide is concerned with questions of meaning on all levels.

Now I would like to consider what I take to be the fundamental elements of suicide: first, the issue of entrapment and despair; then, the quest for meaning, that is for a future, especially an immortalizing future; and, finally, what I call the "suicide construct."

Evidence is well recorded on the subject of entrapment and despair. One has the sense that there is no way out other than killing oneself. Here I want to stress the distinction between depression and despair. The two are treated as though they were the same; they are not. In terms of the preceding paradigm, depression tends to involve loss and a sense of separation, and the experience of the other two death equivalents, stasis and the fear of disintegration, as well; and also brings out elements of anger and protest. Despair functions more on the ultimate level that I described. In despair, one feels unable to maintain or envision any larger human connections of significance—any ongoing link in the great chain of being. And interesting research shows that people can be depressed, and exhibit the very symptoms that we know to be characteristic of depression, without despairing of their future. These people can feel helpless without feeling futureless.[13] While depression and despair tend to merge, the element of despair is central to suicide. The most difficult situation is one in which both of these elements are strong. But the despair is the critical element, with or without manifestations of depression.

In terms of despair and the sense of impaired larger human connection, one can say that the suicide can create a future only by killing himself. That is, one can reawaken a sense of psychic action and imagine vital elements beyond the present only by deciding upon and carrying through that suicide. Although this may appear to be a paradox, and observers have called it irrational or a "psychosemantic fallacy," such judgments may obscure the matter. At issue is the individual experience of the symbolizing process, within which radically negative expectations of the future call forth a desperate, indeed deadly, assertion of self and future. One kills the "dead self" in order to break out of the despair.

The other two fundamental elements of suicide that I wish to stress have been largely neglected: the quest for future-oriented meaning; and the suicide construct. On the issue of meaning, Leslie Farber has written that the suicide is a sadly deluded figure, because instead of finding one's life, one ends it.[14] But for some people, the act of ending one's life is the only way of finding it: for instance, Ludwig Binswanger wrote of the suicide of his famous patient, Ellen West: "Only in her decision for death did she find herself and choose herself."[15] And Antonin Artaud, the revolutionary dramatist, wrote: "If I commit suicide, it will not be to destroy myself but to put myself back together again. . . . By suicide I reintroduce my design in nature, I shall for the first time give things the shape of my will."[16] While Binswanger had more than a touch of the romantic, and Artaud was mad as well as gifted, they articulate the powerful theme of suicide as self-completion, as the only means of appropriately locating oneself in the "design" of the cosmos. This theme is present in every suicide, however agonizing or demeaning the circumstances. That is why the Jungian psychoanalyst James Hillman could speak of suicide as an "urge for hasty transformation . . . the late reaction of a delayed life which did not transform as it went along."[17] One can observe this quest for meaning most clearly in what Emile Durkheim called altruistic suicide. Yukio Mishima is a case in point. He publicly asserted his intent to kill himself in order to revitalize the martial principles of Japanese culture, immortalized from early days but increasingly abandoned in the face of what he considered harmful modern and contemporary influences. We shall see that Mishima combined this quest for larger meaning with elements of personal despair, and that both are likely to be present in every suicide. Where the one—either the despair or the larger meaning—seems to predominate, there are likely to be quiet manifestations of the other.

The third element, the suicide construct, addresses the question why some people kill themselves and others with similar psychological motifs do not. One beginning answer is the existence, often from early life, of the concrete possibility of killing oneself as an active ingredient of psychological experience. The suicide construct can be culturally transmitted, as in the case of the premodern Samurai instilled from early childhood with imagery of meeting certain situations honorably by killing oneself in specific ritual fashion. The Christian missionary's anticipation of martyrdom could entail a parallel suicide construct.

There can also be family transmission of a suicide construct, as in the common clinical impression that suicide is more of a danger when parents or close relatives have committed suicide. This is sometimes seen as hereditary influence, but psychological transmission is probably much more important. Contained in the suicide construct is a central idea: "Suicide is an option—something I can do in my life, something I've seen done, a possibility for me."

A. Alvarez, in his interesting study of suicide, tells of his personal experience with a suicide construct. As a child he had become aware that both parents had on some occasion put their heads in the gas oven, which seemed to him "a rather splendid gesture . . . something hidden, attractive and not for the children, like sex." Over the course of his life, when things would go badly, he would say to himself, "I wish I were dead"—muttering it "unthinkingly," as automatically as a Catholic priest tells his rosary. "IwishIweredead . . . IwishIweredead . . . IwishIweredead." And then one day, in a moment of illumination, "I heard the phrase as though for the first time," and shortly afterward made a serious suicide attempt.[18]

In the case of Ellen West, there is also a powerful suicide construct. Binswanger pointed out that two of her uncles had committed suicide, and a third was "severly ascetic"; a younger brother was briefly hospitalized for "a mental ailment with suicidal ideas"; and both of her parents were subject to severe depressions (including, in all probability, significant suicidal ideation). Ellen West herself grew up with a romanticized feeling about death itself and as a child would be disappointed when a fever would go down. She wrote poetry extolling death and was entranced by the sentence "Those whom the Gods love die young."[19] She killed herself at the age of thirty-two, after several unsuccessful attempts—including pills, jumping out of a window and in front of cars, and self-starvation.

She had previously been hospitalized and was considered a suicide risk. To her husband, Binswanger explained that he could assume responsibility for his patient if she were on a closed ward. But Ellen West did not want to be on a closed ward, and her husband refused to put her there. She wanted to leave the hospital and to kill herself—as, when the decision was made to release her, she did. In anticipation of doing so, she seemed happy and even in a celebratory mood. She was, according to her husband, as if transformed.

One can say that by taking hold of her death in this way, Ellen West experienced, however briefly, a sense of vitality. She found a larger sense of meaning in her violent conquest of the despairing meaninglessness in which she had lived. So all-consuming had been her suicide construct that killing herself was the *only* meaning toward which her life could strive.

The suicide construct can have a certain situational importance, as in a pattern of suicidal contagion that has sometimes been noted. In one important study, there was a virtual epidemic of suicide in a group of mental hospital patients, after a disturbing series of upheavals and turnovers among the staff.[20] There was surely a breakdown in imagery of connection and intensification of despair among these patients. But we may also postulate a spreading intensification of the suicide construct, of the idea in each mind that one might actually kill oneself.

Yukio Mishima is worth returning to here because he illustrates, in the most vivid way, all of these elements at work. In fact, his suicide was so vivid and flamboyant that it had strong elements of caricature. Mishima was a highly talented novelist, considered on more than one occasion for the Nobel Prize, who in November 1970 performed a florid version of ritual Japanese self-immolation, or *seppuku*. Gaining entrance, by means of a pretense, to a Self Defense Force (army) headquarters in Tokyo, Mishima kept the general there hostage and, after making an abortive speech to the men below, retired to an inner room and disemboweled himself. He was then beheaded by one of his followers of the Shield Society, a group he had formed as a private army whose named derived from the traditional Japanese concept of serving as a shield for the Emperor. Mishima's suicide note was his manifesto, in which—in the name of ancient forms of emperor-centered military and cultural glory—he exorted the Japanese to take up arms against contemporary Western and commercial influences on Japan. He wrote, "Let us restore Nippon to its true state, and let us die."[21]

At first view Mishima's actions seem to exemplify suicide in the service of larger, prospective meaning; certainly the immortalizing reach is loud and clear. Yet when one looks more closely, one can also find strong elements of despair and, above all, a lifelong suicide construct.

There is a quality of absurdity in the sequence of events: the "kitsch" uniforms (patterned after those of the Meiji era of the late nineteenth century), the men's mocking responses to his balcony speech, and the difficulty his followers had beheading him. The absurdity reflected Mishima's own inner chaos, including longstanding sexual conflict as a bisexual, increasing feelings of emptiness, and mounting despair over declining creative power and diminishing appreciation of his work by the Japanese public. The greater his sense of decline, the more he engaged in external display—in what some have called public stunts—including death-dominated theatrical literalism, display of his body (he had taken up body building, Japanese fencing [*kendo*], as well as Western boxing), acting in films, and melodramatic rightest political stances.

But all along, Mishima was bound by his extraordinarily powerful suicide construct. He had spent most of his early childhood, until the age of twelve, in the sickroom of his elderly grandmother. For many years she was considered to be dying and would depend upon only the young Mishima to give her medicine and tend to her needs. In an autobiographical novel of his, she becomes a love object—she and death itself. Mishima also tells how, instead of fantasizing about little people, about elves and gnomes (or *kappas* in Japan), he fantasized about little diseases which went about. He wondered which disease creature was more fatal than the others.[22]

Mishima's most persistent fantasy from early childhood was of the martyrdom of St. Sebastian, in which there is both a homoerotic attraction and an erotic attraction to death. As an adolescent and young adult during the Second World War, Mishima embraced the death-dominated aesthetics and politics of the Japanese romantic school of literature and equally romanticized right-wing militarized politics. Yet when he was called up to serve in the military—synonymous with expectation of death—it turned out that he did not want that death after all. His actions in fact could be called a form of malingering in his encouragement of doctors' suspicion of tuberculosis, when he had nothing more than a temporary cold. He spent the rest of his life seeking the romantic, immortalizing death he had lacked the courage to embrace as a late adolescent during the war. He eventually staged the suicide he had been seeking throughout his adult life. His immortalizing commitment to Japanese glory was very real to him, even as it combined with elements of despair and his lifelong suicide construct.

Suicide and Contemporary Threat

After this exploration of individual suicide in a social and historical context, can we now say something more about historical or social suicide? Here one must start with the increasingly documented recognition, at least on the part of Americans, of the threat of extermination:[23] the widespread experience of what I call the "imagery of extinction." I call my general conceptual study *The Broken Connection* because I view this imagery of extinction as a source of a major rent in our psychic tissues.[24] To be sure, we do not consciously entertain possibilities of our extinction during most of our waking hours; but that image is now with us at differing levels of awareness and with periodic waves of intensity—with us in ways we are just beginning to grasp. Does that broken connection between life and death affect our relationship to suicide?

Alvarez thinks it does, and speaks of a sharp increase in suicide among artists and writers. He draws upon my Hiroshima material to construct a thesis that the artist has become entrapped in the threat of meaningless mass death and can find no language, no imagery, with which to express that existential state or to escape from that entrapment. This British writer speaks of the overwhelming "pressure to discover a language adequate to this apparently impossible task, . . . an artistic language with which to grasp in the imagination the historical facts of this century . . . the dimension of unnatural, premature death." In struggling to break out of the shared suppression of feeling, the collective psychic numbness, the artist (Alvarez tells us) becomes a "scapegoat" who "puts himself at risk and explores his own vulnerability . . . testing out his own death in his imagination."[25] They move toward "a suicide of the imagination" if not toward the act itself in their Sisyphean struggle to create (and here Alvarez quotes a Hiroshima survivor) "language which can comfort guinea pigs who do not know the cause of their death."[26]

But we must also ask, What about the rest of us? What about the shared struggle with imagery of radical futurelessness, precisely the struggle that haunts the artists Alvarez discusses. What does that fear of literal human end, of nothingness, do to our overall relationship to suicide?

We do not know the answer to that question. It is hard to tell whether there is an actual increase of suicide in our time, and if there is, whether this imagery of extinction plays a significant part. The variables involved are, in every sense, difficult to control. But we can and should raise questions. Does perceived nuclear futurelessness contribute to the kind of despair and impaired human connection that we know to be part of individual suicide? Does the image of collective nuclear murder/suicide contribute, however indirectly, to the formation and the broad or even "contagious" dissemination of suicide constructs?

These questions contribute to our uneasy fascination with the mass suicide-murder of about 950 people in Guyana in 1978. Jim Jones, the leader of the People's Temple movement, who set the process in motion, looked upon the event as a form of "revolutionary suicide"—that is, collective suicide for an immortalizing purpose that the group could not achieve in life. There was also deep underlying despair: people leaving the group, a threatening investigation by U.S. congressmen, a sense of increasing criticism and pressure from every side. And Jones associated the group's own apocalyptic impulses with parallel images of nuclear threat, undoubtedly used manipulatively but at the same time genuinely experienced. What was most peculiar to this group was a collective suicide construct, really a suicide theology formulated by Jones. Hence the rehearsals of collective suicide in readiness for the occasion of its enactment, should a situation arise in which that enactment became the best or only expression of the group's immortalizing mission. Yet these elements of suicide were not originally visible in a movement that called forth, at least at its beginning, considerable idealism concerning racial harmony and communal living. What haunts us about the Guyana episode is our fear that it prefigures a more massive nuclear suicide/murder that could result from a sequence of events, partly initiated by what is perceived as idealism, but increasingly out of human control.

Finally, can we make life-enhancing use of this recognition of potential connection between suicide and nuclear threat? The death-related psychological issues raised by nuclear threat could help us considerably in our continuous struggle to grasp and cope with the elements of individual suicide. Still more important, what we learn in our explorations of individual suicide, if applied wisely, might well contribute to the desperately needed imaginative efforts to confront imagery of nuclear extinction, on behalf of rejecting and preventing that fate.

17

The Concept of the Survivor

Here I wanted to bring together general ideas of the survivor I had evolved over the fifteen years or so following my work in Hiroshima. I gave an earlier version of this essay at the Conference on Holocaust honoring Elie Wiesel, sponsored by the City University of New York and the National Jewish Conference Center, in November 1977.[1] *I give special attention to what I call "death guilt," because that subject has been so much misunderstood and argued over. And I am concerned with stressing both the uniqueness of the Holocaust perpetrated by the Nazis and at the same time the existence of certain common principles that connect virtually all survivor experience.*

ONE APPROACHES the task of writing about the Holocaust knowing that it is virtually impossible to convey the experience, to find words or concepts for the extremity of its horror. We are faced with the paradox of making an effort to understand, in terms of human feeling, the most anti-human event in human history. The European Holocaust after all was invented by, and consumed, human beings. Its very extremity has something to teach us about our more ordinary confrontations with death and violence.

The word *holocaust,* of Greek origin, means total consumption by fire. That definition applies, all too literally, to Auschwitz and Buchenwald, and also to Nagasaki and Hiroshima. In Old Testament usage, there is the added meaning of the sacrifice, a burnt offering. That meaning tends to be specifically retained for the deliberate, selective Nazi genocide of six million Jews—retained with both bitterness and irony (sacrifice to whom and for what?). I will thus speak of the Holocaust *and* of holocausts: the first, for the unique Nazi project of genocide; the second, to suggest certain general principles concerning the totality of destruction as it affects survivors. From that perspective, holocaust means total disaster: the physical, social, and spiritual obliteration of a human community. *To observe common psychological responses of survivors, however, in no way suggests that the historical events themselves can be equated.*

Those of us who undertake this task face two additional problems. One is the inadequacy of ordinary psychological concepts and yet the necessity to find connections between the extreme and the ordinary in our experience. Another is the nature of the investigator's own involvement—that combination Martin Buber called distance and relation.[2] On the part of psychological investigators there has been too much distance and not enough relation, a tendency to negate or minimize survivors' experiences, largely in response to our own psychic numbing. Yet there is also the danger of the kind of uneasiness before survivors that causes the investigator to romanticize or glorify their ordeal and thereby to divest it of its unsavory dimensions. Either stance—spurious neutrality or compensatory glorification—diminishes the survivor and interferes with our understanding both of what is particular to his or her ordeal and of what insight it may reveal about our own psychological and historical condition.

What follows draws upon my experience, direct and indirect, with survivors of four different holocausts: Hiroshima, where I lived and interviewed survivors over a period of six months in 1962;[3] the Nazi death camps, through others' studies and the writings of survivors and my own recent work with survivors in connection with research on Nazi doctors; the Vietnam War, through intensive work with returning veterans from 1970 through 1973; and the Buffalo Creek flood disaster of 1972, through work with survivors in West Virginia from 1973 through 1975.* Precisely

* This last event involved corporate negligence of a criminal order: the depositing of coal waste in such a way that an artificial dam was created, and the refusal to undertake the necessary repair of the dam despite repeated insistence by the miners that it would burst. That is exactly what happened early on a February morning, and within a matter of minutes, a small valley (or "hollow") was totally inundated with black, sludge-filled water; 125 people were dead and more than 5,000 homeless. The two subsequent law suits were both settled out of court with substantial awards.[4]

because these four events differ so greatly—the last in particular being of a separate order from the other three in terms of size and historical significance—the fact that the survivors share certain psychological responses takes on added importance.

After a few comments about attitudes toward death and holocaust, I will discuss a general perspective on survivors from the standpoint of these four holocausts and then will remark briefly on the position of the professional investigator of holocaust. These issues have long been of concern to me personally—as psychiatrist, Jew, and human being.

Contemporary Death and Holocaust

Yeats once said, very simply, "Man has discovered death." In America that discovery is a new one, and we have to remind ourselves that death has been around for a long time. Encountering the subject everywhere, in public and private discussion, we are confronted with what at times seems almost a media hype. What, then, is the nature of this rather odd discovery? And why do we "discover" it now?

Some cautionary skepticism is in order. In our society no sooner is a need expressed than it is shouted from the rooftops, proclaimed, disseminated, and devoured until its original impulse can be lost. And, perhaps predictably, there has been an impulse to turn death over to the "experts," clerical or psychiatric. Nevertheless there is a legitimate quest for death awareness, one long overdue in our society. There is serious medical and psychiatric work with dying patients and equally serious concern about the whole range of death-related issues among philosophers, social and psychological theorists, and other writers.

If we seek psychohistorical reasons for this outpouring of interest in death, at least five come to mind. First, there is a rebound reaction from what may well be the most extreme denial of death that any society has ever evolved. While denial of death seems to be characteristic of advanced industrial society in general, it is perhaps especially so in U.S. society: in the "Forest Lawn syndrome," for example, we bury not just the dead but death itself under the cheerfully manicured grounds of cemeteries.

A second reason—one that I greatly emphasize—has been the involvement of much of twentieth-century history with death by holocaust.

There has been a slow seepage into consciousness of the imagery of Nazi death camps and, for Americans, our own atomic bombings and the threat of future nuclear holocaust, the war in Vietnam in general, and My Lai in particular. We professionals are not immune to such influences and are in fact creatures of our history not only in our methods of study but in what we choose as the objects of study, and this may be especially true of psychohistorical work.

A third reason for the outpouring of death imagery, I believe, is rapid historical change or pressures toward such change. At such moments, the breakdown of existing symbolic forms may be accompanied by an explosion of death imagery. In turn, this contributes to the collective imaginative impulse to create new or altered forms, as clearly happened in the late Middle Ages and Renaissance in the West, and the Meiji Restoration, in the late nineteenth century, in Japan, when it was modernized with the Emperor Meiji as a central figure.

Still another important influence is that of the mass media, with their capacity to disseminate, instantly and ubiquitously, any viable set of social images, including those involving death (see chapter 1, pages 18–19). We know all too well how such images can be trivialized by the media, but we may well underestimate the depth of their impact. This duality was apparent, for instance, in the televising of the Vietnam War. On the one hand the war became unreal, on the order of a John Wayne film, in ways that contributed to the national numbing. On the other hand, troubling images of meaningless slaughter broke through that numbing or at least contributed to doubt and guilt-tinged discomfort.

Finally, technological feats in medicine and science take us to the borders of life, raising questions about its origins and endings. Organ transplants and other methods of technologically maintaining or prolonging life, when combined with knowledge of genetic engineering, leave new questions (or new versions of old questions) about the nature of life and the meaning of death. We think more about death partly because we are in a position in which we must make more decisions about it, and partly because (and this is true of all five influences) we sense that life and death are increasingly out of joint.

We have struck a number of devil's bargains about these matters in our culture. For a long time the unspoken arrangement was: celebrate only that which is youthful; keep silent about death; maybe it will go away. Next it became permissible to speak about individual death and dying but not about grotesque, massive death, not about holocaust. Now holocaust is increasingly discussed, but mainly in terms of the past, much less in relationship to future potential holocausts or to our own capacity for mass murder. Here the arrangement may be greatly affected by heavy international investments, financial and psychological, in nuclear power as well as weaponry.

We may also have devised a new devil's bargain around our descriptions of the process of living through holocaust—something on the order of a domestication or cleansing, so that it is all right to talk about human strengths but not about degradation. Indeed, my own profession may well have contributed to this tendency in its general neglect of the impact of adult trauma, and especially of the "massive psychic trauma" observed in holocaust.* In any case, there are converging tendencies to divest the survivor experience of some of its psychological horror. These tendencies reflect a society's concerns with, and resistance to, death.

The Holocaust Survivor

Who is a survivor? A survivor is one who has encountered, been exposed to, or witnessed death and has himself or herself remained alive. Albert Camus, in his Nobel Prize acceptance speech of 1957, spoke of "twenty years of absolutely insane history." In this speech he asked a terrible rhetorical question: "Do you know that over a period of twenty-five years, between 1922 and 1947, seventy million Europeans—men, women and children—have been uprooted, deported, killed?" (The "Do you know" means, Do we let ourselves remember? Do we permit ourselves to feel?) One might well repeat the question for the ensuing three decades, in relationship to Asians, Africans, and Latin Americans who have suffered similarly. Camus viewed such things, in the words of one of his biographers, "as a scandal that he himself finds impossible to evade,"[6] and was referring to our landscape of holocaust, from which literature must emerge and life be lived. On that basis (and without in any way equating ordinary life to the experience of holocaust), we all have in us something of the survivor and witness.

Here, as in his other work, Camus expressed the survivor's potential for confronting the death immersion and for seeking from it a measure of

* The situation is partly redressed by a reform in nomenclature that gives recognition to "traumatic neurosis" (or "traumatic syndrome"), but there still seems to be an unwillingness to provide a special diagnostic category for "massive psychic trauma."[5]

insight. But a contrasting response is also possible, one of cessation of feeling or sustained psychic numbing—the response of most ordinary people to the death immersions of their time. This numbed response can be viewed as a second scandal of our time, the scandal of our failure to be scandalized by man-made holocausts, by mass murder.

A few more distinctions. An actual survivor of holocaust undergoes a totality of psychological responses that cannot be duplicated in ordinary experience. Yet separate elements of that death immersion do make contact with general psychological principles. If there is one thing Freud taught us, it is that no single psychological tendency, however extreme or disturbed, is totally alien from "normal" psychic function. So we must study survivor experience both in its uniqueness and in its connection with the rest of human life. It follows that survivors vary enormously in their capacities and inclinations—many extraordinary in their life-power, others capable of destructive behavior, each bringing a particular mixture of virtues and faults to a shared ordeal.

In previous writings, I have described five psychological themes in survivors, which I want to relate now to the four holocausts I have defined.

The first theme is the *death imprint* with its related *death anxiety*. Involved here are *indelible images* not just of death but of grotesque and absurd (that is, totally unacceptable) forms of death. In Hiroshima, the indelible image was likely to include grotesque shapes of the dead and the dying, as immediately encountered after the bomb fell—scenes described to me seventeen years later and yet so immediate in tone that I felt myself virtually in the midst of them. With Nazi death-camp survivors, the imagery can include many forms of cruel memory—the smoke or smell of the gas chambers, the brutal killing of a single individual, or simply separation from a family member never seen again. Vietnam veterans' images were of the bodies of close buddies blown apart and of the slaughter of Vietnamese civilians. Buffalo Creek survivors described the terrifying advance of the "black water" and people disappearing in it. In all four cases, imagery included something close to the end of the world, and "end of time," the destruction of everything. There can be a thralldom to this death imagery, the sense of being bound by it and of seeing all subsequent experience through its prism. The survivor may feel stuck in time, unable to move beyond that imagery, or may find it a source of death-haunted knowledge—even creative energy—that has considerable value for his or her life.

The second category is that of *death guilt*—frequently termed *survivor guilt* and much misunderstood. Death guilt is epitomized by the survivor's question, "Why did I survive while he, she, or they died?" Even before one can ask this question, the beginnings of the process take shape through the indelible imagery mentioned earlier. Part of a survivor's sense of horror is the memory of one's own inactivation—helplessness—within the death imagery; of one's inability to act in a way one would ordinarily have thought appropriate (save people, resist the victimizers, etc.), or even to feel the appropriate emotions (overwhelming rage toward victimizers, profound compassion for victims). I have come to think of this phenomenon as a sense of "failed enactment," and describe it in *The Broken Connection*.[7] Death guilt begins, then, in the gap between that physical and psychic inactivation and what one feels called upon to do and feel. That is one reason the imagery keeps recurring, in dreams and in waking life.

Also contained in this imagery is the survivor's sense of debt to and responsibility toward the dead. These feelings of debt and responsibility are related to guilt, both psychologically and etymologically. One must, of course, be careful to distinguish psychological guilt (a form of self-condemnation or a feeling of badness concerning what one has or has not done) from moral and legal guilt, which involve ethical and social consensus in judgments concerning wrongdoing. Nowhere is the distinction more important than in the case of survivors of holocaust. Theirs is a form of *paradoxical guilt,* one of the many undeserved residua of their experience and perhaps the most ironic. The irony becomes still more bitter in view of the fact, which has been repeatedly observed, that survivors are likely to feel more guilty than do their victimizers.

Death guilt can be expressed in dreams. The dream may "replay" the holocaust, as in the case of a Buffalo Creek survivor who dreamed of "the truck full of bodies . . . [and of] running, or trying to get hold of someone to help them out of the mud." Or in the dream, the survivor may join the dead, as in the case of a woman in Buffalo Creek who dreamed of a close relative, killed in the flood, appearing with a white dress and holding out her hand, asking the dreamer to follow her "back into a hole that looked like a mine." It did not take long for the dreamer to recognize that she was being asked to join the dead.

The sense of guilt can be especially strong concerning the death of close relatives and friends; but in Hiroshima, survivors repeatedly told me of their sense of being stared at accusingly by the eyes of the *anonymous* dead. Here, as in all extreme situations, feelings of guilt and shame merge. That finding also suggests an evolutionary function of guilt, its importance for human ties in general and for maintaining individual responsibility for *sustaining* others' lives.

Freud emphasized the dangers of guilt, especially unconscious guilt. At the end of *Civilization and Its Discontents,* he suggested that this emotion is so dangerous that, in its relationship to potential aggression (emanating, he thought, from the death instinct), it might contribute to the destruction of humankind.[8] But Freud also understood guilt as crucial to the cement of society. I would argue that in our present society the loss of the capacity for guilt, at least under certain conditions, may be the greater human threat. The combination of high technology and elaborate bureaucratization permits mass killing with relatively limited experience of guilt—as we know from the Nazi death camps as well as the atomic bombings of Hiroshima and Nagasaki, and those technologies were relatively primitive by current standards.

Guilt need not be pathological but can also be a powerful impetus for responsibility. One can see this tension in much of Elie Wiesel's work. Consider the powerful passage at the end of his first, most fundamental statement of witness, the autobiographical novel *Night.* Wiesel tells how, as a fifteen-year-old boy, he took tender care of his sick father en route to and within Auschwitz, Buna, and Buchenwald. But when temporarily separated from his father, Wiesel was suddenly horrified at his wish that he not be able to find him: "If only I could get rid of this dead weight, so that I could use all my strength to struggle with my own survival, and only worry about myself." And when they are reunited and his father dies in his arms, Wiesel perceives, "in the recesses of my weakened conscience," a feeling close to "free at last!" He described feeling both guilty and "ashamed of myself, ashamed forever." Later, after being liberated and recovering from a severe illness of his own, he looks into a mirror: "A corpse gazed back at me. The look in his eyes, as they stared into mine, has never left me." Finally Wiesel writes, "In every stiffened corpse I saw myself."[9] I have discussed this passage elsewhere, in terms of death guilt and its relationship to the survivor's identification with the dead and the impulse to bear witness.[10] Indeed, here and throughout his writing, Wiesel demonstrates the delicate relationship between death guilt and debt to the dead, and the transformation of death guilt into the anxiety of responsibility.

In recent years, I have tried to distinguish this kind of *animating* relationship to guilt from more *static* guilt patterns. In the case of Vietnam veterans, for instance, I could delineate two kinds of static guilt: a self-lacerating, or *mea culpa* form, in which one constantly proclaims one's own evil in a self-enclosed fashion that permits little change. The second I have called "numbed guilt," the inability to confront one's death immersion, resulting in a pattern of avoidance together with vague but often distressing feelings of uneasiness and, in many other cases, other symptoms as well (including depression, uncontrollable anger, and various bodily complaints). A more animating relationship to guilt was achieved by those veterans who could examine their experience and draw from it insight and energy (often related to opposing the war). Although the Vietnam veterans differed from the other three groups of survivors in having been made into both victimizers and victims, much of their struggle with guilt was strikingly related to their survival of buddies' deaths. In any case, these forms of guilt are not limited to war or survival but have much more general applicability for healthy and disturbed human behavior.

The third category of the survivor syndrome is that of *psychic numbing*, or the diminished capacity to feel. In Hiroshima, I was impressed by survivors' repeated statements to the effect that, after the bomb fell, they could see that people were dying, and understood that something dreadful had happened, but very quickly found themselves *feeling* almost nothing. They underwent what a Hiroshima writer described as "a paralysis of the mind," a dysfunction between perception and emotional response.[11] I came to recognize psychic numbing as a necessary psychological defense against overwhelming images and stimuli. In such extreme situations, one is simply unable to experience "ordinary" emotional responses and maintain either sanity or anything like adaptive physical and psychic function. The process is on the order of a temporary and partial deadening as a way of avoiding actual physical or psychological death. But psychic numbing can readily outlive its usefulness and give rise to later patterns of withdrawal, apathy, depression, and despair.

I encountered parallel patterns among Vietnam veterans in rap groups and individual interviews. Many described their recovery as something like "learning to feel." In Buffalo Creek, two and one-half years after the flood, the remaining community seemed to experience, at best, a half-life. As one man put it, "I feel dead now. I have no energy. I set down and I feel numb."

But the most extreme and prolonged struggles with numbing took place within prisoners in Nazi death camps. The process was epitomized in the *Muselmänner*, a term used for those who had become numbed to the point of being robotlike or "walking corpses," so that, as Primo Levi once wrote: "One hesitates to call them living: one hesitates to call their death death, in the face of which they have no fear, as they are too tired to understand."[12] (*Muselmann* is the German word for Moslem and came into being under the false assumption that Moslems are indifferent to their environment.) When I asked death-camp survivors how they managed to survive, some answered, "I lost all feeling." (Hiroshima survivors made similar comments, such as: "I became insensitive to human death.") But it would seem that in massive death immersions such as these, one's survival requires numbing that is extensive but never total; one has to maintain sufficient vitality of thought and emotion to evaluate the greatest dangers in one's environment and pursue whatever forms of self-protection and mutual help are available on behalf of survival.

I have mentioned my own struggles with numbing in connection with my Hiroshima work (see chapter 4, pages 52–53). The anxiety occurred when I shifted from general discussions with people *about* the atomic bomb to intensive individual interviews during which survivors would describe, in excruciating detail, what it was like to *experience* the atomic bomb and its aftermath. I came to describe my sequence from overwhelming anxiety to a measure of comfort in the interviews as selective, professional numbing. I do not think I became insensitive to the suffering described to me, but I did develop sufficient distance from it to enable me to conduct the study. A certain amount of numbing is probably necessary in most professional situations—in the midst of an operation a surgeon cannot afford to experience fully the consequences of failure—but it is surely excessive in our society and in our century. So great is the diminished emotion in professionals that it well may be that becoming a professional is in itself part of still another devil's bargain in which one ceases to feel much about the central—the most threatening—questions of our time.

Most malignant are patterns of diminished feeling in actual or potential victimizers. I have been concerned with the patterns of numbing involved in the creation and use of nuclear weapons—both in relationship to the Second World War U.S. atomic bombings and to universal contemporary attitudes toward such weaponry. In my work with Nazi doctors (see chapters 6 and 14) I was able to learn a great deal about perverse nuances of psychic numbing within the overall Nazi movement, especially in relation to the killing of Jews.

I use the term *numbing* rather than the older *repression,* for the latter suggests the act of *forgetting* images and ideas or their exclusion from consciousness and relegation to the realm of the unconscious. *Numbing,* by contrast, suggests the cessation of what I call the formative process, the *impairment* of the human being's essential mental function of symbolization. The term refers to an incapacity to feel or to confront certain kinds of experience, due either to the blocking or to the absence of prior imagery that would enable one to connect with such experience. Thus there is an essential separation of image and associated feeling. This I take to be more the problem of our present age of numbing.

A fourth category has to do with survivor's sensitivity toward the counterfeit or *suspicion of counterfeit nurturance.* On one level, the problem can be understood as a question of dependence and autonomy: the survivor feels the effects of his or her ordeal but frequently resents help offered because to accept is perceived as a sign of weakness. Perhaps more fundamentally the issue has to do with the environment of moral inversion—

the counterfeit universe—the survivor has lived through. In Vietnam, for instance, the counterfeit universe consisted of what I called an "atrocity-producing situation," which was so structured that the slaughter of civilians came close to being a psychological norm.

The fact that a holocaust is man-made has crucial bearing on this sense. One Buffalo Creek survivor declared, "I call this a disaster, not a flood. This wasn't a natural flood." Another man said, "Governor [Arch A.] Moore said it was an act of God but God wasn't up on that slate dump with a bulldozer."

The massive level of killing and dying in the Nazi death camps and Hiroshima created ultimate moral inversion. Living and dying were divested of moral structure and lost all logic. Entrapped in such a world, one is torn between the impulse to reject totally its counterfeit structure and the necessity to adapt to that structure and even to internalize portions of it in order to survive.

Following the death immersion, the survivors' sense of a counterfeit universe may well continue. This sense seems confirmed when they realize that others view them as in some way carrying the taint of the holocaust—as persons to be feared and avoided as though they and the taint were contagious. The survivors can be a reminder not only of death but of the grotesque violation of life characteristic of the holocaust they experienced, and can thus be a subjected to a "second victimization." Even worse, they may in some cases inwardly accept this social response and feel themselves to be enduringly tainted.

These conflicts can lead to patterns of distrust in human relationships, mutual antagonism, and the sense that much of the world around one, even life itself, is counterfeit. Alternatively, survivors can transcend these conflicts and achieve an enhanced sensitivity to falseness, to counterfeit behavior of any kind, and an equally enhanced appreciation of what is authentic and fundamental in relationship to living and dying.

The fifth and final category is the survivor's *struggle for meaning,* for a sense of inner form. Survivors of Nazi death camps have been called "collectors of justice." They seek something beyond economic or social restitution—something closer to acknowledgment of crimes committed against them and punishment of those responsible—in order to re-establish at least the semblance of a moral universe. The impulse to bear witness, beginning with a sense of responsibility to the dead, can readily extend into a "survivor mission"—a lasting commitment to a project that extracts significance from absurdity, vitality from massive death. For many Jewish survivors of the Nazi Holocaust, the survivor mission took the form of involvement in the creation of the state of Israel.

Such matters, however, can become complex and tragic. I believe that much of the intensity of conflict in the Middle East has to do with rival survivor missions: that of the Jews in response to surviving the Holocaust, that of the Arabs in response to surviving long-standing European imperial domination, and that of the Palestinian Arabs in surviving their loss of homes and land. Of course, such survivor emotions have been used politically in various ways, but my point is that they are potent forces in international affairs.

In Hiroshima, bearing witness could extend into survivor missions of conveying to the world, through various peace groups, the nature of atomic weapons. Antiwar Vietnam veterans found their witness and mission in telling the truth about the war they had been sent to fight; one could say that they found their significance in revealing the very meaninglessness of their war.

Survivor emotions can be important in the midst of war as well. The night before the My Lai massacre, the "combat briefing" was combined with a funeral ceremony for members of the company who had died horribly in mine explosions, and especially for a much-admired, fatherly, older sergeant.[13] (See chapter 4, page 54ff.) The men were survivors bereft of meaning, and pressured by their higher officers to find that meaning in "body counts," to "bear witness" by means of killing Vietnamese. Hence the impulse in real survivors to "false witness."

Whether witness is false or true, it involves struggles with grief and mourning. Where death occurs on the scale of Nazi genocide or atomic bombings, survivors are denied not only the physical arrangements of mourning (the grave, the remains, the place of worship) but also the psychic capacity to absorb and feel these deaths, to do the work of mourning. This aborted mourning can proceed to the extent that a survivor's existence can turn into a "life of grief." Impaired mourning becomes equated with a more general inability to give inner form—again significance—to the death immersion, and therefore to the remainder of one's life. The survivors may then be especially vulnerable to various psychic and bodily disturbances, as well as to impaired formulations of their experience. Unresolved, incomplete mourning results in stasis and entrapment in the traumatic process. Survivors require expressions of grief and mourning if they are to begin to derive from their experience its potential for some form of illumination.

The Professional Investigator of Holocaust

Those of us who approach survivors and seek to understand holocaust have a part in this process as well. The professions have a dismal record in relationship to holocaust. More often than not they have lent themselves to a denial of its brutalizing effects. In psychiatry, organically minded practitioners have tried to ignore the effects of massive psychic trauma by insisting that psychiatric disturbance stems primarily from biological inheritance. Some psychoanalysts have contributed to this charade by similarly limiting significant trauma to the first few years of life. Fortunately, sensitive and concerned psychiatric and psychoanalytic voices have strongly contested those assumptions. My impression nevertheless is that the healing professions as a whole maintain a distance from these issues that keeps them in considerable ignorance.

My work in Hiroshima convinced me of the immorality of claiming professional neutrality in the face of ultimate forms of destruction. And I have discussed ways in which my Vietnam work (see chapter 5) led to a re-examination of professionalism and the concept of "profession." We need a model of the professional that balances technique with carefully thought-out ethical principles. Here I am convinced that we are helped by a life-continuity paradigm (see chapter 1), as opposed to an instinctual one, in our efforts to understand survivors' sustained struggles with threats to physical and psychological existence, and to grasp the nature of the psychological universe created by holocaust.

We may be limited in our capacity to do so. But as professionals of any kind, as feeling human beings, we had better try. For only by understanding more of what happens to victims and survivors, and of what motivates victimizers, can we begin to imagine the future holocausts that threaten us, and thereby take steps to avoid them.

18

The Survivor as Creator

This is a companion piece to the previous essay. But it stresses less the pain than the creative possibilities of the survivor. In that sense it attempts to evoke a certain human resiliency, a capacity for regaining, and even enhancing, one's life-power after the most devastating survivor experience. I published it originally in the American Poetry Review, *and received a number of warm letters from poets who identified their work with aspects of the survivor I wrote about. My sense is that virtually all literature contains elements of the survivor experience, feelings close to those I have been describing. But the three authors I explore here—Camus, Grass, and Vonnegut—have not only been special for me but have lived out, and articulated, much of twentieth-century survival.*

WE ARE SURVIVORS in this age," Saul Bellow's Herzog writes in one of his unsent letters, "so theories of progress ill become us. . . . To realize that you are a survivor is a shock. At the realization of such election you feel like bursting into tears." Herzog goes on to suggest that from history's endless succession of wars, revolutions, and famines, "perhaps we, modern mankind (can it be!), have done the nearly impossible, namely, learned something."[1]

Exactly what mankind—and Herzog—may have learned remains ambiguous. But whatever it is, the survivor knows such lessons to be bound up with the dialectic between life and death, with "dying" and being "reborn." Much of this volume deals with what could be called a survivor ethos, one that has been thrust into special prominence by the holocausts of the twentieth century. The holocausts have imposed upon all of us the series of immersions into death that mark our existence. Our literature is beginning to make clear that we are survivors not only of holocausts that have already occurred but of those we imagine or anticipate as well.

Surviving holocaust makes one vulnerable to deformations, dislocations, and imaginative impediments. The hard-won knowledge of death that both defines and plagues one tends to be fragmentary at best and half articulate, yet is precious in the extreme. It takes shape from the survivor's struggle to grasp his or her experience of death immersion and render it significant. Only by such a formulation can the survivor cease to be immobilized by the death imprint, by death guilt, and by psychic numbing. That is, in struggling to reorder one's own experience, one can contribute to the general historical reordering so widely craved. And these psychological emanations—from past holocausts and their survivors, from anticipated holocausts and their imagined survivors—reach everyone. The painful wisdom of the survivor can, at least potentially, become universal wisdom.

What I am suggesting is that to touch death and then rejoin the living can be a source of insight and power, and that this is true not only for those exposed to holocaust, or to the death of parent or lover or friend, but also for those who have permitted themselves to experience fully the "end of an era," personal or historical.

In groping toward an understanding of the survivor's struggle for form, we turn naturally to the experience of the artist, and to what I shall broadly term the "literature of survival." The artist is a prophet of forms. And when forms are in radical disarray, the artist suggests patterns of reordering, even if in the process he or she may seem to contribute further to the disarray. For it is the artist's task, one insufficiently noted, to reveal the exquisite details of the experience of desymbolization.*

* Desymbolization, as I use the term, means breakdown of viable relationships with symbols and symbolic forms. It is an impairment in the "psychic action" of the "formative process," and tends, therefore, to be associated with severe manifestations of psychic numbing. Desymbolization is most extreme in schizophrenia.

Albert Camus: The Gentle Survivor

We could draw upon any of the arts, but a philosophical artist such as Albert Camus is especially revealing because he tells us what he is doing as he does it. While this approach can at moments subvert the subterranean source of the art, it has its own special historical value. Compared with some of his literary successors, Camus seems a relatively gentle kind of Second World War survivor. His Nobel Prize acceptance speech of 1957 is, among other things, a proclamation of a literature of survival that had already existed through the "twenty years of absolutely insane history" he spoke of (see chapter 17, page 235).

Camus saw as the "task" of his generation—or what we could call its survivor mission—that of "keeping the world from destroying itself." But much of the force of this public vision derived from personal experiences in the Resistance during the Second World War, as epitomized by the death of his comrade-in-arms, also a writer and close friend, René Leynaud. As Camus later wrote, "In thirty years of life no death reverberated within me like this one." He also spoke of "paltry excuses of those who remain alive," and, throughout his work, of his own "temptation of hatred [which] had to be overcome"; of his sense of loss ("that strength of love which has been taken from us forever"); and of his and his generation's struggle to construct "an art of living in times of catastrophe in order to be reborn by fighting openly against the death-instinct at work in our history."

Camus' stand on survival emerged from this particular way of applying his imagination—as evolved through his individual-psychological experience—to the holocausts of his time. In noting, as we did, Camus's sense of outrage and "scandal," we may say that the scandal includes not only these millions of deaths but the act of living on in the face of them. And though the scandal is diminished by ethical acts that render the deaths significant, and though Camus, as much as any writer, extolled life in his lyrical evocation of the Algerian sun and sea and its "invincible summer," he never lost his sense that there was something scandalous about having survived so much.

Caligula[2] is Camus' most vivid rendition of the absurd survivor, and one of the most important plays ever written about the aberrations of the survivor state. Formally the epitome of the just ruler (living by the principle that "the only mistake one makes in life is to cause others suffering"), Caligula is suddenly transformed by the death of his sister, Drusilla. He had loved her, and with "more than brotherly feelings," but what overwhelms him is neither guilt nor loss per se but the realization that the world lacks order or meaning, that "men die and they are not happy," and that "men weep because . . . the world's all wrong."

Caligula embarks upon a systematic course of victimization and murder, of rewarding evil and punishing good, and a general perversion of all values by which he and his subjects formerly lived. We can understand his actions as illustrating Rilke's principle that "killing is one of the forms of our wandering mourning." What Caligula mourns beyond even his sister is a lost bond with higher powers, a lost sense of immortality. He kills in order to achieve a new transcendence, convinced as he is that "there's only one way of getting even with the gods; all that's needed is to be as cruel as they." He wants what is unattainable—the omnipotence of *literal* immortality. He must continue to kill in order to perpetuate the illusion that he can obtain such immortality: "When I don't kill I feel alone." Hence his dying words, "I'm still alive!"

Camus explains Caligula's ways as being "unfaithful to mankind through fidelity to himself." This fidelity in rebellion against death and dislocation has in it a quest, however misdirected and pathological, to overcome the broken connection so intolerable to this kind of the absurd survivor. Caligula is not redeemed; but by revealing the most extreme consequences of the unformulated survivor state—the passage from the absurd to the omnipotent survivor—he carries us toward insight.

In *The Stranger*,[3] a single murder reveals a similar attempt to recover a sense of vitality. Meursault is incapable of mourning for his dead mother; he feels nothing and cannot "shed a single tear." When shortly afterward in a somewhat murky altercation he shoots an anonymous Arab, Camus is making a connection between impaired mourning and murderous violence. Meursault is brought to legal justice and condemned to death as much for his seeming inhumanity at his mother's funeral as for the crime itself.

In a dramatic scene with a priest in his death cell, Meursault angrily condemns the priest's clichés and unconvincing promises of immortality. In feeling himself, and imagining his mother to have felt, "on the brink of freedom, ready to start life all over again," Meursault realizes the absurd survivor's liberation in the face of death by means of what Camus calls "lucidity." For him lucidity means not only clarity, consciousness, and truth, but (as suggested by the word's Latin roots) a state of being luminous, fused with light, and thereby transcending the rote and prosaic without recourse to false gods. Yet this lucidity and (in Camus' words) "the extra life it involves" depend "not on man's will but on its contrary, which is death."

The book ends with a ringing defiance of all ethical hypocrisy: "For all to be accomplished, for me to feel less lonely, all that remained to hope was that on the day of my execution there would be a huge crowd of spectators and that they should greet me with howls of execration." In that sentence the absurd survivor becomes an insurgent.

The insurgent survivor is epitomized by Camus' two most celebrated heroes, the rebel and the plague physician. Camus meant his rebel[4] or insurgent survivor to be more radical than even a conventional revolutionary because he is more fundamentally critical, subversive, and formative. There is no revolution to be, once and for all, achieved; there is permanence only in questioning and insurgency. The insurgent survivor rebels, to be sure, against injustice, murder, and suffering—against victimization of any kind. But he also rebels, Camus tells us, against the core of human existence, the fact of death. His "rejection of death," however, is his "desire for immortality and for clarity." What he rejects, in other words, is meaningless or formless death; what he seeks through his rebellion is transcendence by means of ever-renewed human forms. "If nothing lasts, then nothing is justified," he reasons, so that "to fight against death amounts to claiming that life has a meaning, to fighting for order and for unity."

At bottom, then, the insurgent survivor is a form-seeker and a form-giver. His quest "to learn to live and to die, in order to be a man, to refuse to be a god," goes a step beyond absurdity into form. The insurgent seeks to re-establish a sense of immortality that is both biological and creative, and to do so through "the movement of life" and "its purest outburst." When Camus insists, "In the light the earth remains our first and last love," and that with living justice, "our brothers are breathing under the same sky" so that "there is born that strange joy which helps one live and die, and which we shall never again renounce to a later time"—he is presenting us with a survivor mission to live in autonomous connection rather than surrender ourselves to a totalistic vision of the future. He is making a plea for an immortality that is symbolic and fluid rather than literal and fixed.

As a giver of forms the insurgent survivor must perforce become a healer. Dr. Rieux, the central figure of *The Plague,*[5] is called upon to provide both medical and spiritual therapy. His antagonist is not only the plague itself but the more general evil the plague stands for—"the feeling of suffocation from which we all suffered and the atmosphere of dread and exile in which we lived." But knowledge and memories—rejection of illusion, connection with the past, and lucidity toward the present and future—count for much. And the survivor's special knowledge of death, and simple formulation of duty to life, provide rebellious courage and healing power.

The progression from first- to second-generation literature of survival is presaged in Camus' own shift (in such later works as *The Fall* and *The*

Renegade) from compassionate insurgency to acerbic misanthropy. It is the progression from Camus' searching irony to the outlandish mockery of Kurt Vonnegut and Günter Grass. Rather than bemoan our dislocation, this literature of mockery (a more accurate and comprehensive term, I believe, than "black humor") seizes that dislocation with ebullience and even joy. It extends the principle of gallows humor to society (or non-society) at large. Gallows humor mocks the death that awaits one and, in its combination of rebellion and laughter, at least suggests the existence of a more humane order. The literature of mockery views all of contemporary history—and perhaps humanity itself—as moribund if not already dead. Mockery then provides a kind of literary "wake": a vigil or "watch" over the dead social body prior to burial, a means of expressing anguish and of crying out against the cruelly haphazard gods of death and loss, but at the same time a form of libation and release, and at least in some cases a celebration of life in the midst of death.

We gravitate naturally to the mocking and mocked anti-hero who, whether a mere figure of our impotence or a man thrust into greatness despite himself, evokes not our cosmic order (as a tragic hero does) but our cosmic disorder.

In this literature, death and madness are respected; what is savagely mocked is the "sanity" of everyday life, which dissolves the significance both of death and of the human quest for immortality. The central point about mockery is that it *confronts* the phenomena involved, our situation, and ourselves.

In our age of madness, Warren Miller tells us in his novel *Looking for the General,*[6] madness itself becomes not only an expectation but a "duty": "I mean that: *duty*—of the same to pursue madness, to pursue, search, seek out, claim or beg for themselves a tiny portion of that manna, even the merest smudge of that magic dust, sweet pollen that clings to madness's bird-body, gilding feathers, touching breast's filmy down with its flowery gold powder." Madness is a duty, that is, not only because of the unacceptability of what passes for sanity but because the mad state itself provides a form of transcendence. The literature of mockery seems to be telling us that the "manna" or "magic dust" of madness may represent the liberating core of our survivor wisdom. Inevitably the literature of mockery is ambivalent toward its madness. William Carlos Williams's statement, "The pure products of America go crazy," could be interpreted to mean "are driven crazy and destroyed" or "become crazy as the only path to wisdom." Or to put the problem in the form of a question: If those we call "normal" are (according to wiser standards) really insane, does that mean that those we call "insane" are a source of knowledge and health?

Above all, madness becomes equated with a renaissance of fantasy and the rediscovery of the childlike wonder of play. There are German myths of the end or near-end of the world in which the only survivors are children, who re-create the world through play. Children's play provides the imaginative forms that constitute the evolving mind, and the psychic sense of life. But over the course of lived history, such play becomes a more grim business, suffused as it is with the sobering lessons of years of accompanying unplay. This unplay—with its mixture of injustice, unpleasantness, and necessity—enters prominently into a formulation of self and world that must forevermore accompany whatever playfulness is retained. The mocking survivor has a mixed memory, and memory is the essence of the survivor as creator. Again Herzog: "But I, with my memory—all the dead and the mad are in my custody, and I am the nemesis of the would-be forgotten."

Kurt Vonnegut: Duty-Dance with Death

Kurt Vonnegut identifies himself directly as a survivor of holocaust and brings a special kind of bite to the literature of mockery. His two great external themes are Dresden and Hiroshima. His more general themes are death-dealing stupidities carried out by human beings, and, beyond those (as he puts it in his introduction to *Slaughterhouse Five*), "plain old death." "Duty dance," part of the sub-subtitle of *Slaughterhouse Five,*[7] is an accurate description of Vonnegut's imaginative enterprise.

In *Mother Night,*[8] an earlier novel, Howard Cambell, as survivor of Nazism and much else, can only conclude, "All people are insane. They will do anything at any time, and God help anybody who looks for reasons." And in the same vein: "I've lost the knack of making sense. I speak gibberish to the civilized world, and it replies in kind." Here survivor wisdom lies in recognizing how impaired our post-holocaust formulations of the world really are, how lost we are in our "gibberish"—a message that, at least in Vonnegut's hands, becomes a powerful formulation of its own.

In *Cat's Cradle,*[9] Vonnegut directs his formative gibberish to Hiroshima. The life-giving force in this book, its mocking formulation, is "Bokononism" a collection of "bittersweet lies" put together by a black adventurer who finds himself cast adrift on and enchanted by the little Caribbean Isle of

San Lorenzo. There he "cynically and playfully invented a new religion." In a Bokononist poem, Vonnegut is specific about the principle of formative gibberish:

> Tiger got to hunt,
> Bird got to fly;
> Man got to sit and wonder, "Why, why, why?"
> Tiger got to sleep,
> Bird got to land;
> Man got to tell himself he understand.

But we have to turn to Vonnegut's great survivor novel, *Slaughterhouse Five*, for a sense of the exalted possibilities of mockery. *Slaughterhouse Five* is less about Dresden per se than it is about a state of mind evoked in Vonnegut by the destruction of that city. Vonnegut is therefore talking about war and holocaust, and about the human tendency to accelerate the arrival and demean the process of "plain old death." The novel is a survivor's effort to make sense—or anti-sense—of a world dominated by every variety of holocaust and every variety of numbing.

The key to the "telegraphic schizophrenic"—that is, the condensed-mad style and content of this book—is the recurrent phrase "So it goes." This is the Tralfamadorian shrug-commentary on all deaths, since the inhabitants of that planet believe that "when a person dies he only *appears* to die." Vonnegut uses the phrase all through the book with a combination of gaiety and terror, as a form of mocking witness to man's unfeeling murders, to his equally unfeeling survival of those murders, and to precisely the resignation the phrase suggests. "So it goes," then, unifies the diverse filmlike flashes that make up the book's sequence as Billy Pilgrim moves back and forth between his family and optometry office in Illium, New York, wartime Germany, various psychiatric hospitals, and the planet of Tralfamadore. For Billy himself is a kind of death guide for twentieth-century man.

Slaughterhouse Five is about feeling and not feeling, about remembering and not remembering, about looking and not looking back, about dying and not dying, about living and not living. Vonnegut is right there with Billy all through the book. He has Billy suggest, as "a good epitaph for Billy Pilgrim—and for me too. EVERYTHING WAS BEAUTIFUL, AND NOTHING HURT." The little tombstone containing the epitaph is that of Billy, Vonnegut, Nixon, all of us—the tombstone of all who half-live in our present age of numbing.

Günter Grass: Drumming the Grotesque

It is hard to say how much Vonnegut's work has been influenced by Grass's early classic in the post–Second World War literature of mockery, *The Tin Drum,*[10] but the two authors have a great deal spiritually in common. Instead of the clipped, bittersweet apocalypse in Vonnegut's work, Grass gives us an elaborately convoluted—one could even say, epic—form of the mocking grotesque.

The story is told, or rather drummed out, by an inmate who considers his mental hospital bed "a goal attained at last . . . my consolation." He is none other than Oskar Matzerath, dwarf drummer and literary original who, according to his stepmother (and first mistress) "don't know how to live and . . . don't know how to die." He is, however, a genius at surviving.

Oskar, again in the tradition of the literature of mockery, is both all-knowing and hopelessly regressive in his consuming urge to return to that hallowed place under the skirts of his potato-gathering grandmother. But his regression is always brilliantly in the service of subversion, so that on his third birthday he makes the fatal decision to grow no more. The key to Oskar's perennial survivals is his tin drum. The drum not only permits him to resist his impulse to scurry back to the womb but is also his means of recording his own history and history in general. The drum is incorruptible and resists Oskar's attempts to forget segments of his own past. Its most fundamental purpose is social and ethical:

> For it is not only demonstrations of a brown hue that I attacked with my drumming. Oskar huddled under the rostrum for Reds and Blacks, for Boy Scouts and Spinach Shirts, for Jehovah's Witnesses, the Kyffauser Bund, the Vegetarians, and the young Polish Fresh Air Movement. Whatever they might have to sing, trumpet, or proclaim, my drum knew better.

The drum "knew better" because its immortal vision transcends these ephemeral collectivities.

Grotesque form, visionary drum, and miraculous glass-shattering thus enable this diminutive mocking survivor to expose and outlast the absurd history normal adults have created. Oskar's survivals include not only the most extreme manifestations of absurd evil but of the human being's hypocritical and conventional attraction to that evil.

Grass concretizes the survivor ethos in Oskar's witnessing of individual deaths around him. Oskar's grandfather, his mother, and his mother's lover each die in ways that epitomize both the person and the epoch. Oskar's archetypal death encounter inevitably takes place with the demise of his father, Matzerath, who embodies all that Oskar despises but is himself caught up in. Matzerath dies by choking on his Nazi party badge. But Oskar concludes (with characteristic honesty) "that he [Oskar] had killed Matzerath deliberately," that Matzerath had choked both "on the Party" and "on me, his son," and that, in any case, he [Oskar] "was sick of dragging a father around with him all his life."

The themes of fatherlessness and father-son reversal—reminiscent of Sartre (for fatherlessness and the protean style, see chapter 1)—are partly a reflection of dislocation and moral inversion, partly a call to liberation. Oskar's father's funeral is the occasion for a "decision" to start growing again; and although for Oskar this leads to still greater deformation, we can see in the decision a rarely acknowledged side of the survivor ethos—the survivor's capacity to experience the death he has witnessed as a form of release and new beginning.

However undisinfectable life and death may be, however Oskar may appear to be unable to mourn his losses or find significance in the face of them, his gift of mockery keeps him nonetheless oriented toward the living. But Oskar's ultimate strength lies in his infinite flexibility. Our little hero, attaining near the end of the book a mad-grotesque form of maturity, can contemplate his future with protean exuberance: "Yet so many possibilities are open to a man of thirty."

The protean journey must include recurrent visits with terror and evil—with the Black Witch. Protean (contemporary) man (or woman) is pursued, to be sure, by terror and evil, by his own betrayals, and has no choice but to live in the memory and expectation of holocausts. But one can also know transcendence. For Oskar certain enduring objects and memories take on immortal qualities, including "the secret parts of a few women and young girls, my own pecker, the plastic watering can of the boy Jesus . . . my drumsticks, from my third birthday on . . . my umbilical cord, as I sat playing with it." The journey is precarious, replete with disaster, but also exuberant, open, and (here is the hope) endless.

Pornographic Confrontation

Grass's style of grotesquerie takes us directly to still another—in a way, ultimate—literature of survival—the pornographic confrontation. Involved here is the use of underground images, publicly forbidden but close enough to virtually everyone's inner life to be privately (or semi-privately) shared.

When Geoffrey Gorer first spoke of the "pornography of death," he referred to the contemporary habit of offering fantasies of extreme violence to mass audiences. Gorer saw this pornography as more or less pathological, arising from our unhealthy repression of death imagery, just as ordinary (sexual) pornography on a large scale reflects widespread sexual repression. Gorer's view is the psychoanalytic one: repressed ideas never disappear but re-emerge in harmful distorted form; therapy consists of uncovering that which has been repressed so that it can be dealt with in more conscious, rational ways. But if, as I believe, the problem is less repression of death than impairment in the general capacity to create viable forms around it, the pornography of death takes on a somewhat different function. It represents an exposé of our distorted views of death, an extreme rendition of our state of desymbolization. Pornography then becomes a means of revelation by excess. Through what Gabriel Marcel called the "provocative nudity of death," pornography may provide a necessary insight into our condition which is indispensable to, and ultimately inseparable from, the new forms for which we hunger.

Much of Norman Mailer's work is directed at this kind of pornographic confrontation. What may appear to be wallowing in violence can in fact be a form of exploring the excessive—the pornographic—dimensions of death. *An American Dream*[11] is a novel with a special concern with the death encounter not at all grasped by most of its critics. The book is an account of a survivor's experiential journey following his wartime killing of four Germans—an act that showed him equal to the death encounter but at the same time left him with a permanent death imprint, an awesome realization that "death was a creation more dangerous than life."

At moments Rojak (the central figure in the book) experiences a survivor's sense of having conquered death, but mostly he feels overwhelmed by death anxiety, by "a private kaleidoscope of death" that cannot be relieved by his theoretical insight (he is a teacher of existential psychology) that "magic, dread and the perception of death are the roots of all motivation." To still his anxiety, he challenges and courts death, becomes preoccupied with suicide and murder. Rojak's act of murdering his wife is an effort to overcome his own fear of extinction, stave off suicide, reassert his mastery over death, achieve in the act of murder a sense of transcendence, and absorb some of the immortal power of his wife's evil (later he has a fantasy of eating her flesh).

A key arena for pornographic confrontation is what is usually called the "theater of the absurd" but is better termed the "theater of the dead." One could speak here of Jean Genêt and Eugene Ionesco, of earlier influences of Antonin Artaud and Bertolt Brecht, and more recent developments of Jerzy Grotowski and the Living Theater. But I think the key figure for our time is Samuel Beckett. "The living are dead . . . and the dead live," a feeling expressed by Heinrich Böll's disintegrating artist-clown,[12] could well sum up Beckett's world. It is a dead universe, or rather a universe in which life has become so numbed as to be more dead than death.

One could draw upon any number of Beckett people from his plays or stories or musings, but he is most explicit in his play *Krapp's Last Tape.*[13] More than just an incongruous and pathetically humorous figure, Krapp is a man neither dead nor alive. What characterizes his existence is constant self-survival *and no more.*

The sixty-nine-year-old Krapp can live only through one old tape recording to which he continually returns, seeking out that moment of love described on it. But the thirty-nine-year-old Krapp on that tape had come to the same conclusion—the refrain of a lost youth, meaning lost life, expressed throughout the play, along with a denial that he would have it otherwise. The play ends with Krapp staring motionlessly before him and the tape running on "in silence." Beckett's pornographic confrontation is that of a special twentieth-century form of death in life, a form of total numbing in which mechanical recordings, echoing a series of arrivals, replace the act of living.

A common theme runs through Camus' gentility, Grass's grotesquerie, Vonnegut's death-dance, Tadeusz Borowski's unspeakable ironies (in his searing stories of Auschwitz, *This Way for the Gas, Ladies and Gentlemen*), Dr. Strangelove's nuclear insanity, and Beckett's death in life. They all tell us that civilization—human life itself—is threatened, dying, or dead: that we must recognize this death or near-death, pursue it, record it, enter into it, if we are to learn the truth about ourselves, if we are to live. This capacity for intimacy with (and knowledge of) death in the cause of renewed life is the survivor's special quality of imagination, his or her special wisdom. But how can that wisdom be shared? Can survivors be mentors to the world?

In connection with my Hiroshima work, for instance, I have been asked such questions as, How can you be at all certain that it will be useful? Couldn't it bring about further numbing? Or worse, encourage a large-scale shelter program in order to be properly prepared for nuclear war? Or, simply, so what?

My answer has to do with the human capacity to bring imagination to bear upon the unpalatable truths of our historical situation, to expand the limits of imagination on behalf of our survival. If one is to overcome psychic numbing, one must break out from the illusions supporting that numbing and begin to "imagine the real." One must learn to do what has heretofore not been possible for us: to imagine nuclear disaster.

Hiroshima's relationship to the outside world has mainly to do with the imagination. The gap between technology and imagination remains formidable, as is evident in the relative poverty of general creative response. Alain Resnais's film *Hiroshima Mon Amour* (1959), the novel *Black Rain* by Masuji Ibuse, the images conveyed by John Hersey in his pioneering journalistic pilgrimage, and my own psychological study have all had some effect in narrowing the imaginative gap.

The problem, then, is not only calling forth end-of-the-world imagery but in some degree mastering it, giving it a place in our aesthetic and moral imagination. It is not only futile to try, as much of the world does, to dismiss images of Hiroshima and Auschwitz from human consciousness, but the attempt deprives us of our own history, of what we are, and thereby blocks our imaginations and prevents us from creating new forms. We need Hiroshima and Auschwitz, as we need Vietnam and our everyday lives, in all of their horror, to deepen and free that imagination for the leaps it must make.

19

Art and the Imagery of Extinction

I wanted to include at least one example of the give-and-take of an interview. I chose this dialogue with Bonnie Marranca, a gifted young theater critic and editor, because she raised the right questions, and because theater and film have meant so much to me personally. Through family connections, I grew up close to what we used to call the "legitimate theater" and to a socially conscious strand of that wonderful American theater invention, the "musical comedy."

But the dialogue (arranged for publication in the Performing Arts Journal, *which Marranca edits) is less about theater as such than about the overall artistic problem of responding to and creating from imagery of the "end." In that sense, the theater and the arts in general would seem to have to take a special lurch toward nothingness, which is why Beckett's name figures prominently in the discussion.*

I have retained here a few statements similar to those made in other essays, because I wanted to apply them more broadly to art, literature, and theater. My explorations are all too fragmentary, at best suggestive of a few directions of possibility. But the artists themselves will have the important say on these matters; I will continue to learn from them, in ways that I hope can maintain the conversation.

Can you outline a particular kind of character, in film or theater, who offers a psychological profile of a person living under the threat of nuclear war and possible extinction?

I don't think the theater can be expected to have caught up with a "character of extinction," if there is such a character. The terrible problem for art is that an artist is asked to create a narrative or a set of symbols around our own collective and total demise. We resist the narrative, understandably, and it's a tough one to enter, artistically.

In my work I take three dimensions that you can roughly connect with postmodernism, or with our contemporary situation. The first is the breakdown of traditional symbols and of modern parallels or developments of those symbols; the second is the mass media revolution; and the third is imagery of extinction or threat of extinction. This last is the most difficult for art to confront, and I don't know if it's really been represented yet. But maybe the way art has begun to confront it in the theater and elsewhere has been through increasingly radical discontinuity.

You mean in terms of narrative?

Yes, in narrative that hardly exists or is circular or recurrent rather than continuous or linear; in terms of characters who feel cut off from a past or future. If you're cut off from a future, your past is threatened also.

I don't know whether I could suggest the particular kind of character because it's always difficult to figure which came first and what, in effect, people are reacting to. But I think there are some manifestations of new feelings and responses in the theater. For example, take a piece like Satyagraha, *the opera that Philip Glass and Connie De Jong created, also the ACT company from Buffalo under Joseph Dunn, and some of Meredith Monk's work. I think these are examples of a new expressionism or a holistic approach to theater. Some of the expressionistic work we're seeing now could be a different kind of spiritualism. And it's not the same as German expressionism.*

Well, I wrote a piece a few years ago called *Survivor as Creator* in which I took up three writers: Camus, Vonnegut, and Grass. Each saw himself as a survivor, and creatively, a survivor has to imagine that death encounter in order to create past it, to stay in it and use it, yet move beyond it. There the artist and the writer parallel and anticipate some of the thinking and politics necessary to stem the nuclear threat. You must imagine what the end of the world is, as Jonathan Schell tries to do in his book *The Fate of the Earth,* in order to prevent it.

For me, then, the problem is to get a handle on this, and the psychological handle is death and the continuity of life and the larger symbolization of human connectedness, or the "symbolization of immortality." So the theater has the task of expressing, symbolizing, and representing how, in the face of or threat of extinction, one imagines human continuity. Perhaps that spiritual theater or expressive theater you mention is one way of imagining it.

Or turning away from it—

Something in terms of feeling is happening that's important—after the decades of numbing that followed the Second World War, the numbing is beginning to break down. That's got to affect the theater, too. It's a breakdown of the kind of collective arrangement, collusion, and "not-feeling"—especially not feeling what happens at the other end of the weapon, and especially what might happen to us. People are afraid. When I talk to audiences now, kids at colleges are frightened, sometimes at secondary schools, and ordinary audiences. The polls show that most Americans fear and even expect a nuclear war in the not too distant future. That's new. There's a movement now toward awareness or a shift in consciousness, which is quite hopeful.

One of the things you mention in The Life of the Self *is a human hunger for an evolutionary leap, that it will produce a new kind of art. Do you see a manifestation of this new art?*

Not really. Now I question what I wrote. Yes, there's an appropriate moment where an evolutionary leap would be parallel to the technological leap, and perhaps that evolutionary leap would be parallel also to this incredible demand on artists and on all of us that we imagine the end of the world. People have been thinking of the end of the world for a long time. Every kind of millennial imagery and major religion represents the end of the world in some way, but there's a distinction between that millennial imagery where it fits into a system of belief and structure, and millennial imagery that has to do with the nuclear holocaust. In Christian religion, God will punish all sinners and there'll be a judgment day after which everything will begin again. Not so, now, when it's a matter of doing ourselves in with our own tools in an absolutely meaningless way.

For an artist, that kind of end of the world is a very demanding artistic requirement, so we can't expect artists to move suddenly into an evolutionary leap any more than anyone else can. Incidentally, A. Alvarez in his book on suicide claims that recent increased incidence of suicide among artists—and he means writers and painters and artists broadly defined—has to do with reaching a point where it's impossible to find meaning or words that express life's continuity in the face of extinction. He draws upon my Hiroshima work to make this argument. Therefore artists shout more loudly or more desperately but can't get through with the words or the images they need, and that's why they become desperate.

But isn't there another side of the issue: more and more people wanting to be artists? I don't mean necessarily that the average person wants to drop his or her career to become a painter or a writer. But you do find people—and I find them often outside of the city—taking up painting or creative writing, and it's become a major involvement. It's a much more philosophical impulse than, say, a leisure-time activity.

If meaning is harder and harder to come by, and the ordinary symbolic structures are crumbling, they're burdensome rather than liberating. One can feel the increasing appeal of art because art is constantly trying to resymbolize, express symbols; and probably art does thrive, or at least increase its energy, where there is a threat to the existing structure. For instance, there was the extraordinary resurgence of German literature, film, and theater after the Second World War.

The problem is what artists do when becoming artists, and maybe it's only a certain extremely brave and talented vanguard that really moved toward this kind of abyss, or challenged it, and then faced the kinds of issues that Alvarez writes about, or that I write about, too. Or, there's a sense in which there's absolutely nothing you or I or any artist encounters in everyday life or art that's totally caused by nuclear weapons or the threat of extinction, because we still have our work and our struggles with our love lives, our children and our parents and our marriages and friends. On the other hand, there is nothing in our lives that is not affected by the threat of extinction. I guess it's that double life we all live in which the artist has to create. And I think that's quite possible.

In the 1970s there were a lot of plays on the subjects of cancer and death, plays such as The Shadow Box, Whose Life Is It Anyway?, *and* Wings. *We've also seen simultaneously disaster films and an exceptional amount of violence. Would you say that, while these things are not about the nuclear-power issue, they are manifestations of paranoia about destruction and death?*

Absolutely. As soon as you have the threat of imagery of extinction, death and life are out of kilter, and that's why I called a recent book *The Broken Connection:* the connection between the two is radically threatened. That feeds back into what Vonnegut calls "plain old death." We're creatures of our own history and so we're influenced in what we think and study about. This is true in all of the arts, with a great focus on death in the 1960s and 1970s, and the nuclear threat creates or contributes to that preoccupation with death.

America has been notable in repressing death and maybe reaching the most radical form of denial of death that any culture has ever "achieved." So there's a kind of rebound reaction here along with the nuclear threat and some other influences, with a great sense in America that it's now discovered death. Twenty years ago nobody in America ever talked about death because as a young culture we're not supposed to die. It's Europeans and Asians who die. All of a sudden Americans are talking about nothing but death, it's the way Americans embrace things. But with that—again that's the seeming trivialization of the mass media—something happens, some kind of struggle with death and with pain that has been taking place in America is expressed. The plays you mentioned reflected that. They can go just so far, though, can't they?

Because they drift into sentimentality. And they create a vogue for certain kinds of death plays or cancer plays, and young playwrights follow the lead—and then there are a rash of plays on these topics. I'm more interested in the shape of "character" and how that can change. For example, at the turn of the century, and in the 1920s and 1930s, there was a certain type of character, the hysterical woman. You see this in Artaud, in Witkiewicz, Strindberg, Musil, to name a few. Now that kind of Freudian character doesn't exist. Except for some remnants, say, in Tennessee Williams and others. I want to pin you down and see if you can create a model of the contemporary character.

The hysterical character you're talking about began to disappear twenty or thirty years ago. To have a hysterical character you need a whole life pattern, a full individual. Even if that woman or man has gone a little berserk, it's still a life that's relatively intact and has a beginning and a middle and an end, or a sequence. We don't have that now. Freud believed in reason and in cause and effect, and in a linear sequence to lives, and of course we still live around those principles. But here I think art does move ahead of everyday life, and has, in contemporary theater and films.

There's a kind of transition between Freud and proteanism, shape-shifting, multiple selves without a linear process, that's more representative of a contemporary character. And in between somewhere as a transitional or connecting figure is the character of identity struggle. You find them in Arthur Miller and Williams, for example, some of the American playwrights who are transitional, Freudian in their influence, but they're also a little post-Freudian in no longer portraying straight neurosis. Strindberg is straight neurosis with hysteria or whatever, but with Williams and Miller it's a lot about identity and confusion and who one is. That isn't the question Freud asked. That's the question Erik Erikson asks. Freud asked, What does one do with one's instinctual drives, and how does one tame them and become human or live a human life? Erikson asks, How does one maintain a sense of sameness over incredibly shifting environments and themes and influences? That's the question Williams and Miller and a lot of other playwrights are asking. The protean or postmodern question is perhaps, How does one maintain a sense of vitality and life-continuity in the face of the threat of extinction, and in the face of the breakdown of all the symbols by which our lives are organized?

Didn't absurdism dramatize those feelings in the postwar period, with playwrights like Beckett, Adamov, and Ionesco?

Beckett is very much asking the question of identity, but he does it beyond identity, he's very much in the realm of extinction. Beckett's radically constricted characters accentuate by contrast the richness of life. I take from Beckett not a positive message, that would be putting it too strongly, but a great imaginative vision that is very much touched by extinction, but is a little bit beyond it. Beckett is the best example still of a theater that does something with extinction. He's the only one I can think of who we can really talk about as having a profound sense of the imagery of extinction or death in life, yet preserving that notion of continuity. You mentioned Ionesco. He certainly explores and plays with some of these issues, he's a little more concrete. He talks and writes in his journals about the threat to life continuity, but he doesn't transmute them as powerfully as Beckett, and his plays are more limited or cerebral. Maybe that's why when we read and see Beckett he does something for us that nobody else does, because he has really immersed himself in this ultimate image of extinction and come up from it.

In an interview we published with Susan Sontag around 1977 or so, she mentioned something Joe Chaikin had said about Beckett, which is that the problem for Beckett is what to do the next minute. It's a profound, concise statement. That's not the problem in Ibsen, if you know what I mean.

Ibsen assumed that a life would be led and that it would reach its conclusion, that there would be old age unless there was some kind of tragedy.

But we begin to see Beckett's vision in Chekhov, whose sentimental side is, unfortunately, what is stressed in most productions, and yet he dramatizes broken conversation, society falling apart, inertia.

With Chekhov, yes, society is falling apart and his relationship to time takes a new direction. Chekhov is not worried about what happens the next moment. He's worred about what you do now in your life when all the fundamental structures no longer pertain. Part of the power of Chekhov is that, along with the symbols and values breaking down, there's an odd timelessness created because there are no meaningful actions to interrupt the flow of time. Chekhov's characters try desperately to carry out meaningful actions, but they never quite succeed. I don't know of another playwright who gives us that odd suspension of time, or timelessness, because something that is supposed to happen never does and never can happen because people are not hooked into time in a meaningful way.

The question of time is interesting. During the 1960s, a lot of the experimentation in theater had to do with space. I felt it coming that at some point in the last five years or so there would be a switch to time and to narration. In fact, with the rise of autobiography and more interest in writing as a craft, the theater is moving again toward narration and use of writers, back toward dealing with time. I think we've gone through our experimental theater period when there was an attempt to control the environment or space.

If there is a return in the theater to the writer and the experience of time, it might partly parallel the return in painting to the figure, but if it's to be at all powerful, it's got to do that along with retaining considerable doubt and absurdity or worse, some of the influence of extinction. One thing that is crucial to this, both predating but reinforced by the threat of extinction, is the use of absurdity, and then more intense developments of absurdity in the form of extreme mockery.

As opposed to satire, or do you mean the grotesque?

The grotesque has always been with us, and that has to do with the threat of death and the threat of unacceptable death. Maybe the grotesque is especially a modern genre, but it's still not new. Irony requires a strong sense of self because it must reflect on itself in order to be ironic. Absurdity slips off that a little bit, and a lot of theater and modern art, particularly contemporary art, has to do with a kind of absurdity that I think has to do with death. Mockery is absurdity with a lot of doubt about the self. When you mock something, you take a look at someone else's self or claim to a self and do something with it. You're not clear about your own self, you're not self-observing in the way that genuine irony is. If there's to be a return to more formal elements of the theater, it has to have some of that edge of mockery, absurdity, doubt about the flow of time along with a reinstatement of it.

There's been a resurgence in comedy, not only in the theater world but also in the art world. There have been a lot of stand-up comedy people, a renewed interest in the clown performer, and the New Museum recently had a show on humor in art. It's often more like television comedy, only a bit more arch. Nevertheless, it's comedy, and comedy is classically considered a form about self-survival or about limited achievement, as opposed to tragedy, which is about unlimited goals. When you think about popular, contemporary playwrights, you think of someone like Christopher Durang who's mocking Catholicism and bourgeois family life. Or, in film, you think about someone like Woody Allen, whose work exemplifies the humor of disjointed, contemporary characters on the edge. Would you agree?

Yes. Woody Allen is a good example. He is constantly self-absorbed, he's worried about his body and what it does or doesn't look like and what it will or won't do, and his precious little sense of self in this world in which the self takes such a beating. But underneath that, what gives Allen power is the more primal fear of coming apart, disintegrating. And the way of evoking humor, quite wonderfully at times, humor and connection, because he does, I think, rather touchingly, portray love. *Annie Hall* is a good example in which the contemporary sense in all of us of falling apart is embodied by Allen, and he moves into and through it, and beyond into a self-mocking rendition of it. The self-mockery is central—obviously, it's Jewishness universalized—and then beyond into something like love. *Annie Hall* does say something about love; if not permanently or enduringly or perfectly, love is still possible in the face of this threat of disintegration.

Do you watch much television?

My television is limited to special programs, sports and news, and occasional pornography. From what I've seen I guess there's a lot more death and an extremity in comedy-situational dramas and soap operas. Soap operas are a lot more serious and have a lot of death, mourning, fear, neurosis, and trouble in them. They're struggling with a mass cultural rendition of what we've been talking about, and that's difficult.

In discussions about violence on television, I find myself a little reserved. Most television violence is very exploitative, horrible, and harmful psychologically. The trouble is that people need some kind of rendition of violence in order to register and reflect the threats as well as the inner violence they're feeling, in order to avoid recourse to actual violence.

In The Broken Connection *you quote Franz Fanon, who talked about the "shared violence" that a culture goes through providing "therapeutic knowledge." What you're saying is that an audience, or American audiences who watch television, need to go through this violence to express what they cannot do in reality. Do you mean psychologically or physically?*

Well, psychologically, and creatively, perhaps, touching on the actuality of violence. It's a problem of art, though, because nobody would want to prohibit any rendition of violence in any art form. The problem is it's really bad art, so the violence becomes exploitative, and I think violence is the issue where good art and bad art make such a profound difference.

Did you see Route 1 & 9? *It's a brilliant piece, and the only one in years that really divided an audience. It's about nihilism and images of death and life, and social violence. . . . You've written on the Living Theatre—do you think their work is useful violence?*

I think it has been. I guess something like the Living Theatre finds a metier, works in it, then loses it. In those years it had something to say about violence—the late 1960s—and it did connect violence in our lives with some kind of transmuting process of the theater. The moralistic approach to the question of violence flattens it, and reduces it to a simple cultural good and evil, and misses the whole point.

A good example of the border of this in film is the *Dr. Strangelove* theme. It's very literal, it's about nuclear weapons, but consider the end of that film where the pilot goes roaring down with the bomb, straddling it like a horse and yodeling in a great expression of triumph. It's a brilliant mockery of the whole nuclear madness; on the other hand, there is more than a suggestion of a kind of ultimate nuclear high—going down with the bomb. And that's attractive to some people.

Isn't this what you refer to as "nuclearism"?

Yes, and in the book I did with Richard Falk, *Indefensible Weapons,* I have a whole section on what I call "nuclear fundamentalism." I take this up again as an ultimate nuclear "high," but nuclearism is the ultimate fundamentalism in regard to the weapon. There are a lot of people seeking "high" states through fundamentalist religious or political movements, and I think they have a fairly direct relationship to nuclear threat.

In his In Search of the Primitive, *Stanley Diamond talks about the problem of violence in contemporary culture, that unlike tribal times we don't have rituals to exorcise this lingering need for violence.*

Violence in my theory—I develop this in *The Broken Connection*—all violence probably, and this is the irony of violence, is in the service of more life. "More life" is a phrase used by Ernest Becker. There's a search for vitality behind the expression of violence. For instance, in initiation rites, which can be quite violent, with scarification or other assaults on the body, violence is in the service of a death and rebirth ritual—initiation. That channels tremendous anger, rage, and fear and transmutes their energy into some sort of adult constructive work or pastime, like hunting, or whatever adults do in a particular society, and adult rules and rituals around which the society is built. The theater doesn't have sufficient power in our culture to be an initiation rite, but I think people can experience through powerful theater something parallel to that.

In the last fifteen years or so there's been a strong movement toward what Richard Schechner and Victor Turner, among others, refer to as "interculturalism": it brings social anthropology into theater, creating a kind of global theater field in which all communication is seen as one kind of social drama or another. There's been a lot of talk in all this about shamanism, ritual, healing, and other rites. I think there's a significant need among many theater people in the world to turn away from theater in the conventional sense while at the same time viewing all human activity as a theatrical paradigm.

That has parallels with what I would call an experiential mode. When it is strong, it looks for premodern truths and premodern sources of psychological power. Also, this gets complicated. Take the figure of the shaman and its many-sidedness. The shaman is a key figure both for premodern human power and power over death, which is what a shaman had as a precursor of the physician and as a kind of priest. The shaman is a figure of life power and of death power. He or she is a kind of ideal figure to go back to because shamans touch upon magic and that life/death axis. But I find myself now confronting the negative side of shamanism—my work with Nazi doctors and the shamanistic legacy is what the Nazis called upon in a murderous way to enlist doctors in the killing process—and probably some of the interest of the theater in anthropology and shamanistic ritual has to include its murderous capacity or the murderous or more negative use of magic, though the premodern shaman could never begin to approach the modern physician enlisted by Hitler.

I think that when the future is threatened, one reaches backward, and rightly so. I speak of the mode of restoration that can be a form of reaction or a reactionary mode. Reactionary—if you try to restore a past of perfect harmony that never was, something like the Moral Majority. On the other hand, you do need elements of restoration. You've got to look back and see what the shaman really was like and then combine this with very contemporary motifs where you feel some fundamental threat to human continuity, so it makes sense.

Often what they're doing really goes way beyond art; it's more a way of life, really, and it seems almost religious. What Grotowski is doing is also beyond any expression of art. The reports of his rituals in the woods or his theater of sources sound a lot like what I remember in the 1960s—"T" groups and retreats and group encounters. What is problematic about some of these manifestations is the authoritarian male figure involved in all of this—the guru aspect.

That reminds me, certain elements of the late 1960s and early 1970s had a tyrannical authoritarian component and expressed that totalistic component in the name of liberation. It usually had to do with a demand to liberate the body, and certain rituals and arrangements of the group were immediately and totally legislated by the leader. I have an aversion to that—how can I describe it?—an allergy to any kind of totalism. What we're also talking about is a severing of the experiments of the self from what we consider theater, from the discipline of creative performance, from the discipline of creating an experience that can be shared by an audience and that has some relationship to a tradition.

Since you mention it, there is a trend to do performances without spectators. Alan Kaprow has done this kind of work in California, and this is what Grotowski is doing now, and sometimes Barba. It's an attractive idea to a lot of people. This boundary between the spectator and the performer is largely breaking down, and who knows where it's going to go? My feeling is that those people interested in linking cultural anthropology to theater, while often meaning well, assume too many universalities for the audience and the artist. I question the feelings and the assumptions they have about the theatrical experience. There is something too ordered in the anthropological view of the community, and contemporary society is not like that.

One can have a kind of retrospective wisdom. It's hard to make a judgment of how much that tradition is being struggled against and how much it's been abandoned, and it is a critic's own kind of personal judgment about it. I would sense that the anthropological theater has lots of possibilities, but it just depends on what one is doing, and it has a responsibility to the tradition of the theater even, and especially, as it breaks off from it. You can make your most extraordinary innovation by being grounded to some degree in your tradition.

Can you apply the notion of being "grounded in tradition" to the ability of today's artists to use successfully the imagery of death that's all around us, to turn it into life-generating imagery?

Yes. I think that people seek discipline—you can't impose classical authority on them anymore because even mentorship and discipleship, or learning and teaching, have different dimensions now. But one needs rigorous teaching and learning still. You can't be grounded in the theater or in any other art form without a period of real study. It requires a disciplined exposure toward what is known and what has been learned over decades and centuries in the theater. Then, when you have that—as a sensitive writer, director, or performer in the theater—you can connect that grounding and relate it to life/death issues that are imposed upon us. Grounding can give one the strength and courage and innovative potential to immerse oneself in the terrifying imagery of extinction and death-haunted issues that we have to face.

What kind of theater then do you envision that faces these issues?

A theater with elements of a struggle back toward and forward from ritual. A theater that struggles with nothingness and beyond and that has to be post-Beckett. It's hard to be influenced by Beckett without being drowned by him. A theater that is concerned with death but not narrowly and not necessarily concretely, but with what death symbolizes, and with different forms and dimensions of death and its grotesquerie but that transcends it. A theater that can imagine the end of the world and create beyond that.

A theater then that can imagine the end of the world but that also believes in tomorrow.

Exactly. Therefore it's a theater of faith. It can be a religious faith or a kind of secular faith—it has to be for many of us—but you require faith, and faith is something that always goes beyond evidence, but not totally without evidence, in the idea of a human future. But, in order for the faith to be powerful, it really has to immerse itself into precisely what threatens the human future, but it's got to do that in its own way, and that way is hard to come by.

Do you think that, because theater is built on the notion of representation, it has a special power to help an audience go through a catharsis—to go through that way in the experience of the performers?

For instance, Joanne Akalaitis's *Dead End Kids* is a relatively more focused work about the nuclear and radiation issue. It's the most successful play on that issue because it uses a lot of contemporary imagination, very protean in spirit, it's death-haunted but mocking while joyous and humorous, with a lot of gallows humor, which to me is a great plus. Humor is liberating, deepening, pedagogic in the best sense; a theater without humor at all is worthless. The more threatening and serious things get, the more humor is needed. There are different kinds of humor, and of course it's the quality of the humor that's important. If you only stay in the death immersion without the humor, you're in some degree perhaps getting pornographic.

Joe Chaikin always seems able to combine death and humor in his work. But he is out of fashion now with audiences who are more used to highly imagistic or technological work. The thing he provides that no one else involved in group work does is the evocation of real emotion, and he's always been able to do that. That's the problem some people have with Chaikin. They're not used to seeing genuine sentiment anymore.

Yes, he seemed to be in his earlier work, and probably is now, too, on the edge. The issue of emotion becomes very important. Another way of putting it is, emotion is a form and you need formed feeling in the theater. Experiments in the late 1960s, 1970s, and some today, too, have difficulty giving form to feeling and therefore giving it depth, and feeling becomes all too forgettable, or transient. Perhaps a man like Beckett is committed because his way as an artist can be taken as a commitment to the world. That means stepping over a line in which one relates one's life to dealing with the world in some important way, as opposed to simply stepping back from it. And that may be an issue for the theater from now into the future, I don't know.

I think it's a kind of Sartre-like drama, which you talked about, a special kind of theater of commitment, of ethics.

But now the Sartre-like question has to be altered. Yes, it's a similar question but it's already a different time, because it's infused with extinction, which gives it a kind of mixture of terror and amorphousness, and a greater imaginative requirement. It gives it a more wild and extreme dimension. The theater can't shy away from that either, but that grounding I spoke of may give it the freedom to be wild or extreme.

But, dealing specifically with death imagery, it's beyond humor, it's beyond the comic wildness, say, of an Innaurato or a Durang, but actually dealing with death and felt emotions, getting back really to a classical drama.

It may be possible that one can embody the nature of nuclear threat in other metaphors. The limitless symbolizing capacities of the human mind are the same source of either dooming us or saving us. It's that same gray matter that constantly re-creates and symbolizes, and it's very hard to imagine how to subsume human extinction to some artistic or theatrical metaphor. The art generally suffers, and the theater suffers in the effort, as you know. It needn't literally be a death-haunted play about nuclear weapons or about actual death and destructiveness.

There has been a school of theater, an extreme kind of realism primarily by French and German writers, the "theater of everyday life." Perhaps even in some cases with those kinds of plays the attention to detail is more of an involvement in the life process.

Yes, it could be, and it's the power of realism of a certain kind. And any worthwhile realism, so-called, or focus on everyday life has to be touched by madness and the imagery of our time.

It will be interesting to see if we go back into a period more like absurdism or like the period between the wars when there was the greatest experimentation, and perhaps some of the strongest questioning of representation in the theater. But the most recent movements have been realism, back to naturalism—but a kind of flat, stylized naturalism without the heavy psychology. Kroetz, Botho Strauss, David Storey, some of the early Edward Bond is like this. It hasn't been a movement that's influential here because Americans are more into the psychological factor of character and less formalistic and artificial dramatic techniques of stylization. Part of that has to do with the lack of class consciousness, I think.

If the realism is too bound to a kind of old-fashioned version of itself, then the theater is holding on tightly against the threatening images. But art can't follow rules, it sometimes has to be antihistorical. And in my terms some of this realism would be moving back into a restorationist mode almost with a vengeance, almost with a caricature, and it may have to abandon that. Something will be learned in the process.

At a time now, when people are moving more and more toward art because that kind of experience fills some void in their lives, I think the culture is moving toward seeing itself as spectacle, in terms of seeing its citizens as performers in a way. The media has caused this to a certain extent, but I think it's also a human development. Maybe now we can begin to discover again what it means to go into the theater and go through certain experiences as a culture, which is what live actors should do to live audiences.

I think so, too. An awful lot of people are now "imagining the real," in Buber's phrase. The "real" is the threat of nuclear holocaust in the most extreme way. It's a terribly demanding and difficult thing to imagine. But with more and more people forced into making that imaginative effort and never fully organized in an orderly way, that means more and more people are open to art in the best sense, art that has the courage to do something like that.

The fact that this numbing could break down is what I take to be a significant beginning shift in consciousness. It's what I call a movement from a fragmentary awareness to a struggle for formed awareness. The struggle has two sides: one, cognizance of actual danger, being wary; and the other, awareness in the way that theater and artists and visionaries have always understood it, the sense of special insight or vision. There's a struggle for awareness on both of these levels that's more widespread in the culture now, and that I think enhances the possibility of a theater that can say something. Because the theater becomes part of this awareness, of this dreadful but possible moment in our culture, it can also have an audience to join in that process.

20

Toward a Nuclear Age Ethos

The ten principles I enumerate in this chapter emerged from various talks I have given before a variety of audiences, mostly either on campuses or under sponsorship of the doctors' movement. They emerge also from personal struggles and are another example of my sense of the inseparability of the psychological from the moral. The principles seem to me very simple and obvious; they have perhaps become even more ordinary—because more broadly accepted—since I first articulated them during the early 1980s. A more prudent man would reduce the number to nine or extend them to eleven, so as not to be accused of listening to voices from on high. Actually I have heard a few voices, but not from on high. Anyway, I stick to the ten.

WE ARE in the midst of a significant but tortured shift in consciousness concerning the nuclear threat. At precisely such a time we would do well to consider what might be an appropriate set of convictions—appropriate psychologically and in terms of life enhancement. The ten principles

I wish to elaborate are simple ones, already adopted by a growing number of people.

1. *We face a new dimension of destruction—not a matter of disaster or even of a war—but rather of an end: an end to human civilization and perhaps humankind.*

This concept violates our ingrained mental constructs concerning human continuity: though we can imagine particular cultures being impaired or even destroyed, we expect humankind to heal itself sufficiently to survive. But the findings of a possible nuclear-winter effect concretize the idea of a nuclear end, and, however grim, serve the imagination in the difficult task of looking into the abyss in order to see beyond it.

2. *We reject that nuclear end. We commit ourselves to the flow and continuity of human life and to the products of the human imagination.*

We find little solace, for instance, in the idea of a "divine spirit" or a "Buddha mind" continuing after a nuclear war. However sublime these images, they are expressions of the human imagination. Theologians of all religions must question the morality of asserting any principle of spiritual survival in the event of the annihilation of humankind.

To reject the nuclear end, we need to experience the nurturing vibrations and affirmations of everyday human life. To contribute to maintaining the world, we need to affirm our connection with that which has gone on before and that which will go on after what we know to be our finite individual life span.

3. *We either survive or die as a species. Nuclear weapons create a universally shared fate—a technologically imposed unity of all humankind.*

I have described this message of shared fate as applying both to individuals and nations, especially the two superpowers. The United States and the Soviet Union are simultaneously terrorists and hostages. As in the case of an airplane hijacked in flight, the terrorist's use of his or her own weaponry will kill that terrorist as certainly as it will any hostages.

This shared fate highlights as nothing else does the pragmatic dimension of nuclear-weapons issues and of survival itself. At the same time it can throw us back on not just individual but collective humanity, on an evolving ethic of mutual responsibility, and help disseminate psychological and moral currents contributing to the evolution of a species self (see chapter 9). As pragmatism and moral imagination combine, the United States and the Soviet Union may be able to think less in terms of "the enemy"—the real enemy to both is nuclear extinction—and more in terms of committed partnership in survival.

4. *We believe that collective human power can bring about change, awareness, and ultimately human survival.*

If one looks only at expanding nuclear stockpiles and at the dubious mutual assumptions supporting that buildup, the image of collective human power on behalf of survival grows dim indeed. But, on the other hand, there has been an extraordinary and unanticipated recent shift in world consciousness to revulsion toward nuclear weapons, awareness of their destructive power, and demand for their radical reduction. This protest is a form of collective human rights: the right not to be extinguished as a species, the right to bring up children without nuclear fear and futurelessness, and the right to reclaim from the nuclear priesthood—those who make decisions of ultimate life-and-death consequence—a reasonable degree of control over one's own destiny, which in the United States could be thought of as a return to Jeffersonian democratic principles.

This struggle incorporates different dimensions of the human repertoire. It requires a capacity for reflection and rigorous thought to produce new ideas for coping with unprecedented combinations of threat. It requires passion, which may include some of the emotions of the traditional warrior spirit transmuted into militant actions against the nuclear threat and on behalf of nonviolence and human survival. Above all, a spirit of healing is required, to draw an ever-broadening spectrum of people into the struggle and to keep attitudes and actions commensurate with life-enhancing goals.

The human insistence upon imagining a future gives powerful psychobiological support to this protest. Indeed, precisely the capacity to do so contributed centrally to the evolutionary emergence of our species. Imagining a future was crucial to our becoming human and continues to prod us toward efforts to maintain collective human life.

We need be neither optimistic nor pessimistic about that human future; rather, we must hope. Hope means a sense of possibility and includes desire, anticipation, and vitality. It is a psychological necessity and a theological virtue, a state that must itself be nurtured, shared, mutually enhanced.

5. We believe that a key to that life power lies in the renunciation of nuclearism—of the dependency upon, and even worship of, nuclear weapons.

Psychologically, as we have seen, nuclearism includes so great an attachment to the weapons as to count on them for safety or "security"; for solving strategic, political, and social dilemmas; even for keeping the world going. It is the ultimate human irony that we embrace our potential agents of extinction as a means of maintaining human life.

Nuclearism is an ideology that requires a series of deadly illusions concerning control and limit, preparation, protection, and recovery. Nuclearism derives from both our general tendency to demand the "technological fix" in situations requiring human solutions and even more importantly from the awesome power of ultimate destruction the weapons actually possess. The tendency of strong advocates of nuclearism to reverse themselves at the moment of retirement (see pages 25–26) indicates the strength of institutional nuclearism.

A consequence of the expanding public awareness of the destructive power of nuclear weapons, buttressed by the findings of nuclear winter, is a profound contradiction affecting both policy and mind-set of nuclear strategists. While acknowledging that any nuclear exchange is likely to produce a nuclear end with neither victory nor survival, these strategists have structured the nuclear-weapons buildup to include a nuclear war-fighting option. Many strategists struggle with this inner contradiction, as the research of Steven Kull demonstrates.[1] Given the world-destroying power of existing stockpiles, strategists recognize claims of survivability or of the need for added nuclear weaponry as illusory, and yet may publicly defend those very illusions. Kull points out that they may do so because they think the illusions are required by either the American people or by the Soviet leaders, or by both. But I believe that there may be a less rational psychological process involved: the inner division of doubling (see chapter 14).

Generally, however, the rejection of nuclearism and recognition of its dangers have become widespread. Ordinary people in both nuclear superpowers reject, and indeed consider absurd, the nuclear illusion promulgated by their governments. To renounce nuclearism is to renounce the nuclear illusion and to recognize nuclear weapons as instruments of genocide and that the continuity of human life—hope itself—lies only in prevention.

6. We believe in the possibility of a world without nuclear weapons—a world that directs its energies toward more humane goals and looks to more genuine human security.

To be sure, from the standpoint of the present situation, this conviction sounds utopian. But as a goal to be achieved gradually and incrementally it is more realistic than the present course. That goal, and the general process by which it can be achieved, must first be agreed upon so that nuclear arms control or disarmament is not viewed as a sporadic, disorganized process controlled by "bargaining chips" or "positions of strength." The initial agreement could become part of a continuous process in which there is a sequence of agreed-upon steps toward nuclear disarmament, with very active third-party participation, and continuous monitoring and exchange of information. The nuclear superpowers and the various participating governments could then have a much better chance of exerting pressure on other actual or potential possessors of nuclear weapons to become involved in a similar process. The stance we must take, then, includes both an address to our immediate nuclear-weapons-dominated world and the elaboration of images, plans, and policies beyond present arrangements—a very different stance from "living with nuclear weapons" and accepting long-standing patterns of nuclear buildup.

To contribute to a climate that makes genuine nuclear disarmament possible, ideas about it must be more widely exchanged among Americans. Activists, students, and scholars from among minority groups may be ready to enter the process more energetically now if they can see it to be connected, as it surely is, to questions of social justice. There are also means by which these ideas cross over barriers between the United States and the Soviet Union. The process could come to include reductions in conventional weapons and even explorations of ways to rid the world of the institution of war as such. Shared fate can be the beginning of wisdom.

7. We recognize that our own lives must inevitably and profoundly be bound up with this struggle, so we take the step away from resignation—from "waiting for the bomb"—toward commitment to combating it.

Each person, at some level of consciousness, realizes that there is no individual escape from the question, if only because the bomb envelops all as potential victims. In making the decision to do something of this kind in one's life, however modest, there can be a considerable sense of relief, even liberation. For a great deal of psychological work goes into the conflict over whether one can or should do anything in connection with the nuclear threat.

The step toward commitment may be small, from the stance of having been a sympathetic spectator, or an enormous, conversionlike recognition of what is involved from having permitted oneself to see into the nuclear abyss. Taking that step relieves one from self-deception even as one assumes new responsibilities. In overcoming resistance and admitting to our minds knowledge we wish we did not possess, that knowledge, rather than remaining only the darkest of shadows, becomes a basis for truthful thought and constructive action.

8. In these personal, individual efforts, we seek to connect our everyday working professional existence and creative concerns with the struggle against nuclear weapons.

People need no longer be workers, teachers, or students from nine to five Monday through Friday and anti-nuclear advocates on an occasional evening or weekend: they are at all times both. Professional activity of any kind should be informed by the nature of the nuclear threat, and approaches to that threat require whatever professional knowledge can be mustered. More than that, each in this way can proceed toward unification of the self.

Just as scientists and doctors have attempted to draw from their professional knowledge and experience to inform and deepen the anti-nuclear movement, so can every profession, academic discipline, or working tradition do the same. Architects, workers on assembly lines, medieval historians, policemen, and ministers—all can bring significant aspects of their experience and tradition to the struggle to maintain human life.

Indeed, one of the great scandals of our time is the paucity of human and material resources mobilized to cope with the absolute question of our time. That situation is beginning to change, though ever so slightly. There are stirrings of a more general, extraordinarily overdue, cultural response from the sciences, the arts, academia, the professions, and popular cultural sources.

9. In participating in this struggle, we do not embrace doom and gloom—hopelessness and despair—but rather a fuller existence.

In confronting a genuine threat, rather than numbing ourselves to it, we experience greater vitality. We feel stronger human ties. We turn to beauty, love, spirituality, and sensuality.

There is a distinction between depression and despair. Depression is usually reactive, having to do with a sense of loss, or in this case threatened loss. Depression has a certain symptom complex: one slows down, has less energy, withdraws from people, and may have varying degrees of guilt and anger. Yet depressed people, as stated earlier (see chapter 16), are not necessarily hopeless about the future, and may in fact anticipate recovery and a return of vitality. Despair, on the other hand, involves hopelessness and absence of larger human connection. Moments of depression are inevitable; they are part of being human. Despair can be more serious and can be managed only by reasserting human ties, both in immediate life relationships and in shared anti-nuclear struggle. Despair is overcome when we begin once more to believe in, and act on, a human future.

10. In struggling to preserve humankind, we experience a renewed sense of human possibility; we feel part of prospective historical and evolutionary achievements.

A culmination of this overall ethos is a higher self-regard. We feel more authentic in our life and work—as physicians or clergy, as scientists or artists, as teachers or students, as human beings alive to ultimate threat and hopeful in working toward a future beyond that threat.

NOTES

[Dates in brackets refer to the original publication date of a title.]

Introduction

1. A. G. Mojtabai, *Blessed Assurance: At Home with the Bomb in Amarillo, Texas* (Boston: Houghton Mifflin, 1986), p. 181.

Chapter 1. *The Future of Immortality*

1. See *Thomas Merton on Peace,* ed. and with an introduction by Gordon C. Zahn (New York: McCall Publishing, 1971); and Thomas Merton, *The Hidden Ground of Love* (New York: Farrar, Straus, Giroux, 1985).
2. William Faulkner, interview on "The Art of Fiction," *Paris Review* 12 (1956): 28–32.
3. William Faulkner, from *Faulkner in the University* (Charlottesville: University of Virginia Press, 1959).
4. Carl Jung, *Modern Man in Search of His Soul* (New York: Harcourt Brace, 1936), 129–30.
5. Maryse Choisy, *Sigmund Freud: A New Appraisal* (New York: Philosophical Library, 1953), p. 5; and Max Schur, *Freud: Living and Dying* (New York: Basic Books, 1972), pp. 50–51.
6. Otto Rank, *Beyond Psychology* (New York: Dover Books, 1958), p. 64.
7. Robert Jay Lifton, *Death in Life: Survivors of Hiroshima* (New York: Basic Books, 1982 [1967]).
8. Marghanita Laski, *Ecstasy: A Study of Some Secular and Religious Experiences* (Bloomington: Indiana University Press, 1961).
9. William James, *The Varieties of Religious Experience* (London: Longmans, Green, 1952).
10. Robert Jay Lifton, *Revolutionary Immortality* (New York: Norton, 1976 [1968]). See also Lifton, *Thought Reform and the Psychology of Totalism* (New York: W. W. Norton, 1961).
11. From Richard Ellmann, *James Joyce* (New York: Oxford University Press, 1982 [1959]), p. 57.
12. Robert Jay Lifton, "Protean Man," in *History and Human Survival* (New York: Random House, 1970), pp. 311–31.
13. Theodore Solotaroff, review essay on Sartre, *Bookweek,* 25 April 1963.
14. Jean Paul Sartre, *The Words* (New York: George Braziller, 1964), p. 19.
15. Saul Bellow, *The Adventures of Augie March* (New York: Viking Press, 1953).
16. Tony Tanner, *City of Words: American Fiction, 1950–1970* (New York: Harper & Row, 1971).
17. Jerome Hamilton Buckley, *The Turning Key* (Cambridge, Mass.: Harvard University Press, 1984).
18. Joseph Campbell, *The Hero with a Thousand Faces* (New York: Meridian Books, 1956 [1949]), pp. 15, 337.
19. Betty Jean Lifton and Eikoh Hosoe, *A Place Called Hiroshima* (New York and Tokyo: Kodansha International, 1985).

Chapter 2. *Is Hiroshima Our Text?*

1. Robert Jay Lifton, *Death in Life: Survivors of Hiroshima* (New York: Basic Books, 1982 [1967]), pp. 22–23.
2. Ibid., p. 54.
3. Robert Jay Lifton, *The Broken Connection: On Death and the Continuity of Life* (New York: Basic Books, 1983 [1979]), p. 174.

Chapter 4. *Vietnam—Beyond Atrocity*

1. Seymour M. Hersh, *My Lai 4: A Report on the Massacre and Its Aftermath* (New York: Random House, 1970); and *Cover-up: The Army's Secret Investigation of the Massacre at My Lai* (New York: Random House, 1972). See also Richard Hammer, *One Morning in the War: The Tragedy at Son My* (New York: Coward-McCann, 1970); Martin Gershen, *Destroy or Die: The True Story of Mylai* (New Rochelle, N.Y.: Arlington House, 1971); Robert Jay Lifton, *Home from the War—Vietnam Veterans: Neither Victims nor Executioners* (New York: Simon & Schuster, 1973), chap. 2; and Richard Falk, Gabriel Kolko, and Robert Jay Lifton, eds., *Crimes of War: A Legal, Political-Documentary, and Psychological Inquiry into the Responsibility of Leaders, Citizens and Soldiers for Criminal Acts in Wars* (New York: Random House, 1971).
2. Hammer, *One Morning*, p. 136.

Chapter 5. *The Postwar War*

1. Robert Jay Lifton, *Home from the War—Vietnam Veterans: Neither Victims nor Executioners* (New York: Simon & Schuster, 1973).
2. Robert Jay Lifton, *Death in Life: Survivors of Hiroshima* (New York: Basic Books, 1982 [1967]).
3. Robert Jay Lifton, "Experiments in Advocacy Research," in *Science and Psychoanalysis*, vol. 21, ed. J. H. Masserman (New York: Grune & Stratton, 1972), pp. 259–71, n. 1.
4. Lifton, *Home from the War.*
5. R. Glasser, *365 Days* (New York: George Braziller, 1971).
6. Robert Jay Lifton, *Thought Reform and the Psychology of Totalism: A Study of "Brainwashing" in China* (New York: W. W. Norton, 1961).

Chapter 6. *Medicalized Killing in Auschwitz*

1. See Robert Jay Lifton, *Death in Life: Survivors of Hiroshima* (New York: Basic Books, 1982 [1967]); and Lifton, *Thought Reform and the Psychology of Totalism: A Study of "Brainwashing" in China* (New York: W. W. Norton, 1961).
2. Robert Jay Lifton, *The Broken Connection: On Death and the Continuity of Life* (New York: Basic Books, 1983 [1979]); and Lifton, *The Life of the Self: Toward a New Psychology* (New York: Basic Books, 1984 [1976]).
3. R. Hilberg, *The Destruction of the European Jews* (New York: New Viewpoints–Franklin Watts, 1973), rev. and definitive ed. (New York: Holmes & Meier, 1985); R. Rubenstein, *The Cunning of History* (New York: Harper-Colophon, 1978); and H. Arendt, *Eichmann in Jerusalem: A Report on the Banality of Evil* (New York: Viking, 1963).
4. Dr. Ella Lingens-Reiner, personal communication.
5. Ella Lingens-Reiner, *Prisoners of Fear* (London: Gollancz, 1948), pp. 1–2.
6. Adolf Hitler, *Mein Kampf* (London: Hutchinson, 1969 [1925–26]).
7. Quoted from Frank diary in Hilberg, *The Destruction of the European Jews*, p. 12.
8. Ibid.

9. J. P. Stern, *Hitler: The Führer and the People* (London: Fontana/Collins, 1975), p. 70.

10. Ibid., p. 77.

11. S. Bloch and P. Reddaway, *Psychiatric Terror: How Soviet Psychiatry is Used to Suppress Dissent* (New York: Basic Books, 1977).

12. J. Marks, *The Search for the "Manchurian Candidate": The CIA and Mind Control* (New York: Basic Books, 1979).

13. J. Reston, Jr., *Our Father Who Art in Hell: The Life and Death of Jim Jones* (New York: New York Times Books, 1981); and Robert Jay Lifton, "The Appeal of the Death Trip," *New York Times Magazine*, 7 January 1979, pp. 26–27, 29–32.

14. United States v. Karl Brandt et al., Case no. 1, Trials of War Criminals Before Nuremburg Military Tribunals (1946–49), vols. 1 and 2. See especially vol. 1, pp. 8–17, for the indictment, and pp. 27–74, for the opening statement of the prosecution.

15. The description of doctors' activities is based on interviews with former Nazi Auschwitz doctors and with former prisoner doctors, plus the following major sources: R. Hoss, *Commandant in Auschwitz* (New York: World, 1960), including supplementary statement, "The final solution of the Jewish question in the Auschwitz concentration camp," appendix 1; and "Die nichtärztliche Tätigkeit der SS-Ärzte im K. L. Auschwitz" (The Nonmedical Activity of SS Doctors in the Concentration Camp Auschwitz), *Hefte von Auschwitz*, no. 16 (Auschwitz Museum, 1975), pp. 75–77 (the *Hefte* is a rich source of related materials). See also materials of Frankfurt Auschwitz trial of 1963–65 in "Proceedings against Mulka and others, and English summary of that trial," in B. Naumann, *Auschwitz: A Report on the Proceedings Against Robert Karl Ludwig Mulka and Others Before the Court at Frankfurt* (New York: Praeger, 1966); *Przeglad Lekarski*, a journal published by the Medical Academy of Krakow (many articles have been translated into English by the International Auschwitz Committee and published in Warsaw); and H. Langbein, *Menschen in Auschwitz* (Vienna: Europaverlag, 1972).

16. Descriptions of experiments are based on interviews with former Nazi doctors and former prisoner doctors; with survivors who had worked on medical blocks, including a physical anthropologist who had assisted Mengele in measurements on twins; and with other survivors who had themselves been subjected to these experiments and "research studies." See also A. Mitscherlich and F. Mielke, *The Death Doctors* (London: Elek Books, 1962); M. M. Hill and L. N. Williams, *Auschwitz in England: A Record of a Libel Action* (New York: Stein & Day, 1965); Y. Ternon and S. Helman, *Les Médecins allemands et le national-socialisme* (Paris: Casterman, 1973); Y. Ternon and S. Helman, *Historie médecin SS* (Paris: Casterman, 1970); F. Bayle, *Croix gammée contre caducée: Les Expériences humaines en Allemagne pendant la deuxième guerre mondiale* (Imprimerie Nationale à Neustadt [Palatinat], Commission Scientifique Française des Crimes de Guerre, 1950); and various Red Cross documents, published at Arolsen (West Germany) and Geneva, such as L. Simonius, "On Behalf of Victims of Pseudo-Medical Experiments: Red Cross Action," *International Review of the Red Cross* (Geneva: 1973).

17. The most complete documentation of this sequence, and especially of the Nazi "euthanasia" project, can be found in the Heyde trial documents, compiled at Limburg/Lahn and Frankfurt in 1959–60. See also Ernst Klee, *"Euthanasie" im NS-Staat: Die "Vernichtung lebensunwerten Lebens"* (Frankfurt/M.: S. Fischer, 1983); K. Dörner, "Nationalsozialismus und Lebensvernichtung" (National Socialism and the Extermination of Life), *Vierteljahrshefte für Zeitgeschichte* 15(2): 121–52; G. Schmidt, *Selektion in der Heilanstalt 1939–1945* (Stuttgart: Evangeliches Verlagswerk, 1965); H. Ehrhardt, *Euthanasie und Vernichtung "lebensunwerten" Lebens* (Stuttgart: Ferdinand Enke Verlag, 1965); G. Sereny, *Into That Darkness: From Mercy Killing to Mass Murder* (New York: McGraw-Hill, 1974); Y. Ternon and S. Helman, *Le Massacre des aliénés* (Paris: Casterman, 1971); and F. Wertham, *A Sign for Cain: An Exploration of Human Violence* (New York: Macmillan, 1966).

18. K. Binding and A. Hoche, *Die Freigabe der Vernichtung lebensunwerten Lebens: Ihr Mass und ihre Form* (Leipzig: F. Meiner, 1920).

19. G. Mosse, *Toward the Final Solution: A History of European Racism* (New York: Howard Fertig, 1978).

20. Ibid., pp. xv–xvi.

21. M. H. Kater, *Das "Ahnenerbe" der SS 1935–1945: Ein Beitrag zur Kulturpolitik des Dritten Reiches* (Stuttgart: Deutsche Verlags-Anstalt, 1974). See also the medical case cited herein, in the footnote on page 81.

22. R. Ramm, *Ärztliche Rechts- und Standeskunde; Der Arzt als Gesundheitserzieher*, 2nd, rev. ed. (Berlin: W. deGruyter, 1943).

23. This material comes from interviews with physician survivors. See also E. A. Cohen,

The Abyss: A Confession (New York: W. W. Norton, 1953); O. Lengyel, *Five Chimneys: The Story of Auschwitz* (New York: Ziff-Davis, 1947); W. Fejkiel, "Health Service in the Auschwitz I Concentration Camp/Main Camp," *Przeglad Lekarski,* English trans. (Warsaw: International Auschwitz Committee Anthology, vol. 2, part 1, 1979, pp. 4–37); R. J. Minney, *I Shall Fear No Evil: The Story of Dr. Alina Brewda* (London: William Kimber, 1966); G. Perl, *I Was a Doctor at Auschwitz* (New York: International Universities Press, 1948); and Lingens-Reiner, *Prisoners of Fear.*

24. I discuss Dr. B. in much greater detail in *The Nazi Doctors: Medical Killing and the Psychology of Genocide* (New York: Basic Books, 1986), chap. 16.

25. Alexander and Margarete Mitscherlich discuss overall Nazi tendencies toward derealization in *The Inability to Mourn* (New York: Grove Press, 1975). For general explorations of psychic numbing in extreme situations, see also Lifton, *Broken Connection;* and Lifton, *Death in Life.*

26. W. Ryan, *Blaming the Victim* (New York: Vintage, 1976).

27. L. S. Dawidowicz, *The War Against the Jews 1933–1945* (New York: Holt, Rinehart & Winston, 1975), p. 149.

28. M. Eliade, *Cosmos and History: The Myth of the External Return* (New York: Harper Torchbooks, 1959).

29. E. Becker, *Escape from Evil* (New York: Free Press, 1975); and Lifton, *Broken Connection.*

Chapter 8. *The Inability to Mourn: Alexander and Margarete Mitscherlich*

1. Alexander and Margarete Mitscherlich, *The Inability to Mourn* (New York: Grove Press, 1975).

Chapter 9. *The New Psychology of Human Survival*

1. William F. Vandercook, "Making the Very Best of the Very Worst: The 'Human Effects of Nuclear Weapons' Report of 1956," *International Security* 11 (Summer 1986). (Subsequent quotations are from this typescript unless otherwise specified.)

2. Philip Green, *Deadly Logic: The Theory of Nuclear Deterrence* (Columbus: Ohio State University Press, 1966).

3. The Harvard Nuclear Study Group: Albert Carnesale et al., *Living with Nuclear Weapons* (Cambridge, Mass.: Harvard University Press, 1983), p. 253.

4. A. P. Mojtabai, *Blessed Assurance: At Home with the Bomb in Amarillo, Texas* (Boston: Houghton Mifflin, 1986), pp. 167–68.

5. Ibid., p. 164.

6. Ibid., p. 171.

7. E. P. Thompson, ed., *Star Wars* (New York: Pantheon, 1985), p. 26.

8. Ibid., p. 27.

9. Steven Kull, "The Mind-Sets of Defense Policy Makers," *The Psychohistory Review* 14 (Spring 1986): 21–37. Quotation on p. 28.

10. Definitions of idolatry are taken from *American Heritage Dictionary, Oxford English Dictionary,* and *V. Firm and Encyclopedia of Religion* (New York: The Philosophical Library, 1945).

11. Kull, "Mind-Sets of Defense Policy Makers."

12. Ibid.

Chapter 10. *The Nuclear Illusion*

1. Ruth Adams and Susan Kullen, eds., *The Final Epidemic: Physicians and Scientists on Nuclear War* (Chicago: Educational Foundation for Nuclear Science, Inc./University of Chicago Press, 1981).

2. Robert Jay Lifton, "Beyond Nuclear Numbing," *Teachers College Record* 84 (Fall 1982): 15–29.

3. Robert Jay Lifton, *Death in Life: Survivors of Hiroshima* (New York: Basic Books, 1982 [1967]).

4. Edward Teller and Allan Brown, *The Legacy of Hiroshima* (Garden City, N.Y.: Doubleday, 1962), pp. 244 ff.

5. Herman Kahn, *On Thermonuclear War* (Princeton, N.J.: Princeton University Press, 1961), p. 86.

6. Jonathan Schell, *The Time of Illusion* (New York: Alfred A. Knopf, 1976).

7. See Michael Carey, "The Schools and Civil Defense: The Fifties Revisited," *Teachers College Record* 84 (Fall 1982): 115–27.

8. Robert Jay Lifton, *The Broken Connection: On Death and the Continuity of Life* (New York: Basic Books, 1983 [1979]).

9. Teller and Brown, *The Legacy of Hiroshima.*

Chapter 11. *Beyond the Nuclear End*

1. Lester Grinspoon, ed., *The Long Darkness* (New Haven, Conn.: Yale University Press, 1986).

2. Robert Jay Lifton, *Death in Life: Survivors of Hiroshima* (New York: Basic Books, 1982 [1967]), p. 23.

3. Ibid.

4. M. Hachiya, *Hiroshima Diary* (Chapel Hill: University of North Carolina Press, 1955), pp. 54–55.

5. Y. Ota, *Shikabane no machi* (Town of corpses) (Tokyo: Kawado Shobo, 1955), p. 63.

6. Hachiya, *Hiroshima Diary*, pp. 4, 5, 37.

7. Daniel Paul Schreber, *Memoirs of My Nervous Illness*, ed. and trans. Ida Macalpine and Richard A. Hunter (London: Wm. Dawson, 1955 [1903]), pp. 84–88.

8. Macalpine and Hunter, *Memoirs*, p. 55.

9. Harold F. Searles, *Collected Papers on Schizophrenia and Related Subjects* (New York: International Universities Press, 1965), pp. 488–89, 497.

10. Lifton, *Death in Life*, p. 27.

11. E. Rabinowitz, "Five Years After," in *The Atomic Age*, ed. M. Grodzins and E. Rabinowitz (New York: Basic Books, 1963), p. 156.

Chapter 12. *Prophetic Survivors*

1. Gar Alperovitz, *Atomic Diplomacy: Hiroshima and Potsdam* (New York: Simon & Schuster, 1965).

2. William L. Lawrence, quoted in Robert Jay Lifton, *The Broken Connection: On Death and the Continuity of Life* (New York: Basic Books, 1983 [1979]), p. 371.

3. William L. Lawrence, *Men and Atoms* (New York: Simon & Schuster, 1959), pp. 116–19.

4. Ibid., p. 197.

5. In Norman Moss, *Men Who Play God: The Story of the H-Bomb and How the World Came to Live with It* (New York: Harper & Row, 1968), pp. 20–21.

6. Edward Teller and Allan Brown, *The Legacy of Hiroshima* (Garden City, N.Y.: Doubleday, 1962), p. 180.

7. Ibid., p. 244.

8. Carl von Weizsäcker, quoted in Robert Jungk, *Brighter than a Thousand Suns* (New York: Harcourt, Brace, 1958), p. 81.

9. See Philip M. Stern, *The Oppenheimer Case* (New York: Harper & Row, 1969); and Stern, "Foreword," in *In the Matter of J. Robert Oppenheimer* (Cambridge, Mass.: MIT Press, 1970).

10. See Alice Kimball Smith, *A Peril and a Hope: The Scientists' Movement in America 1945–47* (Chicago: University of Chicago Press, 1965).

11. See Nuel Pharr Davis, *Lawrence and Oppenheimer* (New York: Simon & Schuster, 1968).

12. Martin J. Sherwin, *A World Destroyed: The Atomic Bomb and the Grand Alliance* (New York: Alfred A. Knopf, 1975), p. 219. See also Lifton, *Broken Connection*, pp. 422–23.

13. Nuel Pharr Davis, personal communication.

14. Letter of Robert Oppenheimer to James Conant, in Stanley A. Blumberg and Gwinn Owens, *Energy and Conflict: The Life and Times of Edward Teller* (New York: G. P. Putnam, 1976), p. 207.

15. Jungk, *Brighter than a Thousand Suns*, p. 49.

16. Leo Szilard, "My Trial as a War Criminal," reprinted in Leo Szilard, *The Voice of the Dolphins and Other Stories* (New York: Simon & Schuster, 1961 [1949]), pp. 75–86.

17. Leo Szilard, "The Voice of the Dolphins," in Szilard, *Voice of the Dolphins*, pp. 19–71.

Chapter 13. *Dreaming Well: Frontiers of Form*

1. Robert M. Laughlin, *Of Wonders Wild and New—Dreams from Zinacantán* (Washington, D.C.: Smithsonian Institution Press, 1976), p. 3. (The first epigraph to this chapter is from the same source.)

2. See Robert Jay Lifton, *The Broken Connection: On Death and the Continuity of Life* (New York: Basic Books, 1983 [1979]), pp. 38–39 and 38n.

3. *Oxford English Dictionary.*

4. Lifton, "Youth and History: Individual Change in Postwar Japan," in *History and Human Survival* (New York: Random House, 1970), pp. 30–32.

5. Ibid., pp. 73–75.

6. Robert Jay Lifton, *Home from the War—Vietnam Veterans: Neither Victims nor Executioners* (New York: Simon & Schuster, 1973), pp. 222–23.

7. Michael Casey, "On Death," *Obscenities* (New Haven: Yale University Press, 1972).

8. Lifton, *Home from the War*, pp. 180–81.

9. Harrison Kohler, "Victory," *Winning Hearts and Minds: War Poems by Vietnam Veterans*, ed. Larry Rottman, Jan Barry, and Basit T. Paguet (Brooklyn, N.Y.: First Casualty Press, 1972), p. 44.

10. Lifton, *Home from the War*, pp. 110–21 for remaining quotations from Vietnam veterans.

11. See Robert Jay Lifton, *The Nazi Doctors: Medical Killing and the Psychology of Genocide* (New York: Basic Books, 1986), chap. 16.

12. Lifton, *Nazi Doctors*, p. 306.

13. See Lifton, *Nazi Doctors*, chap. 16.

14. Howard P. Roffwarg et al., "Ontogenetic Development of the Human Sleep-Dream Cycle," *Science* 152 (1966): 604–16, 612.

15. In Erik Erikson, "The Dream Specimen in Psychoanalysis," *Journal of the American Psychoanalytic Association* 2 (1954): 17n.

Chapter 14. *Doubling: The Faustian Bargain*

1. Paul W. Pruyser, "What Splits in Splitting?," *Bulletin of the Menninger Clinic* 39 (1975): 1–46.

2. Ibid., p. 46. See also Jeffrey Lustman, "On Splitting," in *The Psychoanalytic Study of*

the Child, vol. 19, ed. Kurt Eissler et al. (New York: International Universities Press, 1977), pp. 119–54; and Charles Rycroft, *A Critical Dictionary of Psychoanalysis* (New York: Basic Books, 1968), pp. 156–57.

3. See Pierre Janet, *The Major Symptoms of Hysteria* (New York: Macmillan, 1907); and Janet, *Psychological Healing* (New York: Macmillan, 1923). See also Leston Havens, *Approaches to the Mind* (Boston: Little, Brown, 1973), pp. 34–62; and Henri F. Ellenberger, *The Discovery of the Unconscious* (New York: Basic Books, 1970), pp. 364–417.

4. Sigmund Freud and Josef Breuer, *Studies on Hysteria*, vol. 2 of *Standard Edition of the Complete Psychological Works of Sigmund Freud*, ed. James Strachey (London: Hogarth Press, 1955 [1893–95]), pp. 3–305.

5. Edward Glover, *On the Early Development of Mind: Selected Papers on Psychoanalysis*, vol. 1 (New York: International Universities Press, 1956 [1943]), pp. 307–23.

6. Melanie Klein, "Notes on Some Schizoid Mechanisms," *International Journal of Psychoanalysis* 27 (1946): 99–110; and Otto F. Kernberg, "The Syndrome," in Kernberg, *Borderline Conditions and Pathological Narcissism* (New York: Jason Aronson, 1973), pp. 3–47.

7. Henry V. Dicks, *Licensed Mass Murder: A Socio-Psychological Study of Some SS Killers* (New York: Basic Books, 1972).

8. See, for example, Erik H. Erikson, *Identity: Youth and Crisis* (New York: Norton, 1968); Heinz Kohut, *The Restoration of the Self* (New York: International Universities Press, 1977); Henry Guntrip, *Psychoanalytic Theory, Therapy and the Self* (New York: Basic Books, 1971); and Robert Jay Lifton, *The Broken Connection: On Death and the Continuity of Life* (New York: Basic Books, 1983 [1979]).

9. William James, *The Varieties of Religious Experience: A Study in Human Nature* (New York: Collier, 1961 [1902]), p. 144.

10. Rank's two major studies of this phenomenon are *The Double: A Psychoanalytic Study* (Chapel Hill: University of North Carolina Press, 1971 [1925]); and Rank, "The Double as Immortal Self," in Rank, *Beyond Psychology* (New York: Dover, 1958 [1941]), pp. 62–101.

11. Rank, *The Double*, pp. 3–9; Rank, *Beyond Psychology*, pp. 67–69. On "Der Student von Prag," see Siegfried Kracauer, *From Caligari to Hitler: A Psychological History of the German Film* (Princeton, N.J.: Princeton University Press, 1947), pp. 28–30.

12. E. T. A. Hoffmann, "Story of the Lost Reflection," in *Eight Tales of Hoffmann*, ed. J. M. Cohen (London, 1952).

13. Rank, *Beyond Psychology*, p. 98.

14. Ibid.

15. On Rank's "artist-hero," see Rank, *Beyond Psychology*, pp. 97–101.

16. Rank, *The Double*, p. 76.

17. Ibid.

18. Rank, *Beyond Psychology*, p. 82.

19. Michael Franz Basch, "The Perception of Reality and the Disavowal of Meaning," in *Annual of Psychoanalysis*, vol. 11 (New York: International Universities Press, 1982): 147.

20. Ralph D. Allison, "When the Psychic Glue Dissolves," *HYPNOS-NYTT* (December 1977).

21. The first two influences are described in George B. Greaves, "Multiple Personality: 165 Years After Mary Reynolds," *Journal of Nervous and Mental Disease* 168 (1977): 577–96. Freud emphasized the third in *The Ego and the Id*, vol. 19 of *Standard Edition of the Complete Psychological Works of Sigmund Freud*, ed. James Strachey (London: Hogarth Press, 1955 [1923]), pp. 30–31.

22. Ellenberger, *Discovery of the Unconscious*, pp. 394–400.

23. Margaretta K. Bowers et al., "Theory of Multiple Personality," *International Journal of Clinical and Experimental Hypnosis* 19 (1971): 60.

24. See Lifton, *Broken Connection*, pp. 407–9; and Charles H. King, "The Ego and the Integration of Violence in Homicidal Youth," *American Journal of Orthopsychiatry* 45 (1975): 142.

25. Robert W. Rieber, "The Psychopathy of Everyday Life" (Manuscript).

26. James S. Grotstein, "The Soul in Torment: An Older and Newer View of Psychopathology," *Bulletin of the National Council of Catholic Psychologists* 25 (1979): 36–52.

27. See Robert Jay Lifton, *Home From the War: Vietnam Veterans—Neither Victims Nor Executioners* (New York: Basic Books, 1984 [1973]).

28. Rudolf Höss, quoted in Karl Buchheim, "Command and Compliance," in *Anatomy of the SS State*, Helmut Krausnick et al. (New York: Walker, 1968 [1965]), p. 374.

29. Christian de La Mazière, *The Captive Dreamer* (New York: Saturday Review Press, 1974), pp. 14, 34.

30. John H. Hanson, "Nazi Aesthetics," *The Psychohistory Review* 9 (1981): 276.

31. Sociologist Werner Picht, quoted in Heinz Höhne, *The Order of the Death's Head: The Story of Hitler's S.S.* (New York: Coward-McCann, 1970 [1966]), pp. 460–61.

32. Rolf Hochhuth, *A German Love Story* (Boston: Little, Brown, 1980 [1978]), p. 220.

33. Rank, *Beyond Psychology,* p. 68.

34. Koppel S. Pinson, *Modern Germany: Its History and Civilization,* 2d ed. (New York: Macmillan, 1966), pp. 1–3. (Last phrase is from Nietzsche's *Beyond Good and Evil.*)

35. Ronald Gray, *The German Tradition in Literature, 1871–1945* (Cambridge: Cambridge University Press, 1965), pp. 3, 79.

36. *Faust,* quoted in Pinson, *Modern Germany,* p. 3.

37. Gray, *The German Tradition,* pp. 1–3.

38. Walter Kaufmann, *Goethe's Faust* (New York: Doubleday, 1961), p. 17.

39. Thomas Mann, *Doctor Faustus: The Life of the German Composer Adrian Leverkühn as Told by a Friend* (New York: Alfred A. Knopf, 1948 [1947]), p. 243.

40. Ibid., pp. 249, 308.

41. Rank, *The Double.* See also Robert Rogers, *A Psychoanalytic Study of the Double in Literature* (Detroit, Mich.: Wayne State University Press, 1970).

Chapter 15. *Cults: Religious Totalism and Civil Liberties*

1. Robert Jay Lifton, *Thought Reform and the Psychology of Totalism* (New York: W. W. Norton, 1961).

2. Robert Jay Lifton, "The Appeal of the Death Trip," *New York Times Magazine,* 8 January 1979, pp. 26–27, 29–31.

3. Albert Camus, *The Fall* (New York: Alfred A. Knopf, 1957), p. 120.

4. Ibid., p. 8.

Chapter 16. *Suicide: The Quest for a Future*

1. Robert Jay Lifton, Shuichi Kato, and Michael Reich, *Six Lives/Six Deaths: Portraits from Modern Japan* (New Haven, Conn.: Yale University Press, 1979).

2. H. Scott-Stokes, *The Life and Death of Yukio Mishima* (New York: Farrar, Straus & Giroux, 1974).

3. K. Menninger, "Psychoanalytic Aspects of Suicide," in *A Psychiatrist's World: Selected Papers of Karl Menninger* (New York: Viking, 1959), pp. 332, 338, 346.

4. K. R. Eissler, *The Psychiatrist and the Dying Patient* (New York: International Universities Press, 1955), pp. 64–67.

5. J. G. Frazer, *The Fear of the Dead in Primitive Religion,* vol. 2 (London: Macmillan, 1936).

6. G. Zilboorg, "Suicide Among Civilized and Primitive Races," *American Journal of Psychiatry* 92 (1936): 1361.

7. J. Campbell, *The Masks of God: Primitive Mythology* (New York: Viking, 1964).

8. J. Choron, *Suicide* (New York: Scribners, 1972), pp. 15–20.

9. Frazer, *Fear of the Dead,* p. 157.

10. Sir Thomas Browne, *Religio Medici,* quoted in A. Alvarez, *The Savage God* (New York: Random House, 1972), p. 50.

11. *A Discourse of Death* (London, 1613), quoted in M. D. Faber, "Shakespeare's Suicides: Some Historic, Dramatic and Psychological Reflections," in *Essays in Self-Destruction,* ed. E. S. Shneidman (New York: Science House, 1967), pp. 31–32, 52.

12. R. E. Litman, "Sigmund Freud on Suicide," in *Essays in Self-Destruction,* ed. E. S. Shneidman (New York: Science House, 1967), p. 332. Quotation from Freud, "Mourning and

Melancholia," vol. 14 of *Standard Edition of the Complete Psychological Works of Sigmund Freud*, ed. James Strachey (London: Hogarth Press, 1953–74), p. 252.

13. Harrow et al., "Symptomatology and Subjective Experiences in Current Depressive States," *Archives of General Psychiatry* 14 (1966): 203–12; and A. T. Beck, "Thinking and Depression," *Archives of General Psychiatry* 9 (1963): 324–33.

14. L. Farber, *The Ways of the Will* (New York: Basic Books, 1966), p. 94.

15. L. Binswanger, "The Case of Ellen West: An Anthropological-Clinical Study," in *Existence: A New Dimension in Psychiatry and Psychology*, ed. R. May, E. Angel, and H. Ellenberger (New York: Basic Books, 1958), p. 298.

16. Alvarez, *Savage God*, p. 131.

17. J. Hillman, *Suicide and the Soul* (New York: Harper & Row/Colophon Books, 1973 [1964]), pp. 73, 454.

18. Alvarez, *Savage God*, pp. 267–69.

19. Case description and quotations are from Binswanger, "The Case of Ellen West."

20. Arthur L. Kobler and Ezra Stotland, *The End of Hope—A Social-Clinical Study of Suicide* (Glencoe, Ill.: Free Press, 1964); M. J. Kahne, "Suicide in Mental Hospitals," *Journal of Health and Social Behavior* 12 (1966): 177–86; and Robert Jay Lifton, review of *The End of Hope, Archives of General Psychiatry* 12 (1965): 192–94.

21. Scott-Stokes, *The Life and Death of Yukio Mishima*, p. 43.

22. John Nathan, *Mishima* (Boston: Little, Brown, 1974), p. 21. See also Yukio Mishima, *Confessions of a Mask* (New York: New Directions, 1958).

23. Daniel Yankelovich and John Doble, "The Public Mood: Nuclear Weapons and the U.S.S.R.," *Foreign Affairs* 63 (Fall 1984): 33–46; and Yankelovich, Robert Kingston, and Gerald Garvey, eds., *Voter Options on Nuclear Arms Policy: A Briefing Book for 1984 Elections* (New York: *Public Agenda* and the Center for Foreign Policy Development at Brown University, 1984).

24. Robert Jay Lifton, *The Broken Connection: On Death and the Continuity of Life* (New York: Basic Books, 1983 [1979]), chaps. 17, 18.

25. Alvarez, *Savage God*, pp. 245–46.

26. K. Harada, "Genbaku no Kioku," quoted in Robert Jay Lifton, *Death in Life: Survivors of Hiroshima* (New York: Basic Books, 1982 [1967]), p. 354; and in Alvarez, *Savage God*, p. 262.

Chapter 17. *The Concept of the Survivor*

1. Robert Jay Lifton, "The Concept of the Survivor," in *Survivors, Victims and Perpetrators: Essays on the Nazi Holocaust*, ed. Joel Dimsdale (Washington, D.C.: Hemisphere, 1980), chap. 4.

2. M. Buber, "Guilt and Guilt Feelings," in *The Knowledge of Man: Selected Essays* (New York: Harper & Row, 1966).

3. Robert Jay Lifton, *Death in Life: Survivors of Hiroshima* (New York: Basic Books, 1982 [1967]).

4. Robert Jay Lifton and E. Olson, "The Human Meaning of Total Disaster: The Buffalo Creek Experience," *Psychiatry* 39 (1976): 1–18.

5. H. Krystal, ed., *Massive Psychic Trauma* (New York: International Universities Press, 1968).

6. G. Brée, *Camus* (New Brunswick, N.J.: Rutgers University Press, 1959).

7. Robert Jay Lifton, *The Broken Connection: On Death and the Continuity of Life* (New York: Basic Books, 1983 [1979]).

8. Sigmund Freud, *Civilization and Its Discontents*, vol. 21 of *Standard Edition of the Complete Psychological Works of Sigmund Freud*, ed. James Strachey (London: Hogarth Press, 1961 [1930]), pp. 64–145.

9. E. Wiesel, *Night* (New York: Hill & Wang, 1960), p. 92.

10. Lifton, *Death in Life*, pp. 489–99.

11. Y. Ota, *Shikabane no machi* (Town of corpses) (Tokyo: Kawado Shobo, 1955).

12. P. Levi, *Survival in Auschwitz* (New York: Collier, 1961), p. 82.

13. Lifton, *Home from the War—Vietnam Veterans: Neither Victims nor Executioners* (New York: Simon & Schuster, 1973), pp. 47–48.

Chapter 18. *The Survivor as Creator*

1. Saul Bellow, *Herzog* (New York: Viking, 1964).
2. Albert Camus, *Caligula and Three Other Plays* (New York: Alfred A. Knopf, 1957).
3. Albert Camus, *The Stranger* (New York: Alfred A. Knopf, 1946).
4. Albert Camus, *The Rebel* (New York: Alfred A. Knopf, 1954).
5. Albert Camus, *The Plague* (New York: Alfred A. Knopf, 1947).
6. Warren Miller, *Looking for the General* (New York: McGraw-Hill, 1964).
7. Kurt Vonnegut, *Slaughterhouse Five* (New York: Delacourt, 1969).
8. Kurt Vonnegut, *Mother Night* (New York: Delacourt, 1971).
9. Kurt Vonnegut, *Cat's Cradle* (New York: Delacourt, 1971).
10. Günter Grass, *The Tin Drum* (New York: Pantheon, 1961).
11. Norman Mailer, *The American Dream* (New York: Dial Press, 1964).
12. Heinrich Böll, *The Clown* (New York: McGraw-Hill, 1965).
13. Samuel Beckett, *Krapp's Last Tape and Other Dramatic Pieces* (New York: Grove Press, 1960).

Chapter 20. *Toward a Nuclear Age Ethos*

1. Steven Kull, "Nuclear Nonsense," *Foreign Policy* 58 (Spring 1985): 28–52.

LIST OF ACKNOWLEDGMENTS AND PERMISSIONS

Grateful acknowledgment is made to the following sources for their permission to reprint:

Chapter 2, "Is Hiroshima Our Text?" was originally published in Robert Jay Lifton and Richard Falk, *Indefensible Weapons: The Political and Psychological Case against Nuclearism,* copyright © 1982 by Basic Books.

Chapter 3, "The Hiroshima Connection," was originally published in *The Atlantic Monthly* 236 (5 [4 November 1975]): 83–88. Copyright © Robert Jay Lifton, M.D., The Atlantic, November 1975.

Chapter 4, "Vietnam—Beyond Atrocity," was originally published in *Crimes of War,* ed. Richard A. Falk, Gabriel Kolko, and Robert Jay Lifton (New York: Random House, 1971).

Chapter 5, "The Postwar War," originally appeared in *Journal of Social Issues* 31 (4 November 1975): 181–95.

Chapter 6, "Medicalized Killing in Auschwitz," was originally published in *Psychiatry* 45 (4 [November 1982]). Copyright © 1982 by The William Alanson White Psychiatric Foundation, Inc.

Chapter 7, " 'Decent' People and Evil Projects," originally appeared as a review of *Psychotherapy in the Third Reich: The Göring Institute,* by Geoffrey Cocks, *New York Times,* 27 January 1985. Copyright © 1985 by The New York Times Company. Reprinted by permission.

Chapter 8 originally comprised the introduction to *The Inability to Mourn,* by Alexander and Margarete Mitscherlich. Copyright © 1975 by Grove Press, Inc. Reprinted by permission of Grove Press, Inc.

Chapter 10, "The Nuclear Illusion," originally appeared as "Beyond Nuclear Numbing," in Douglas Sloan, ed., *Education for Peace and Disarmament: Toward a Living World* (New York: Teachers College Press. Copyright © 1983 by Teachers College, Columbia University).

Chapter 11 originally appeared as "Imagining the Real: Beyond the Nuclear End," in *The Long Darkness: Psychological and Moral Perspectives on Nuclear Winter,* ed. Lester Grinspoon. Copyright © Yale University Press, 1986.

Chapter 12, "Prophetic Survivors," originally appeared in *Social Policy* (January–February 1972).

Chapter 14, "Doubling: The Faustian Bargain," was originally published in Robert Jay Lifton, *The Nazi Doctors: Medical Killing and the Psychology of Genocide,* Basic Books, 1986.

Chapter 15 originally appeared as "Cult Formation," in *Cults, Culture and the Law: Perspectives on New Religious Movements,* ed. Thomas Robbins, William C. Shephard, and James McBride (Chico, Cal.: Scholars Press, 1985). Reprinted with permission of American Academy of Religion and Scholars Press.

Chapter 17, "The Concept of the Survivor," was originally published in *Survivors, Victims and Perpetrators: Essays of the Nazi Holocaust,* ed. Joel Dimsdale, pp. 113–26. Copyright © 1980 Hemisphere Publishing Corporation.

Chapter 18, "The Survivor as Creator," was originally published in *The American Poetry Review* 2 (1 [1973]).

Chapter 19, "Art and the Imagery of Extinction," an interview conducted by Bonnie Marranca with the author, appeared in *Performing Arts Journal* 6, no. 3(1982): 51–66.

Chapter 20, "Toward a Nuclear Age Ethos," originally appeared in *Bulletin of the Atomic Scientists* 41, no. 7 (August 1985): 168–72.

Excerpt from "Author's Apology" by T. Carmi, in *Anatomy of a War,* Acum Publishers, 1977.

Excerpt from "Victory" by Harrison Kohler, in *Winning Hearts and Minds: War Poems by Vietnam Veterans,* ed. Larry Rottmann, Jan Crumb, and Basil T. Paquet (Brooklyn, N.Y.: First Casualty Press, 1972).

Philip Levine, excerpted from "Lost and Found," from *Ashes.* Copyright © 1971, 1979 Philip Levine. Reprinted with the permission of Atheneum Publishers.

Excerpt from "The Long Waters" by Theodore Roethke. Copyright © 1962 by Beatrice Roethke, as administratrix of the estate of Theodore Roethke. From *The Collected Poems of Theodore Roethke.* Reprinted by permission of Doubleday and Company, Inc.

Excerpt from "On Death" by Michael Casey, in *Obscenities.* Copyright © Yale University Press 1972. Reprinted with permission.

INDEX